AUGUST

A FATHER AND DAUGHTER'S JOURNEY INTO THE STORM

GALE

BARBARA WALSH

gpp

Guilford, Connecticut

Project editor: Meredith Dias
Text design: Sheryl P. Kober
Layout: Joanna Beyer

ISBN 978-0-7627-8490-5

Printed in the United States of America

10 9 8 7 6 5 4 3 2 1

To my parents, Ronald and Patricia Walsh,
who have always had faith in me

CONTENTS

CONTENTS

PREFACE

August Gale started out as a story about a storm and my seafaring ancestors who were caught in a killer hurricane, a "devil" that descended upon Newfoundland's waters in the summer of 1935.

But it turned out to be much more. The story grew to include my grandfather, a man who created his own tempests and abandoned my father as a young boy. It would have been much easier to just recreate the gale and my Great Uncle Captain Paddy Walsh, but stories have a way of changing course, becoming living, breathing entities.

My grandfather Ambrose Walsh was Captain Paddy's younger brother. Though I tried to exclude Ambrose from the book and focus only on the fishermen who battled the sea, my grandfather's past, his connection to my father and my family, haunted me. I soon learned I had to tell his story, too.

A journalist for thirty years, I had written about killers, rapists, corrupt politicians, and the victims of crimes, accidents, and misfortune. Their stories were often difficult to tell—but they were strangers. I had never written about my family. The thought of writing about my father's pain, his childhood hurt, overwhelmed me. *I trust you,* he repeatedly told me.

Over the past nine years, *August Gale* took my dad and me on several journeys. We traveled to Newfoundland to gather memories from our ancestors and the children whose fathers fought for their lives in a roiling sea. We traveled to Staten Island and Brooklyn, where churches, playgrounds, and rough-and-tumble neighborhoods stirred the memories of my father's turbulent past.

More than 150 people shared their recollections about a hurricane that forever changed a small Newfoundland village in

1935. And scores of my family members—aunts, uncles, cousins, and my father—helped me to understand the grandfather I never knew.

All the events in this book are true, and the characters are real. In some cases, the dialogue was repeated to me by someone who witnessed the event or the conversation. In other instances, I had to recreate dialogue to retell a scene. In preparation, I reviewed hundreds of pages of newspapers, government documents, and hurricane data to confirm facts, details, and personal accounts.

Nine years have passed since my father first told me the story of the August Gale; for nine years I have lived with this story in my heart and in my head. It is time to let it go, let it be told.

As my seafaring friends would say, "Hoist the main, heave the anchor, and let 'er sail!"

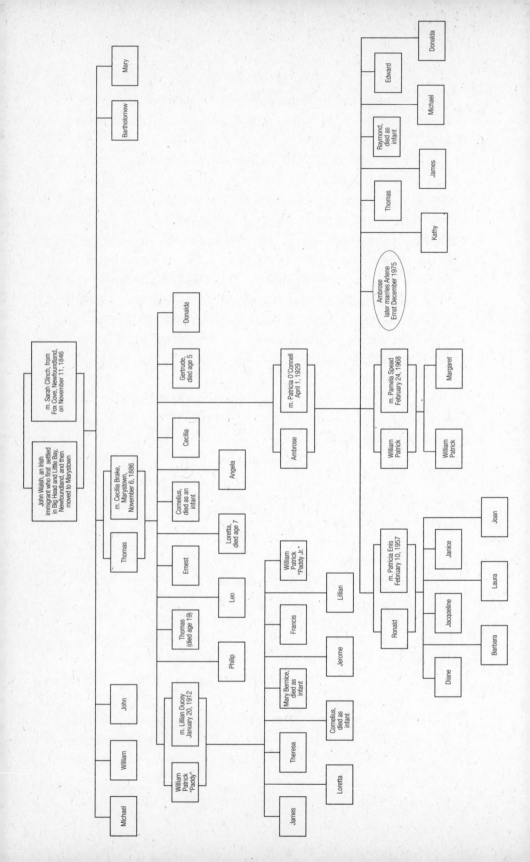

CHAPTER 1

A SUDDEN WIND—BROOKLYN, AUGUST 1935

Ambrose Walsh sits alone on a bench. The pungent odor of fresh fish and the pleasant scent of saltwater waft through the air, reminding the young man of his Newfoundland home. In the distance, the Staten Island ferry chugs across the bay, churning up waves that slap the Brooklyn pier. Ambrose eyes the diminishing ship, his mind drifting like the plumes of steam billowing from the ferry's engine. He is uncharacteristically distracted at this moment, perhaps by the euphoria of his first son's birth, a dark-haired boy born just two weeks ago; or perhaps he is consumed with worry like any other family man, hoping that he doesn't end up in the relief line with his hand out and his pride gone.

A stranger passing Ambrose on this afternoon would admire his ink-black hair, dark eyes, thick chest, and strong arms. His shoulders and back are taut, straight. Though he is only twenty-seven, he can handle himself in a fight or on a job, and in this year of 1935, he needs all of this strength to believe the future holds more than the past. A strange and sudden gust, a warm August breeze, pulls Ambrose from his thoughts. Sheets of newspaper drift in the air and tumble along the pier until they reach the bench where the young man sits. Glancing down at the trash, Ambrose considers letting the wind take it further along the gritty Brooklyn wharf, but the summer breeze rattles the paper as if it were calling, demanding his attention.

Finished with lunch, Ambrose considers returning to work, but something draws him to the newspaper that has remained at his feet despite the wind that swirls around him. He bends to pick up the paper, scanning the front-page stories. A bold headline captures his eye: AUGUST GALE KILLS MORE THAN 40 NEWFOUNDLAND FISHERMEN.

Ambrose is not a man who panics easily, but now fear constricts his throat, making it difficult for him to breathe. He has been gone from his home, the small Newfoundland fishing village of Marystown, nine years. There had been nothing for him in the rural outpost; he never had the stomach for or the desire to battle the sea like his four older brothers. When the demand for exporting cod and salt fish prices began to tumble in the 1920s, Ambrose decided it was time to explore other opportunities.

He had barely turned eighteen when he filled his duffle and hugged his mother, Cecilia, good-bye. "You're too young to be leaving, boy," she'd told him. She didn't like the idea of losing her youngest child, her mischievous "Tom Divil" to a country so far from her village doorstep. Yet she harbored little doubt that Ambrose could charm his way, flash his smile, and endear himself to women and men alike. *And sure now, he wasn't the first of her boys to head for America. Her son Leo had done the same years earlier, like so many Newfoundlanders looking for opportunity and a better life.*

"Don't forget us now," she had scolded. "I'll be praying for you, son."

Ambrose hadn't thought much of Marystown since he arrived at New York City's Penn Station, the enormous train depot that made him dizzy and delighted all at once. Never before had he seen so many people in one place, hurrying in dozens of directions, heads bent with purpose. Ambrose was eager to find his own purpose, a good job, a fair wage. His older brother Leo, who lives in Staten Island, had promised to get him hired at his place of employment, a company called Procter & Gamble. Ambrose had never heard of this American company or its famous Ivory soap, but his brother Leo assured him that a man could do well working for them.

From the moment he arrived, Ambrose has chosen to cut off communications with his Newfoundland family. A man prone to keeping secrets, he now guards the details of his new life, understanding that his silence will make his mother think the worst: that her youngest son is dead or in some horrible trouble. Still, neither he nor his brother Leo sends letters to Marystown about Ambrose. No word about his home in Staten Island or his marriage to Patricia O'Connell, a shy, blonde-haired girl with kind blue eyes.

On this August afternoon, Ambrose has an aching desire to return to Marystown, the rows of houses on the bay, the families bound by blood and sea. The guilt of abandoning his family weighs on him now. He is afraid to read more of the newspaper story, more of the killer gale. A betting man, fond of gambling and playing the horses, Ambrose knows the odds of losing family in this storm are great. Most of his brothers, uncles, and cousins still earn their living from the sea. Surely his oldest brother Paddy was out in his schooner, hoping to make his final catches for the long winter months ahead.

Ambrose allows himself a grin at the thought of Paddy shouting orders to his crew as they prepared to sail from Marystown: "Heave up the anchor, boys!" There would have been singing on the deck, the crew's voices blending together as they heaved the anchor and hoisted the sails. Ambrose knows that nothing thrilled Paddy more than sailing schooners. He lived for fishing from one season to the other. Paddy knew where to find the cod and how to handle the sea when it grew rough.

"You're missing the adventure, boy," Paddy had often chided him. "A man should be at sea. Come out and crew for me. Come and fill yur dory with fish. We'll fight the sea together."

Ambrose had tried to embrace Paddy's love for fishing. Briefly, he considered it, imagined himself hunting cod and sailing schooners, all the while his heart telling him there was no measuring up to Paddy.

Twenty-one years older than Ambrose, Paddy is more like a father than a brother. Ambrose's own father, Tom Walsh, is old enough to be his grandfather, and any fatherly instincts have long been spent on his first eleven children. It was Paddy whom Ambrose had sought as a youngster, longing to be in his presence, wanting what Paddy had: confidence and the courage to face whatever challenges came his way.

Now on this Brooklyn wharf, Ambrose would give anything to hear Paddy tell another story, the two of them sitting beside the kitchen cooker, laughing late into the night.

Ambrose hasn't enough money in his pockets for the fare home to Newfoundland; there is no hope of seeing Paddy or anyone else in his family. He has little doubt that his mother, along with every woman and child in Marystown, is on her knees, whispering the Rosary for the missing men. He cannot say his own prayer, begging God to keep his family safe from the storm. Ambrose has never believed in the Lord no matter how much his mother tried to persuade him otherwise, and he is not about to change his mind now for even the most desperate of causes.

Though the August sun warms his face, Ambrose is bone cold, as if he himself had fallen into icy waters. He is afraid to learn more about this killer storm, yet he cannot ignore the paper pushed to his feet by a sudden wind. His dark eyes scan the report of sunken schooners and scores of missing men. He finds the words that cause him to cry out.

Like his brothers and the generations of Irish ancestors born before him, Ambrose Walsh is not in the habit of revealing his fears or emotions. Yet on this day, as the ferry carries him across New York Harbor to his Staten Island home, he curses and moans. The wild look in his eyes frightens the other passengers. When he arrives at his doorstep, his voice hysterical with grief, his wife, Patricia, hushes their baby, as Ambrose, himself, weeps like a child.

CHAPTER 2

LURED BY THE GALE—MAINE, FEBRUARY 2002

My father is the first to tell me about Ambrose and the August Gale. He shares the story with me one winter evening, realizing that he has never recounted it to anyone since his mother had told it to him forty-odd years earlier. He finds it strange that the story has lain dormant in his mind for so long.

Yet this does not surprise me. My father, Ronald Eugene Walsh, was the baby Ambrose's wife hushed that August afternoon in 1935, the dark-haired son whom Ambrose would abandon eleven years later.

For most of my life, Ambrose was a mystery, a taboo topic. When I was a child, I asked my Nana where Grandpa was. She quickly told me, "He's dead." I do not remember asking more about him. In my seven-year-old mind, I accepted that Grandpa didn't exist. I could not see or touch him; I did not know his name, and no one ever spoke it—not my father, not Nana, nor my uncle. There was no evidence of Ambrose, no photographs of him in our home or my grandmother's.

I was eighteen before I learned my grandfather was alive. The revelation occurred when my older sister Diane and I drove my dad from our New Hampshire home to the airport in Boston, Massachusetts. During the ride, Ambrose's name came up. I do not remember if I pressed my father for details about my grandfather's death, but he suddenly explained, "Ambrose isn't dead. He's living in California with another family."

"He's alive?" I repeated, stunned.

There was little time to ask more questions before we pulled to the airport curb for my father's flight. Grabbing his bags, he hugged us good-bye, and I watched him disappear beyond the airport door.

I turned to my sister, who strangely did not seem as surprised at the news about our grandfather. "Can you believe that Ambrose is alive?"

"I knew he was in California," she replied nonchalantly. "Nana used to tell me about him."

"What? How come no one told me?" I asked, hurt.

Despite my shock over Ambrose and his mysterious California family, my grandfather quickly slipped back into a place best left untouched, forgotten. Asking questions about Ambrose was like touching a hot stove. My five sisters and I knew it would cause pain. During our teenage and college years, random phone calls from our mysterious grandfather stirred my father's anger, leaving him silent, brooding. Occasional books, letters from California were quickly discarded. If anyone dared to utter Ambrose's name, my father fell silent or left the room, unwilling to acknowledge the man he could not forgive. Years before I was born, the guests at my parents' wedding were told that Ambrose was dead. It was easier than answering questions about a man who abandoned his family—twice, on distant American coasts.

Now on this winter evening, my father talks about Ambrose and the August Gale. I fall silent, unconsciously holding my breath, afraid that if I speak, it will stop my father from continuing, from giving me a gift: a story about my grandfather.

We sit, side by side, on my living room couch as a distant foghorn echoes in the woods out back. My father is three years shy of turning seventy. His broad-chested, five-foot-eleven-inch frame is still intimidating, a characteristic that helped him in the amateur boxing ring and in the brawls he fought as a young

Navy sailor, touring the world. Though his hair is gray and thin-ning, decades of yard work and a lifetime of sports have kept my father trim, muscled. His brown eyes hold a newfound soft-ness—a benevolence—and they remind me of my Nana's kind blue eyes. My father has softened in other ways too. During the past few years, he has begun telling me and each of my five sisters after every phone conversation: "I love you." My voice always catches as I return the salutation, understanding that his part-ing words illuminate a shift, an emotional sea change. Though I have never doubted his love, my dad has long guarded and bur-ied his feelings. Now, at the age of forty-four, I am beginning to understand why.

On this February night, his voice is low, mesmerizing, as he shares what he knows about the 1935 Newfoundland hurricane. While my father speaks, his large hands cut the air to empha-size his thoughts. Later I will learn he has his father's hands—Newfoundland hands—strong and suited for hauling cod. He describes how the foreboding newspaper landed at Ambrose's feet carrying news of the deadly storm; how Ambrose feared his hero, his older brother Paddy, was dead.

It is this moment, when my grandfather is most fragile, that he becomes real in my mind. I can hear his sobs and see his face red with pain, and for the first time in my life, I want to know more about him and his family. I press my father for details: "How bad was the storm? Did a lot of our people die? Did Ambrose ever get back to Newfoundland to see his family?"

My father cannot answer these questions. He believes that one of the crew may have lashed himself to the schooner wheel to survive, but he is unsure of what happened to Captain Paddy or any of our other Newfoundland relatives. The scant details are enough to lure my imagination. For most of my journalism career, I have chased stories about strangers. Now the journalist in me wants to chase the storm, resurrect the men, my ancestors, who sailed schooners and relied on God and the wind to carry them home. My father, a lover of history, sea adventures, and a former Navy shipman, is equally intrigued by the story.

"Maybe we can get in touch with some of the family," he says, "and see if they know anything about the storm."

Family? Ambrose's relatives? I silently ask. My father's offer to contact Ambrose's family stuns me into silence. Over the last twenty years, attempts to coax my father to talk about my grandfather have met with little success. Though I did not often try to broach the topic, one occasion stands out in my mind: My dad had flown from his New Hampshire home to visit me and tour the Fort Lauderdale, Florida, newsroom where I worked in the late 1980s and early 1990s. On a warm March evening, we sat in the dark on my patio, a small deck that looked out onto the city's man-made canals. We sipped beer and dined on the only thing I had in my cabinet—a bag of pretzels. Perhaps it was the effect of the second beer on my empty stomach that gave me the courage to try and unearth my father's feelings. "How," I asked, "did you learn to be a good father, when your dad wasn't around to teach you or give you advice?"

My father stared into the dark, past the row of sailboats silhouetted in the city lights. His rocking chair creaked as he pushed it back and forth with the tips of his sneakers. He could not find the words to answer me.

The rigging on the nearby boats rattled and clanged, filling the silence between us. When our words returned, they focused on the newspaper stories I had written that day and my father's plans to play golf the following morning.

Now on this winter evening, my father's offer to contact Ambrose's family leaves me quiet again. I do not question why he is ready to share memories that have remained private for decades. I only know that I am grateful that this conversation about the August Gale has found its way to my living room on this February night. It is well after midnight when we finish talking about the storm and how we might further our research. My father promises to e-mail and call relatives, who can help us learn more. I kiss him on the forehead and bid him goodnight, adding "I love you."

He quickly replies, "I love you, too." Before I head down the hallway to my bedroom, I turn to look at him. He is lost in thought, and I wonder if his mind has drifted back to his child-hood, and his father, Ambrose.

The house is still as I slip beneath my bedcovers. My hus-band, two daughters, and my mother have been asleep for hours. I lie awake in the dark, excited about this story that links me to my father's past and our Newfoundland family. That night, I dream of giant waves and the grandfather I never had the chance to know or meet.

CHAPTER 3

THE KING OF MARYSTOWN—NEWFOUNDLAND, 1935

Paddy Walsh rubbed the coins in his pocket as he walked toward the priest's meadow. The coins had always given him comfort as tokens of his good fortune and the bountiful catches that had provided well for his family. Yet on this August day the sound of the money did not console, but rather unnerved Paddy, reminding him of how little the salt cod was worth.

The schooner captain was not a man who consumed himself with worry, but in this summer of 1935, Paddy was uneasy about the years ahead. At the age of forty-eight, he could still find the fish, hauling more cod than most captains on the southern shores of Newfoundland, yet a full hold meant little when it drew a pitiful price. The smell of the sea pulled Paddy from his thoughts. He eyed the bay that separated the northern and southern shores of Marystown. Wooden houses flanked the dirt paths leading along the water; here the Reids, Brintons, Farrells, Walshes, and Powers made their home, descendants of Irish immigrants who crossed the Atlantic to seek their fortune in a place the Irish called *Talamh an Éisc*, "Land of the Fish."

Like the thousands of Irish fleeing wretched poverty and farms they could not own, Paddy's great-grandfather left one British-ruled country for another. Unable to convince young British men to immigrate to an island known for its boggy land and fog-shrouded seas, the English relied on Irish fishermen and farmers who viewed Newfoundland as a transatlantic Tipperary to settle the colony. By the mid-1800s, much of Marystown and Newfoundland's southern shore was as Irish as Ireland itself.

As the August breeze rippled the water, the bay where Paddy's great-grandfather once moored his schooners was oddly quiet. For as long as Paddy could remember, nearly every family in Marystown had put aside their chores and work to celebrate the Blessed Virgin's ascension into heaven. The rural outport was named after the Mother of God, and none of the five hundred souls who called Marystown home dared tend to their trawls or vessels on the fifteenth of August, a holy day that called for prayer in church and a communal feast in the priest's meadow.

Paddy understood the fishermen's fervent beliefs, but the sight of the empty schooners reminded the skipper of his mounting debt and the money owed to local merchants. The miserable 1930s were nearly half over now, and politicians promised prosperity was around the corner. Yet the only corner Paddy could see was the one that he felt himself boxed into. Despite his threats to local merchants—*Give me the highest price for the fish or I'll kill ye*—the price of cod had begun tumbling not long after the First World War, and with unemployment and poverty crippling the economy in Newfoundland and foreign countries, the salt fish exports dropped like a stone.

Supplying schooners with grub and gear was damn near impossible when the merchants offered a pittance for a quintal of fish. Paddy thought of his younger brother Ambrose's words before he immigrated to the Boston States. "Fishing's too much hard work for too little pay. There's no future in it, Paddy."

Whispers and the jingle of metal pulled Paddy from his thoughts. Small boys walking a few steps behind the captain rubbed pieces of tin in their pockets, wishing for the real coins that Paddy often had. Turning to the boys, Paddy offered a greeting, "Afternoon lads." The youths quickly replied with a polite, "Afternoon, Mr. Paddy."

There were many Paddies among the Irish immigrants in Marystown, but there was only one "Mr. Paddy." Known as "The King of Marystown," William Patrick "Paddy" Walsh followed his own rules both on land and at sea. The boys had heard stories about Paddy from their fathers and other fishermen. They knew you watched your step and your words around Mr. Paddy. Like his four younger brothers, Paddy was a large man. Nearly six feet tall, his chest was blocky, his shoulders broad from decades of rowing dories and pulling cod from the sea. The salt wind and years of drink had also made their mark, leaving Paddy's cheeks red and flushed. His dark eyes held a wildness and unpredictability to them, as if he were perpetually issuing a challenge. And those in town well knew, *ye didn't challenge Skipper Paddy.*

The men who crewed for Capt'n Paddy, Marystown merchants, the law, and the town priest understood: *Paddy had no fear of nothin' or nobody.* Fishermen swapped stories about Paddy like precious coins, retelling their favorites over and over. The law didn't mean much to Paddy. It did not stop him from starting a brawl with a constable who towered over the captain or half murdering a man for swearing in the skipper's house. Following several rounds of drinks, Paddy had nearly punched a fisherman's eye out after the man cursed in the captain's parlor. When the bloodied doryman later filed charges, Paddy confessed to the local magistrate that, indeed, he was guilty of the assault.

The judge, who often enjoyed cards and rum with Paddy, chastised his friend for the crime. "Next time ye would handle yurself differently now wouldn't ye, Paddy?"

"Yes sir," Paddy said tipping his cap, "Next time I'd kill the son of a bitch."

With every exploit and adventure on land and sea, Paddy's legend grew until the people of Marystown and the villages and towns beyond could no longer discern which stories about the "king" were true and which had been stretched like the line on a doryman's trawl.

Still, like most of the fishermen on Newfoundland's southern shore, the boys who followed Paddy on this Lady Day afternoon dared not test the skipper's ire. Careful not to meet Paddy's eyes, they cast a furtive glance at the skipper and raced toward the carnival barker and his lyrical chant: "Try yur chance at the Wheel of Fortune. Five cents for fifty cents."

Children lined up at the wooden wheel, rubbing a nickel or two in their hands, dear few coins their fathers had given them for the garden party. In the shadow of the Sacred Heart Church, boys chased one another in a game of tag. Pennies jingled in their pockets, payment for a paper grab bag that might hold a few special trinkets: a comb, candy, or a bar of soap. Large wooden tubs held every child's delight—ice cream churned with winter ice from the bay and homemade berries.

From long wooden tables, the smell of fudge and homemade apple pies beckoned hungry fishermen. Women outfitted in their Sunday finery, long dresses with buttons of pearl or glass, fussed over their baked goods. Nimble and quick hands arranged pies, cakes, and pots of tea, waiting for customers to buy their offerings. A line of fairgoers stood before Paddy's wife, Lillian, who sold her cakes to eager customers. A petite and proper woman, Lillian was known for her baking and sewing skills. Her goods were always the first to go at the garden party. And Paddy made certain none of Lil's pies went unclaimed.

Across the field, a crowd of fishermen gathered around a large barrel of rum. Dorymen who would soon be rowing miles back and forth to their skippers' schooners stood in tight circles drinking from mugs that were blessedly full. Tom Reid, Paddy's second hand, sipped his liquor and listened to the voices that grew increasingly louder. Tall and blocky like Paddy, the two men could have been brothers. Reid had fished with Paddy for many years, and despite their occasional brawls (fueled by too much rum or moonshine made in the woods), Reid counted himself lucky to be aboard Paddy's schooner. The winters weren't as rough when the skipper returned to Marystown with his boat weighted down with cod. There was likely to be a bit of salt pork on the table, butter for the bread, and maybe even sugar for the tea. *Aye, Paddy can be a rough character, but a skipper has a rough job,* Reid thought. *He's got to command his crew and know everything about the seas, how to handle the waves when they grow to mountains, how to keep clear of the sunkers, and how to find the best fishing grounds. He worked ye hard, but he always found the fish.*

"Yis b'ys," drink up, Reid and the men told one another. There would be no rum in the dories, where their calloused hands would soon be busy baiting and hauling trawl and pulling on the oars from dawn to dusk. The fishermen were anxious to make their catches before the long, dark months ahead. But they also knew it was the start of hurricane season, when tropical storms roared up the North Atlantic and descended upon the Bay of Fundy and the Grand Banks.

It was bad luck to talk about the August gales, but each of the fishermen had heard the stories that were told and retold by those who sailed the sea. They had heard the tales about the gale of 1873 that struck the sea off Nova Scotia and Cape Breton, claiming more than five hundred Canadian and American fishermen. The tide on that August evening rose higher than it had in twenty-four years. Ships as large as a thousand tons, and boats as small as thirty tons, foundered or sank. Scores of fishermen were found dead, lashed to their schooners' rigging or drowned in their decks below. Hundreds more were swept off vessels and met their watery grave. In the days following the storm, dead bodies rolled in with the tide; dories and derelict boats washed ashore, empty and battered with holes.

One hundred more Newfoundland and Nova Scotia men drowned in 1927 when an August gale blew into the Grand Banks with winds of one hundred miles per hour. Captains had never seen the barometer drop so suddenly.

It was as if the devil himself had danced on the waters, surviving fishermen told their sons. *The sea was as smooth as oil. By Gad, all of a sudden there came mountains of water. We pulled on our oilskins and got ready for the boil.*

The wind roared like a freight train. Walls of water broke onto decks, stripping vessels of their masts, dories, and gurry butts. Everything above board disappeared into the briny deep as captains hollered, *It's every man for himself!*

Throughout the small outports, telegrams arrived bearing news of all hands lost. Word came too about the fate of vessels like the *John Loughlin*. The schooner from nearby Placentia Bay had been fishing off Cape St. Mary's with a seven-man crew and a young boy, when the gale breezed up. A day after the storm, a fisherman spied the *Loughlin* bobbing in seas that were still rough and hazy with fog. From the rigging in the schooner's crosstrees, a man hung by his right arm. The corpse dipped in the sea as the boat listed. When the storm winds ceased, fishermen boarded the schooner and cut the sailor from the mast. Captain Albert Loughlin would be the only body found on the vessel. Loughlin's two brothers, the five other crew members, and the small boy had disappeared in the monstrous waves that had risen up beneath blue skies.

The weatherglass was no good when the August gales whirled up the coast. Without radios on board, there was little warning and scant chance of sailing to safe harbors. Fishermen faced the storms with nothing but the small crosses and religious medals they carried in their pockets. Still, there was no use fretting over the hurricanes when there were hungry children at home. Like many of the Irish Catholics, Tom Reid had a large family, six children to feed and clothe. It was a struggle to keep enough food on the kitchen table.

No, Reid told himself, no sense worrying about the gales and the winds that could flip a dory like a matchstick. Reid also took comfort in Paddy's resolve to come home with all hands. *Aye, the Capt'n never left a man behind. No, we never returned to harbor wit' the flag at half-mast. Paddy could be a son of a bitch to work for, but he never lost a man in his twenty-five years as skipper. Despite shipwrecks, storms, t'ick of fog, or treacherous ice floes, Paddy and his crew always made it home.*

Reid shook off the dark thoughts and joined the other fishermen at the rum barrel. Paddy nodded to Reid and grinned at the fishermen who were already unsteady on their feet. As sure as Sunday, Paddy told himself, the fists will be flying before dawn. The Farrells, Fitzpatricks, Brintons, Reddies, and Walshes will be carrying on decades-old feuds over slights suffered by their grandfathers.

Beyond the circle of men, children's voices carried across the meadow, where boys wrestled in the grass. Paddy searched for his own young sons, Frankie and Jerome. The sight of girls outfitted in flour sack dresses, rags mended with the odd button and tattered ribbon, prompted a curse and sigh from the skipper. The boys were no better off with their frayed knickers and caps. The children's gaunt faces told of flour and potato diets, with a bit of fish, if they were lucky. The boggy town graveyard had claimed enough of them, Paddy thought. Their frail bodies couldn't fight off a cold never mind the damned tuberculosis sweeping through the country. With spotty medical care and one doctor for five neighboring villages, few in Marystown hadn't lost a child or youth to disease. Paddy had grieved two of his own, Cornelius and Mary Bernice, babies stricken by pneumonia. His wife, Lil, still mourned the infants who had been buried twenty years past.

The laughter of Paddy's son, Frankie, stirred the captain from his brooding memories. The boy sat in the wooden swing as other lads pushed the box, sending it skyward. Frankie's mouth widened into a grin, causing Paddy himself to smile. The boy didn't laugh often enough, Paddy thought; he's too serious for a child of twelve. Paddy had hoped fishing would loosen Frankie up a bit, give him more courage, confidence. But the lad was just too sensitive. Frankie's stomach had betrayed him on last summer's fishing trip, leaving him ill and retching. *Maybe this trip, me boy, you'll find your love of the sea.*

Paddy had no worries with his older son, Jerome. If anything, the lad had to be reined in. Two years older than Frankie, Jerome would have gladly dropped out of school to fish with his father. *Aye, there's plenty of time for fishing, me son,* Paddy had told him. *Plenty of time.*

Before they headed back to school, Paddy had promised the boys one final summer journey. In less than a week, they'd be heaving the anchor, sailing forty miles east, across Placentia Bay toward Cape St. Mary's fishing grounds. If the weather remained fair, Paddy had promised he'd let his sons set trawl from the dory with the rest of the crew.

Sensing someone's eyes upon him, Paddy turned to face a lone man dressed in black. The customs officer glared at Paddy and spit into the dirt.

"Afternoon," Paddy said. tipping his cap.

The local officer sneered at Paddy and muttered words beneath his breath. Paddy laughed, savoring the memory of the lawman's attempt to search Paddy's boat for liquor. Paddy had just returned from the nearby French island of St. Pierre, where rum was plentiful and cheap. A fifty-mile sail from Marystown, Paddy and other fishermen often smuggled the booze home in the hold of their vessels. The skipper had never paid any taxes on his liquor, and he wasn't about to start now. As the customs officer stepped on board Paddy's boat, he grabbed the lawman by his coat and tossed him into the bay.

"Jaysus, you son of a bitch! I can't swim!"

"I know," Paddy replied.

Paddy watched as the officer flailed in the water, his hands flapping like a puppet gone mad. When it looked like he might go under for the last time, Paddy bent down and pulled the man back onto the wharf.

Now on this August Lady Day afternoon, the customs officer sought revenge. He glared at Paddy and weighed what infractions he might use to lock the skipper up for a good, long spell. Perhaps this evening would provide an opportunity. He smiled at Paddy and muttered "*bastard.*"

Paddy clenched his fists and took quick steps toward the lawman. Before he could strike a blow, the skipper heard his name called across the field. The long black robes of Father John McGettigan slapped the priest's heels as he walked briskly to Paddy. Despite his stout frame, McGettigan moved quickly on his feet. His thick legs would serve him well today when the rum barrel emptied and the fights began.

"Ye ready for a row tonight, Father?" Paddy asked.

"Yes, I could see that you were ready now to pick a fight of your own. Don't you be starting anything, Paddy," McGettigan warned, though the priest knew there was no stopping Paddy, especially if the skipper had a few belts of rum in him. Like many of the Irish in Marystown, Paddy fought for pure devilment and distraction. Idle fishermen meant certain trouble, and McGettigan would have his hands full if Paddy joined in the garden-party brawls.

Of Scottish decent, McGettigan wasn't shy about using his fists to break up fights in his parish. Known as Father John "Bull" McGettigan, the priest had racked up many hours in the boxing ring sparring with his older brother, a heavyweight champion.

McGettigan's boxing skills came in handy on a Lady Day past, when a concerned wife knocked on the rectory door late one evening, pleading, "Father, you've got to come; the men are knocking each other out after drinking too much."

McGettigan grabbed his axe, strode past the brawlers, and splintered the rum barrel to pieces. Called to assuage a drunk during another garden party, McGettigan told the liquored-up fisherman, "Fight me if you want more trouble."

"I cannot hit ye, father, ye being a priest," the parishioner slurred.

McGettigan tore off his white collar and bellowed, "What's yur excuse now?"

Whether it was with his fists or his voice that boomed across the wooden pews at the Sacred Heart Church each Sunday morning, McGettigan ruled the rural outport of Marystown. The sight of the priest terrified children and adults alike. Small boys ran toward the woods if they spied McGettigan walking toward them along the dirt paths, errant husbands received harsh words during church sermons, and unwed pregnant women were married outside at low-tide water mark, publicly shamed.

Instilling the fear of God and pastoring the small community had taken its toll on McGettigan, who grew fond of rum himself. There was little in the fishing village that connected the priest to his privileged upbringing in St. John's, Newfoundland's largest city. Educated in Dublin, Ireland, at All Hallows College, McGettigan hailed from a family of wealth and education. During his seminary schooling, he read fine literature and poetry. He studied Shakespeare, sang tenor in Ireland's elite choirs, and learned how to play the violin and piano.

After he was ordained, he returned to his family home in St. John's, where he served as an assistant priest, enjoying the city's concerts, plays, and fine restaurants—luxuries that were stripped away when he received orders appointing him to Sacred Heart

Church in Marystown. In the village, there was nothing opulent about the hens and sheep that roamed the dirt paths or the pungent smell of drying fish stacked up on wooden stages that lined the shore.

And the well-to-do priest soon learned that parish coffers would suffer among fishermen who could barely feed and clothe their own families. During McGettigan's first mass, the collection box drew thirteen pennies. Thankfully, a few wealthy merchants and fishermen like Paddy contributed more than their share and invited the priest to their homes for Sunday dinners.

"Ye'll be getting a new pulpit when I get me next catch," Paddy had promised McGettigan.

As the afternoon sun slipped behind the clouds, McGettigan eyed his friend. Dark circles rimmed Paddy's eyes, making him look older than his forty-eight years. *How much longer will you fight the sea?* the priest wondered. The skipper had talked about leaving the fishing to his eldest son, James. Over the past decade, James had earned his due. He had sailed with Paddy since he was a young boy, learning to navigate by the stars, the compass, and the glass that foretold foul weather. Paddy had groomed James to captain on his own, taking over the helm from his father. But McGettigan knew pulling Paddy from the sea would be a rough go. The skipper grew ornery when he remained ashore too long.

"We'll be off to Cape St. Mary's next week, Father," Paddy reminded McGettigan. "Send us some of your blessings for fine seas and fair weather."

McGettigan laughed. He knew full well that Paddy did not rely on God to save him in times of peril. When storms blew in, most of the Catholic fishermen stood on the bows of their schooners and made the sign of the cross over the mountainous combers, beseeching the Lord and the Blessed Virgin to calm the swelling seas. But Paddy had no use for crossing the waves. The more the wind blew, the more defiant he became. Paddy often climbed to the top of the mast during a raging storm; his face to the heavens, he would shout, "I'm not afraid of ye!"

The skipper, the priest knew, relished a fight, whether it was with another man, the sea, or the Lord himself.

CHAPTER 4

THE FAMILY STORM UNRAVELS—NEW HAMPSHIRE, 2002

My father hunches over the computer, his two index fingers pecking awkwardly at the keyboard. He sits alone on dark winter nights, searching the Internet for details about the August Gale and his Marystown ancestors. He has little experience or comfort with computers, and his tap, tap, tapping is often punctuated with sighs and curses. But like any project or job he has pursued in the past, he grows obsessed with this task, and for hours at a time, he continues to search.

In part, I know my father does this for me, the daughter who is more comfortable communicating through the written, rather than spoken, word. The second oldest of six girls, I was what relatives called "painfully shy." My mother often joked that I never uttered a complete sentence until high school. I took comfort in books, pen, and paper.

While my reading and writing skills impressed my father, he sought to boost his timid daughter's confidence. Best man for his brother Bill's wedding, he surprised me with a request: "I want you to write the toast for me." Ten at the time, I chose my words carefully, crafting a poem for the occasion. In a crowded reception hall, my cheeks reddened as my father lifted his glass and announced, "My daughter, Barbara, wrote these words." I remember the pride in his voice and the applause. Years later, after high school teachers affirmed my father's encouragement, I pursued a journalism degree. My studies went fairly well until

I flunked a college magazine writing class; I had failed to turn my story in before grades closed. "You'd be better off pursuing photography instead of writing," the professor scolded.

Devastated, I walked along the campus railroad tracks. My writing career was over before it had begun. "I'm changing my major," I informed friends. "I'm no good as a writer." My father thought differently. "You have a gift," he told me. "You're a writer."

Now more than twenty years later, my dad encourages me to tell his family's story, even though this narrative pulls him back to a past he would rather forget. While I continue to work at my newspaper job, my father explores Newfoundland websites hunting for details about the 1935 storm and the schooners that Paddy Walsh and his son, James, sailed so many years ago. Hoping to piece together his family roots, he downloads the Marystown 1921 census. The eight pages of surnames read like the neighborhood tally in an Irish village: Kelly, Farrell, Kilfoy, Flynn, Mallay, Hanrahan, and Walsh. Among the 343 people living on the southern shore of Marystown, there are forty-three Walshes. My father's engineering mind methodically reviews each Walsh household, noting the ties to himself and Ambrose. He marks the pages with a pencil, underlining his grandparents, Thomas and Cecilia Walsh, and their surviving children: William Patrick Jr., Philip, Leo, Ernest, Angela, Cecilia, Ambrose, and Donalda. He circles their ages; in 1921 Ambrose is 13; his older brother Paddy is 34. The census lists Paddy's wife, Lillian, and their offspring: James, Lottie, and Theresa.

Paddy's future children, Frankie, Jerome, Lillian, and William Patrick Jr., are not yet born. Of the seventy-three homes on the southern shores of Marystown, Paddy is one of two families with a live-in servant (the other is a wealthy merchant).

With a bit of luck and his brother's help, my father finds a family member from Marystown: Paddy Walsh's granddaughter.

On a Canadian maritime website, Jamie (Walsh) Willet had posted her e-mail address and a note about her connection to the 1935 storm. Eager to talk with her, my father e-mails his second cousin, who now lives in Florida.

> *Hi Jamie*
> *My name is Ronald E. Walsh. I was born on August 12, 1935, in Staten Island, NY. My father's name was Ambrose. He was your grandfather's brother (21 years younger). My brother, William Patrick Walsh, was born on January 20, 1945. He is named after your grandfather.*

After explaining that he is looking for information on the August Gale and his relatives, he concludes, "I hope to hear from you."

Less than three hours later, Jamie's enthusiastic response, typed in large capital letters, sits waiting in my father's e-mail inbox.

> *DEAR RON. YOU SOUND LKE ME. I AM SO INTERESTED (in our family). WHEN I GO HOME I LOVE MY PEOPLE AND MARYSTOWN. THEY ROLL OUT THE RED CARPET FOR ME.*

Over the next week, Jamie and my father trade e-mails back and forth; Jamie sorts out the confusing list of half uncles, brothers, and sisters, and in between, she informs other Walsh relatives of her sudden connection with Ambrose's firstborn son, Ronald.

In just a few days, my father receives a surprise e-mail. The subject line catches him off guard. He reads the message several times before sharing it with me.

Sliding the piece of paper across my kitchen table, he explains, "This is from Ambrose's daughter."

"Ambrose's daughter?" I repeat, confused about this unexpected note from my grandfather's second family.

I begin reading the words that are crammed in one long paragraph, as if the writer had dared not take a breath, as if she had wanted to share these thoughts for many years.

Ambrose's daughter starts her note with an innocent "Hello," and I wonder if she refrained from using the salutation of "Dear Brother" for fear of offending my father with such an endearing term. Named after Ambrose's sister Donalda, she refers to herself as Donnie. In her opening lines, she explains that she had learned about my father through Paddy Walsh's granddaughter Jamie.

I received an e-mail from Jamie, telling me that she has been speaking to my brother, Ron; I told her I have never met you, but heard about you growing up. I knew I had two half brothers and always have been interested in knowing you, but was always a bit hesitant to do so, considering the situation of our father and what happened so many years ago. I don't understand how a man can leave his family and never look back. I was twelve years old when I found out about you; I am forty-three now.

The youngest of Ambrose's children, Donnie explains that she has four brothers and a sister, Kathy, who is the oldest in the family. Before Ambrose died, he had many misgivings, Donnie says. "One of his worst regrets was the sons he left; he said none of us could ever replace them." My father will later shake his head over Ambrose's sentiment, asking me, "How the hell could he say something so stupid to his kids?"

Ambrose's words stir both anger and sadness in me. Like my father, I cannot understand how he would utter something so callous to his children, yet I wonder how my grandfather's regret tarnished his life and his second family. I consider my father's half sister, my "aunt," who is five years younger than I am and living thousands of miles away, across the country in California. I imagine her carefully crafting her feelings, struggling with her own emotions and guilt. It is clear Donnie has a desire to ease the pain Ambrose inflicted.

I'm really sorry that things happened the way they did. I hope that maybe we can get to know each other. I don't need anything from you, except to know you and your brother; it has been a wish of my sister's and I for a very long time. You have been in our thoughts since the day we found out about you.

Donnie ends her e-mail explaining that she would love to receive a letter from my father, but understands if it is too difficult for him to write her.

"*Just know*," she concludes, "*that you are thought about very much.*"

I wipe tears from my eyes realizing my father's half sister offers the apology Ambrose never uttered. In the months since my father shared the story about the August Gale, he has also begun to share the memories of his childhood. He talks about his feelings in bits and pieces, recreating small snippets of time.

"I thought he was God," he tells me, recounting his early years with Ambrose. "I followed him around like a puppy dog."

I listen to these words closely, imagining my dad as a young boy, shocked by the abandonment of his father, his hero, the most important man in his life. I wonder what Donnie knows about my father. Does she know the details of his childhood in Staten Island and Brooklyn? Does she know Ambrose abandoned my Nana, uncle, and father not once, but twice? I hand Donnie's e-mail back to my father. He studies the words on the page and shares his reaction to her note.

"At first, I thought: Why is she writing to me? What am I supposed to say to her?" He had no interest or desire to talk with Ambrose's second family. Why would he want to talk with the children Ambrose chose over him? Knowing my father's reluctance to even speak Ambrose's name, I figure he will put Donnie's e-mail aside, like the feelings he has buried since he was a small boy.

But my father makes another decision. His voice is soft and low when he speaks. "What the hell. She is my half sister. I think I'm going to write her back."

My father's e-mail is short and to the point. Just as Donnie tried to ease his hurt, he tries to relieve her guilt.

Hi Donnie:

I am extremely impressed with your sensitivity, consideration, and openness in regard to the situation concerning our father. I don't have any bad feelings regarding you, your sister, or your brothers (nor should I). With my father, however, even after all these years, there remain some ill feelings.

I have lived in Pelham, NH since 1960. Born in Staten Island, NY 1935. I am married to a wonderful woman (Patricia), and we are blessed with six lovely daughters. (I am downright spoiled.) We also have eight grandchildren who are the joy of our lives.

Ron

Three thousand miles away, Donnie waits for her half brother's reply. She prepares herself for the possibility that his response will not be positive. She tells herself: *He could say that he just doesn't want to know anything about us. Or he could simply not write back. If I don't hear from him, I'll put this all to rest.*

When Donnie receives my father's e-mail, she squeals with relief and joy. She quickly writes her half brother back: "I feel like this is Christmas."

CHAPTER 5

"'TIS NOTHING BUT WORRY AND WAITING"— MARYSTOWN, AUGUST 1935

Lillian Walsh stood by the parlor window, her eyes focused on the bay below. From the mantel, a clock marked the time and its ticking seemed unnaturally loud, as if reminding Lillian of the hours that remained before Paddy and her sons set sail. She pressed closer to the panes of glass, her eyes following her husband as he walked along the dirt path toward the water and his wharf.

"Off to see how the crew is getting along, fitting out for the trip," he had told her. In a few days, they would all be at sea: Paddy, Frankie, Jerome, and James. It was worrisome enough when Paddy and James were out together on a single schooner, but now they'd be on different boats, James captaining his own vessel for the first time. The thought of it made Lillian sigh. *He's only twenty-three*, Lillian wanted to plead, but she knew better than to try and change Paddy's mind. "James will be fine, Lil," Paddy had reassured her.

"By Gad, he's ready to take the helm on his own. Did I not captain my own schooner at the age of twenty-three from Gloucester to Newfoundland?"

"Yes, ye did," Lil nodded, silently thinking, *But the boat ye sailed back from the Boston States 'twas a fine vessel, and double the size of the fifty-foot schooner James will skipper.*

Since the codfish prices had begun falling, nothing made sense anymore Lillian thought. It was daft to risk your life for fish that were all but worthless. There was little else but the sea to earn your living from; still, Paddy's younger brother Philip had opened a small shop and operated his own fish-drying business. "Why can't you stay on the blessed land, Paddy, like your brother Philip?" she'd asked him that morning. Paddy shook his head and said nothing, his mind lost on concerns he could not share with his wife. Of Paddy's four brothers, he and Ernest were the only two left captaining schooners. *Stuck in the ways of their father and grandfather before them,* Lillian thought. And the two of them as competitive as the day was long. How Paddy hated to hear his younger brother caught more fish than he. Such news would put him in a fierce mood for days. Cursing and muttering like a fiend, he'd be. *Dear God, would ye be certain Paddy hauls more than his brother on this journey? We could do with a bit of peace around the home.*

Footsteps from across the hall drew Lillian from her thoughts. In the dining room, the family maid dusted the piano, gently whisking the black and white keys. Lillian turned to the woman, watching her as she moved about, methodically sliding her cloth along the harp, the glass case filled with china, and the imported dining room chairs. Lillian eyed these gifts that Paddy brought home from his fishing trips or freighting dried cod to Portugal and Spain. She knew she was fortunate to have these treasures. Few houses in Marystown had store-bought goods; most of the fishermen's wives made do with homemade chairs and tables, curtains tied up with a bit of string rather than the thick metal rods that Lillian's plush drapes hung from.

But the luxuries mattered little when Paddy was at sea. Fine furnishings were all but invisible to Lillian then. The only things that drew her attention were the windows and the water below. A few days into her husband's journey, Lillian would set herself by the glass panes, watching, waiting for his return. The longer he was gone, the more she sat, stricken with worry. It seemed she had spent the last twenty-five years of her life looking out one window or another, praying for Paddy's safe journey. Like the other fishermen's wives, she fretted from the moment her husband left until the moment his boat breezed back into the harbor. The relief of seeing his sails on the horizon never failed to make her shudder, the pent-up worry releasing itself like a fever.

Flushed with the warmth of the room, Lillian pushed the parlor window open. A summer breeze carried the smell of fish drying along the shore. For as far as Lillian could see, fish flakes lined the beach. Rows of split and washed cod were laid out on the wooden platforms, waiting to be sold or shipped overseas. On the beach sand, women washed their husbands' catches in cold saltwater tubs. *Their hands were surely numb and raw by now,* Lillian thought. A baby wailed from its makeshift cradle, a bucket set near its mother's side. The infant's cry stirred sympathy from Lillian. *Thanks be the Lord, she and her three daughters had never dipped their hands in a fish barrel.* Nor did they have to contend with menial household chores. With two maids, Lillian and her girls did little cooking, cleaning, or gardening.

She knew her well-to-do status irked some of the other fishermen's wives, who barely had a moment's rest to themselves. She could only imagine their conversations, the words they whispered behind her back. "Did ye see the foxtail fur on her coat? And the fine shoes on her feet? She walks around like the Queen of Marystown, she does."

Lillian understood their jealousies. Most of the women worked from dawn to dusk, scrubbing the cod clean and laying it on the spruce boughs that topped the fish flakes. When they weren't hauling fish to and from the flakes, they were raking hay, planting, and tending gardens. Lord, they worked themselves to the bone, and it still wasn't enough to properly feed and clothe their children.

The silhouette of her daughter-in-law, Lucy, caught Lillian's eye as the young woman walked slowly along the footpath that hugged the bay. Lucy stopped suddenly, took a deep breath and rubbed her broad belly. *The baby was due any day now; there was no changing that fact,* Lillian thought. *What's done is done.* They had been lucky enough that Father McGettigan had married her son James and Lucy in the church. Lucy could barely hide her pregnancy beneath the white gown Lillian had stitched together herself.

Lillian eyed her daughter-in-law's long face; James was not yet at sea, and Lucy looked forlorn already. *Aye, there's plenty years of worry ahead, me girl,* Lillian thought. If she had a penny saved for every minute she spent staring at the sea waiting for Paddy to return, she'd be a rich woman indeed. Now, like most of the women in Marystown, Lucy would likely give birth while her husband was away. Surely, Paddy was only present for a few of the nine children she'd birthed. As Lucy slowly made her way toward the *Mary Bernice,* Lillian shook off a chill. She had heard Father McGettigan chastise women who had gotten pregnant before marriage: "You will have to atone for your sins!" McGettigan bellowed from the pulpit. "Dear Lord, forgive them," Lillian whispered, praying for her son and his new wife. "Forgive them."

The laughter of her two younger boys interrupted Lillian's thoughts. *What in the divil are they up to now?* From the window, she could see Frankie and Jerome wrestling in the meadow. The boys wore the new knickers she had made for their trip. Surely, they'd be tattered before they left town. She had stitched the boys a new set of clothes telling Paddy, "If ye will be going into port anywhere, I want the boys and yourself to wear your Sunday best." Of course, there was another occasion for which the boys and Paddy might need their fine clothes on such a journey, but Lillian pushed those dark thoughts from her mind.

She allowed herself a smile as she watched Frankie and Jerome chase one another in the meadow. *The two of 'em never stopped moving. Thin as spirits they were. It was no use trying to fatten them up; they devoured enough biscuits and beef to feed a grown man. In a few day's time, they'd be eating schooner grub, and it was likely that poor little Frankie would not be swallowing much a'tall as the boat rocked on the swells.* Lillian had hoped he would beg off this trip, but the boy would not disappoint his father, nor did he want the taunts from the local lads, who learned of his seasickness on last summer's journey. "Sissy," they had jeered. "Ye mustn't be Paddy's son after all. Poor little sick lass."

The thought of her boy ill and without his mother's hand to wipe his brow made her own stomach twinge. She knew Jerome would look after his younger brother, but Jerome himself was just a boy of fourteen. "C'mon," he cried to Frankie from the field outside, "let's go see Da. Race you!" Lillian followed their shirttails as they disappeared down the hill. It was just a short journey they were off to, Lillian told herself, a week away before the boys returned to their schooling. "Just a quick trip o'er Cape St. Mary's and Cape Race," Paddy had told her. "Nothin' to worry about."

At least it 'twas just a quick trip. Sure now, it could be worse with her boys dropping out of school to fish in the dories before they turned twelve. Paddy himself and most of the men and boys in Marystown had done the same. "No sense in schooling," the dorymen told their sons. "It's the sea where ye do yur learning. It's the sea that teaches and feeds us."

It's also the sea that takes ye, Lillian thought as she turned back to the window. Frankie and Jerome hollered from the wharf below, "Can we climb the rigging, Da?" Beyond the plum and lilac trees in the front garden, Lillian could see the masts of *Mary Bernice* and *Annie Anita*. The boats looked so small, Lillian thought. In these desperate times, she understood Paddy was lucky to have a vessel to sail, but they were a pitiful sight compared to the grand schooners he had owned in the past. *Mary Bernice* was a fifteen-ton boat and not much longer than fifty-five feet; on her deck, she'd carry two double dories, James, and his crew of four men. Paddy's vessel, *Annie Anita*, was forty tons and a seventy-five footer. She'd carry three dories, along with Paddy, his two young sons, and six men.

Lillian could not help but compare the schooners to the vessels Paddy had captained in the past: *Lillian, Swan, A. Davis*, and *Golden Glow*. Many of them were sixty-ton boats, capable of carrying six dories and fourteen men; they were schooners that could weather storms, rough seas, and trips to the Grand Banks, Greenland, Portugal, and Spain. How she loved the sight of Paddy returning in the *A. Davis*, his hand proudly on the helm and the wind at his back as he headed for his wharf, where he would drop the mainsail in a salute to his wife.

It just about tore him in two to lose that vessel, the last of his grand schooners. A few years past, the merchant's men had come with their legal papers while Paddy was in St. John's trying to settle his debt for the schooner. The creditors had knocked on her door and gruffly told her, "We're taking the *A. Davis*." They were not long gone when the steamer carrying Paddy back home glided into the bay. From the bow of the ship, Paddy glimpsed the *A. Davis* with its sails stretched tight against the wind. His fists flailing in the air, Paddy shouted curses as his schooner breezed toward the sea. If he could have caught the men before they slipped away, he would have killed them. That much Lillian knew.

Now he was left with these two schooners, one of them named after their daughter Mary Bernice, who had died of pneumonia. Lillian understood Paddy's sentiment, wanting to honor the memory of their lost child. *Skippers often named boats after their kin; but sure now, 'twas it not poor luck in naming a schooner after a baby who lay in the cold ground? Could that not bring ill fortune upon those who sailed her?* Misfortune had also fallen upon the vessel's previous crew. Before Paddy bought shares in *Mary Bernice,* she was caught in the 1927 gale; one of her crew had been washed overboard and drowned. *She's already lost a man,* Lillian thought. *What if the* Mary Bernice *is cursed?*

Paddy hushed his wife when she spoke of her misgivings. He had no use for premonitions, but Lillian looked for them in her dreams, in the sky, and in the noises after dark. In the small village of Marystown and its neighboring outports, Lillian was not alone in her beliefs. The superstitions and folklore had traveled across the Atlantic with the Irish immigrants who had made their homes in Newfoundland. The elder women knew the cures that could rid you of headaches and warts, infected sores, and boils. When the May snows fell, they collected and bottled the flakes to rub on tired and sore eyes; potions of kerosene and molasses were blended to soothe a ragged cough. From the graves of pious souls, they gathered pebbles to ease achy teeth; in the woods, they plucked juniper and dogberries for upset stomachs; and from the shores, they picked seashells and seaweed, the makings of a poultice for festering wounds.

They believed in the old ways, and the Marystown Irish heeded the omens and superstitions that had passed from one generation to the next. A fisherman's wife dared not conjure bad luck by calling her husband back once he departed out the door on his journey; she did not wave good-bye for fear a wave would sweep her man to his watery grave. And while their husbands fished the sea, wives took care not to overturn a bread or cake pan, lest they overturn or upset their man's dory or vessel. And never did a whistle pass their lips, for the sound would surely summon a storm at sea. 'Twas understood by all that "a whistling woman and a crowing hen, bring the devil out of his den."

Lillian and the ladies of Marystown guarded against a great many misfortunes, and they kept careful watch for omens of death. A picture or calendar falling off the wall, a moaning dog or a banshee wind, a broken clock that suddenly counted the hour portended a sudden passing of family or friend. Women and children quickly crossed themselves when a single crow flew overhead, warding off the blackbird's bad luck. Few of the young would venture out after dark or into the woods without a bit of bread in their pockets for the fairies or spirits that might cross their path. And how many wives had tokens, dreams of their husbands drowning at sea before they were lost? More than Lillian wanted to count. Her dreams were most vivid when Paddy was at sea. She dreamt of dark shapes, roiling waves, and horses galloping wildly, horses that heralded oncoming storms. When Paddy had shipwrecked *Golden Glow* on his way back from Prince Edward Island, hadn't her dreams haunted her? She heard cries among ragged waves, faceless men screaming.

The storm had blown in suddenly as *Golden Glow* sailed from Prince Edward Island past Codroy on Newfoundland's northwest coast. The winds and waves rammed the schooner onto the rocks, and Paddy and his crew scrambled into their dories, rowing safely to shore. Even Paddy's loyal sea dog floated in on the captain's sea chest. Days later, Paddy returned to Marystown unharmed with another yarn to share, one more story for the old and young lads on the wharves. There was only laughter in his voice as he bragged about boarding the train that took him and his men from the west to east coast of Newfoundland. As Paddy prepared to step onto the train, the conductor eyed the large black dog by his side. "Sorry, Skipper. No dogs allowed on the train."

"He survived the damn shipwreck like the rest of us," Paddy hollered. "He's coming on board." Paddy pushed past the conductor, the dog at his heels.

Paddy did not share the other details with Lil, the ferocious wind that toppled the boat like a toy, or how quickly the schooner sank beneath the water, the sea rushing through the gaping hole in her side. No, he never shared those stories with her; she was left to imagine them on her own, and she had no trouble coming up with those visions. No trouble a'tall. She had counted him dead many times, dreamt of the telegram, edged in black, that would bear the news of his loss. *How many years could he continue?* Lillian wondered. He was nearly fifty now, surely it was time to give up the sea as his two brothers who had left Newfoundland had done. Lillian thought of them now, Ambrose and Leo, both of them living in New York. Ambrose had never taken to the fishing. *Maybe he was the smartest of them all for it,* Lillian thought. Leo had sworn off the sea in 1922 after he and his brother Ernest nearly perished on a journey to Naples to sell a cargo of salted cod. They had left in the middle of September on *The Ria,* promising they'd be home in plenty of time for Christmas. With no word from the schooner, Christmas came and went. Lillian remembered how her younger sister Catherine, Leo's wife, was certain the vessel was lost with all hands. Six months and twenty days passed as the three-masted schooner fought its way through gales and pack ice before returning to Marystown.

Catherine nearly fainted at the sight of Leo. She had already begun mourning his death. When her senses returned, she had words for her husband, "Please God, I can do this no more."

Leo, his face still gaunt and strained from the journey, nodded.

Lillian had hoped the haunted look in his brother's eyes would make some sort of impression on Paddy. But it did nothing of the kind. Paddy had been sailing straight through since Leo's desperate trip thirteen years ago. *Stubborn old man,* Lillian muttered. A whistling teakettle roused her from her thoughts.

From the kitchen, the maid's voice inquired, "Would ye be wanting a cup of tea now, Miss Lil?" Hearing no response, Alice Brinton made her way to the parlor where she found Lillian sitting by the window. The maid took in Lillian's pale fingers, delicate and thin, wrapped around the arm of her chair, gripped as if she were holding on for dear life. Such a small slip of a woman, Alice thought, but she knew Lillian was as strong as the iron anchors that moored the boats in the bay below. No, she never cried or carried on inside or out of her home; she kept her feelings hidden deep beneath her dark eyes. Never did she raise her voice or utter a bad word. Proper as royalty she was. But she would have to be strong and proper now would she not? Being married to Paddy and all. One of them had to present some manners and civility to the children. Still, aside from Paddy's bluster and fondness for the drink, Alice knew Miss Lillian loved the captain like the day was long. Always wanting to be by his side, she was.

The young maid eyed the clock on the mantlel. Nearly an hour had passed while Miss Lil had been gazing out the window. Lost already she is. *A bit early to start fretting over this journey,* Alice thought. *But can't say that I blame the woman. 'Tis nothing for a fisherman's wife but worry and waiting. Sure, the men were gone away more than they were home.* Alice understood Lillian's concern. Her own husband, John, would soon be gone, too. He often crewed for Paddy, his mother's half brother. Alice's husband considered himself fortunate to work for his Uncle Paddy, a skipper who knew the fishing grounds as well as the meadow behind his home. But despite Paddy's keen skills, Alice would fret herself, a mother with three children of her own, and a new baby born last month. Not long after her husband John hugged her good-bye, her own dreams would soon begin, dreams of dark clouds and upturned dories.

CHAPTER 6

VICTORY SHIPS AND A SAN FRANCISCO TEMPEST— MY PARENTS' KITCHEN, APRIL 2003

The refrigerator hums, and the burst of electrical juice is jarring in the still and quiet kitchen. It is nearly one in the morning as my father and I sit alone at the table. I do not remember how or why the conversation began, but for the past three hours, my father has talked about his childhood and his feelings about Ambrose.

Over the past few months, he and his half sisters have been e-mailing back and forth, sharing information about themselves and their lives. Whether it is our research into the August Gale or the messages he writes to Ambrose's daughters, my father's past seems more present now. On this Easter weekend, I listen to his words closely, knowing that he has not shared these emotions since he was a young boy. When he talks, his brown eyes are focused on something I cannot see. He speaks in a fluid stream of memories, as if he himself needed to hear these words aloud. It is the San Francisco trip that prompts my father's voice to rise in anger; what happened there he cannot forgive or forget.

"After he left us in Red Hook, it was bad, but I cannot understand why he called us out to California. How the hell did he think that was going to work? I can never forgive him for that. Jesus," he says, his head shaking with the memory. "What my mother went through."

What about what you went through? I want to ask, but I do not.

A journalist for twenty-five years, I had written many stories about tragedies. I had talked to families who had lost children or loved ones to murders, suicides, and car accidents. I was adept at absorbing their sorrow, their emotions, and conveying them through the written word. Now I was gathering details about my own father's childhood pain, and the thought of asking my dad about Ambrose left me queasy, anxious. There is no distance here; there are no strangers in this story. The interviewing skills that I have honed over the last few decades do not work on this night. Here in my parents' kitchen, I am not a journalist; I am a daughter, overwhelmed by my father's memories, struck silent with my own sadness over his past.

These feelings of grief and concern for my father are new to me. When I think of him, I conjure images of him happy, spontaneously singing Frank Sinatra songs, crooning lines from one his favorite lyrics, "I've got you under my skin . . . New York, New York, these little town blues . . ." In my mind, he is steady, strong, the source of support and encouragement for my five sisters and mother. Years ago, after I graduated with a degree in photojournalism, I announced that I was traveling alone to Ireland to find work. My father did not question why; perhaps he knew I was running from failed confidence and my professor's belief that I would be better off pursuing photography instead of writing. Rather than find a reporting job in Ireland, I worked as a photographer for a weekly paper on the west coast in Galway. I photographed Gaelic football, fishermen sitting on ancient stone quays, tinkers begging for money, small Irish girls dressed like child brides on their First Communions. Taking pictures was easier than writing. There were no deadlines to miss. I was gone a year before returning home and falling into a comfortable job: working for a small weekly paper in the town where I had grown up. I wrote stories and took pictures. It was a role I felt secure in; there were no daily deadlines. When an editor from a nearby city newspaper called wanting to hire me, my gut told me to say no. There would be more pressure, more chances to fail. My father understood my fears. "You can do it," he told me. "Take the job."

My father has always bolstered my courage and understood my frailties. Now for the first time in my forty-five years, I see him as vulnerable, and it is odd and unnerving. He has always been the protector, the provider, but on this spring night as we sit alone, I find myself wanting to change roles with my father. But how does a daughter fix her father's past, repair the hurt inflicted so many decades ago? As the refrigerator hums in the corner of the kitchen, I sit quietly at the table and I fall back on what I have done since I was a small girl: I listen and put my father's words into stories.

I imagine Ambrose's son, a dark-haired child on the playgrounds of Staten Island, following his father's footsteps, eager to be in Ambrose's presence. The boy is too young to understand why Ambrose draws the attention of both men and women alike. The Newfoundland immigrant charms women with his easy smile. Men admire Ambrose's rough nature and enjoy his stories about his seafaring family's Newfoundland home.

Though he has but a sixth-grade education, Ambrose is quick to learn on the jobs offered by his father-in-law, Thomas O'Connell. A builder with an Irish temper and an eye for perfection, O'Connell is not easy to please. But when Ambrose begins working for his father-in-law, painting houses, sanding and shellacking floors, O'Connell is surprised at Ambrose's skill and work ethic. "He's the hardest-working goddamn Newfoundlander I've ever seen," he boasts to family.

Still, something about the dark-eyed immigrant makes O'Connell uneasy, but the builder knows there is little use in voicing his concerns. His daughter Patricia is crazy about Ambrose and refuses to acknowledge any harsh words about her husband.

When the Second World War comes, it brings opportunities for Ambrose with his knowledge of ships and sails. The young man who grew up on fishing wharfs and in schooners earns a job at the Arthur Tickle Engineering Works, repairing the torpedoed Liberty and Victory ships. In charge of the rigging loft, Ambrose supervises eighty men from all walks of life: bookies, tailors, sailmakers, carpenters, and dozens of Newfoundland immigrants. He convinces each of them they have the skills to repair the massive cargo steamships battered by German U-boats. Ambrose's crew learns how to sew rigging ropes and make canvas hatch covers; they master splicing cable two and three inches thick—sturdy wire rigging—that will keep the ships' one-hundred-foot-tall masts and five-ton booms strong and steady.

At the height of the war in 1944 and early 1945, Ambrose and his employees work seven days a week, twelve-hour days, and sometimes around the clock, repairing and rebuilding rigging for the 455-foot-long Victory ships. Pushed to return the cargo workhorses to sea as quickly as possible, Ambrose has little use for laziness or incompetence. Men find themselves knocked to the floor when their boss discovers shoddy work or overhears an insolent remark. The rigging loft crew quickly learns: Ambrose has a sharp temper and powerful punches.

Despite the respect and admiration Ambrose earns at work, the long hours take a toll on his family, which has grown to include another boy, William Patrick, named after Ambrose's brother, Paddy. While his mother tends to the new infant, Ambrose's son, Ronnie, looks for company. Lonesome for his father, he sometimes visits Ambrose on Saturdays. Ten years old now, he grins with pride when his father places his arm around the boy's shoulders and boasts to his crew, "This is my son Ronnie."

Ambrose's workers notice how the boy's face brightens, how the child seems to grow taller in his father's company. Left under the care of the men in the rigging loft, nearby sewing machines clatter as the child watches Ambrose disappear among coils of rope and sheets of canvas cloth.

Months later, when the war ends, Ambrose, like many of the workers at Arthur Tickle, is out of work. The money that once was plentiful is tough to come by. To pay the bills, Ambrose seeks odd painting jobs and is gone now for days and weeks at a time. In between working, he is also secretly meeting with a woman he met while his family vacationed at Long Island's Mastic Beach. Eighteen years younger than Ambrose, Arlene has honey-colored hair and a slim waist. Ambrose spends more and more time with her, and these sudden absences confuse Ronnie. The eleven-year-old boy grows angry and refuses to come in from the playground one evening to say good-bye to his father.

"Your dad was mad that you didn't come see him," his mother tells him.

"So what?" Ronnie shrugs.

In the fall of 1946, Ronnie is a seventh-grader, and Ambrose's second son, Billy, is nearly two years old. During the past year, as money has grown increasingly scarce, they have moved from a rooming house in Staten Island to a one-bedroom apartment in Stamford, Connecticut, to a small apartment in Red Hook, Brooklyn. Their new neighborhood is largely Italian, and Ronnie is singled out for his ancestry, quickly earning the nickname "Irish." With little money coming in, dinners are often onion sandwiches, day-old bread, and whatever the family can buy at the grocery with donations from the local Catholic charity. Patricia's sister, Eleanor, and her husband Eddie live on the second floor of the Red Hook apartment building, and they offer what they can to help, but they have little to give.

While Patricia becomes concerned about Ambrose's time away, it is not her nature to find fault in people; she wants to believe that Ambrose is looking for work when he disappears.

But she also knows that her husband has a gambling problem and that whatever money he earns often ends up in the bookie's hands or spent at the horse races. In between the worrying, she prays at the local Catholic church, The Visitation of the Blessed Virgin Mary, where she sits alone, bathed in the soft light of the stained-glass windows. Beneath the cavernous wooden ceiling that resembles the hull of a boat, she holds her Rosary beads and prays to God, "Please help me take care of my boys."

A month before Christmas, it is cold and dark when Ambrose closes the door of his family's Red Hook apartment and slips into Eleanor and Eddie's secondhand car. In his pocket, Ambrose has $800, an early payment Eddie received from a friend who hired him and Ambrose to paint his house. As his two sons and wife sleep, Ambrose drives to another part of the city and picks up Arlene. In her arms, she holds a baby girl. Ambrose wraps his new daughter in his coat and then drives toward the highway that will take them south. By morning, they will be several hours into their journey to Florida. There Ambrose has set himself up with a job working on a yacht that he will eventually help sail to San Francisco.

When her son wakes, Patricia tells her eleven-year-old boy, Ronnie, "Your father has gone away."

Later that morning she will inform her sister Eleanor, "He's not coming back."

"What are you talking about?" Eleanor will ask. "He stole our damn car and the money for a paint job!"

Christmas comes and there is one present under the tree, a miniature plastic bowling ball set. The name tag says it is for Billy. Ronnie sets up the bowling game for his younger brother, trying to hide his disappointment from his mother. Later, when his friends boast about all the gifts they received, Ronnie brags, too, making up imaginary toys that he found under the tree.

Several months later, they are back in Staten Island in a one-room apartment. Patricia has managed to get a job as a bank file clerk, and with the money she is able to feed and clothe her sons. Ronnie is in the middle of eighth grade when Ambrose calls.

"I miss you all," he says. "Please come to San Francisco. Bring the boys."

"Don't go," Patricia's sister, Eleanor, tells her. "Don't be a damn fool."

Patricia's older sister, Ruth, and her father also urge her not to leave, but the young mother is still in love with the dark-eyed Newfoundland immigrant. She quits her bank job, packs clothing for her two sons, and her nephew, Thomas O'Connell, a boy she has cared for on and off since his birth. She buys tickets for the four of them, fares for the trains that will carry them across the country. Ronnie can tell his mother is happy about her decision and the call from Ambrose; he hasn't seen her smile like this for a long time. He is happy, too.

"We're all going to be together again," he thinks. "My dad wants us back."

They board a train in New York's Penn Station, where Ambrose first arrived from Newfoundland nearly fifteen years past. Pressing their faces close to the train windows, Patricia's boys are eager to begin their journey that will take them more than three thousand miles, from New York to California, to see their father. Over the next day and a half, their train rumbles through the mountains of Pennsylvania and the flattened cornfields of Ohio. Soon they are crossing the Mississippi River, and when they wake up the next morning, the Colorado Rockies are rising straight up before them; forests, canyons, and roaring rivers pass before their eyes. They are far from Brooklyn's busy city streets and the small apartment where their father disappeared on a cold November night.

After traveling three nights and four days, they cross San Francisco Bay, where the city's skyline and the orange Golden

Gate Bridge greet their tired eyes. Ambrose welcomes them at the train station, hugging each of them. With the warm February sun and the palm trees that wave in the soft breeze, everything seems perfect. The cold and hardship of their lives in the northeast are a distant memory. They settle into a one-bedroom apartment in the nearby city of Mill Valley, where Ronnie sleeps on a cot in the living room. The apartment is cramped, but no one seems to mind. Everyone is content to be together again. For a while there are no surprises, no sudden changes, until Ronnie comes home to find his mother caring for a baby girl.

"Whose baby is that?" he asks.

"She belongs to a friend of your father's at work," Patricia tells her son.

Ronnie shrugs and helps his mother change the infant's diaper. He does not know that this is the baby his father had with Arlene, the woman who now lives in an apartment down the hill from their home, the woman who is too overwhelmed to care for her child now that Ambrose is living with his first family.

Each day while Ronnie is at school, Arlene walks up the hill that leads her to Patricia's apartment. Patricia makes tea and the two women talk while Arlene holds her child. Arlene is surprised at Patricia's kindness and her willingness to care for Arlene's daughter. But Patricia has always loved children, particularly babies, and this infant reminds her of her first child, the daughter she birthed stillborn and blue. Patricia still mourns the loss, and she will not let Arlene's infant suffer because of Ambrose's reckless choices. She also knows how upset Arlene must feel to be pushed aside.

"I'm not with her anymore," Ambrose has told Patricia, and she wants to believe him; she also understands she has little choice but to go along. She has moved her family across the country to be with their father again. She cannot afford to upset this reunion.

In the months ahead, Arlene takes her baby back to her own apartment, and Ambrose begins to spend more and more time at the horse races and the bookie joints. Unable to pay rent at their Mill Valley apartment, Ambrose moves his wife, Patricia, his two sons, and his nephew, Tommy, to another small rental in Union Square. Consumed with gambling, Ambrose rarely comes home anymore, and eventually he leaves for good. Ronnie does not understand his father's disappearance, and when he asks his mother, she explains, "Your father is living with another woman in Mill Valley."

Patricia does not share anything more or the fact that this other woman, Arlene, is pregnant again with Ambrose's child. As money grows increasingly scarce, Patricia, her sons, and Tommy move to a cheaper place, this time to a run-down hotel in the Mission District, a working-class neighborhood on the east side of San Francisco. There is one bed in the hotel room where Patricia and her youngest son, Billy, sleep. Each night, Ronnie and Tommy make their beds on the floor with their coats. In the morning, Ronnie rises at 4 a.m. to sell newspapers on street corners, earning what he can to help his mother. As he walks alone in the neighborhood, he sometimes glimpses his father near the bookie shop that is located a few streets away from their hotel. On the last time that he sees his father, Ambrose calls Ronnie to his side. He reaches into his pocket and pulls out a few coins. Tussling Ronnie's dark hair, Ambrose tucks the silver into his boy's hand. "See you later, son."

Ronnie takes the change, the coins cool in his palm. He watches Ambrose's broad back disappear into the darkened doorway. Inside the dimly lit room, there is smoke and shouting, men's voices excited about the horses that could make or break their bets. Alone, Ronnie stands on the street corner and and thinks about his mother. He knows she would not want him to take a nickel from Ambrose's hand. So he keeps the meeting and the money a secret, and for now on this San Francisco street, the thirteen-year-old boy still has hope that somehow his family is going to be okay.

His mother does not share her son's optimism. She knows in her heart there is no hope left; that she cannot rely on Ambrose for the truth, or a few dollars. Desperate for money, she fills out papers so she can collect unemployment. In this city of hills and fog, Patricia is stricken with dread and regret. She spends much of the day in bed crying or sleeping. Her nephew, Tommy, who is now seventeen, is worried about his Aunt Patricia and her deepening depression. He works as a clerk at a local bank and offers her most of his paycheck, but it is not enough to cover the rent and the grocery bills. Patricia rarely leaves the hotel room, and when she does, it is to walk the two blocks to pray in the Mission Dolores Church. The oldest building in the city, the church is named for the presence of a nearby stream, Arroyo de Nuestra Señora de los Dolores, or Our Lady of Sorrows Creek. Here in the whitewashed adobe sanctuary, Patricia cries her own tears as she kneels and asks God again to help care for her boys. Though this time, she does not have enough strength to wait for an answer. She returns to her hotel room where she considers jumping from a window.

The priest from Mission Dolores knows Patricia from her frequent visits to Sunday Mass, and he is familiar with her son Ronnie, who serves as an altar boy and sells newspapers after church. The monsignor feels badly for the young woman from New York, and he has done what he can to give her money for food and rent during her time of need. But he also realizes that Patricia has had a nervous breakdown and her sons are in trouble. He pays a visit to her motel room and knocks lightly on the door. When she rises from her bed, her eyes are rimmed red with tears. The priest offers her a hello and asks in a voice soft and low, "How are you getting on, Mrs. Walsh?"

Patricia does not speak, and her sobs fill the small room. Placing a hand on her shoulder, the priest shares his words slowly, and he tells her as gently as he can, "You've got to get better, Mrs. Walsh, or the state is going to take your children."

The priest's admonishment stirs Patricia from her stupor. Misfortune has already claimed her firstborn, and she will not allow anyone to take another child from her. When money from her older brother is wired to San Francisco, she buys four tickets for the long train ride back to the northeast.

In my mind's eye I envision this scene: my Nana crushed by Ambrose's betrayal, his lies, his decision to call his family out to San Francisco only to abandon them again thousands of miles from their home and their relatives. I consider her pain, the unbearable hurt of being pushed aside again for Arlene. Her shock at learning Arlene was pregnant with Ambrose's second child. Her anger and shame at being duped by Ambrose twice in two years. Her wishing she had listened to her father and her sisters, who warned her not to move her sons across country. How she must have felt later after it all unfolded: A complete fool to have trusted Ambrose. Yet, I know too how blinded she was, how deeply she loved Ambrose; he was her first and only love, and now he has shattered her heart.

She was so pure, so trusting, my Nana. I can understand her wanting to believe Ambrose's words. Wanting to mend her broken family. Wanting a father for her sons.

Billy is four, too young to understand his father's absences. But Ronnie, at thirteen, is just a few years shy of becoming a man himself, of figuring out the world and his place in it. I imagine my father's fury that begins brewing in San Francisco, like a storm gathering strength from the wind and waves. The resentment and pain welling up inside him, the questions that bubble up: Why did my father leave us? Why did he do this? The confounding and tormenting lessons that his role model, his hero, offered.

I cannot fathom the strength of my father's emotions, the power of his feelings. I only understand the wrath I feel for a man I've never met—and those emotions offer me a modest appreciation of how deep my father's feelings must run.

Lost in our own thoughts on this April evening, my father and I are silent, each reliving the past. The refrigerator hums once again, lulling us both in the still house. I glance at the clock that hangs on the wall behind me, surprised to see that it is a few minutes after 1:00 a.m. My movements pull my father back to the present, and he glances at the clock too. He sighs and pushes his chair from the table. "Guess we should go to bed, Barbsie," he tells me, harkening back to my childhood nickname.

I nod and stand myself, reaching up to hug him goodnight. "I love you, Dad."

He softly replies, "I love you, too," before turning down the darkened hallway.

CHAPTER 7

GATHERING A CREW—MARYSTOWN, AUGUST 1935

The salt cascaded from the fish tub like winter snow. Granules skittered across the merchant's wharf, turning the wooden boards white as the schooner crew unloaded their catch from the hold.

Two fishermen grunted as they pulled lines, hoisting a fish tub from the vessel to the dock. Hooked by its iron bail, the large container swung precariously in the air, catching the schooner captain's eye. "Careful with that tub!" the skipper hollered, waving his cap. "Ye spill that fish, I'll split yur head!"

The captain's threats drew laughter from the dorymen who repaired their flat-bottomed boats along the wooden pier. "Aye," one veteran fisherman muttered, "The old man sounds like he could do with a drop of rum after his month out on the Banks."

The dorymen nodded and turned back to their task, scouring every inch of their vessels. They searched the fifteen-foot dories from stem to stern, looking for leaks or cracks between the planks; they checked the lines, straps, tholepins, and buoys, ensuring their boats were seaworthy and prepared for waves that could sink or flip the small dory in the frigid Atlantic Ocean.

A soft breeze swirled around the men as they worked, carrying the ever-present odor of fish that enveloped the village from spring to fall. It rose up from the schooner holds, where layer upon layer of salted fish awaited the market scales; from the cod livers fermenting in nearby puncheons; and from the shore rocks, where discarded entrails enticed seabirds that darted and pitched, fighting over the blood-red remains.

Oblivious to the pungent odors that hung in the warm summer air, captains and cooks stood on schooners alongside the wharf, bellowing orders to their crews as they hauled food supplies onto decks. Barrels of salted pork and flour rolled like thunder toward the fo'c'sle, sacks of peas and sugar, jugs of molasses, and bags of beans passed from one pair of thick hands to another down the stores' hatch.

Across the bay, a dory edged toward the pier. The ferry master pulled his oars, his strokes even and strong, as he transported his passenger from the south to the north side of Marystown. The passenger's broad shoulders caught the fishermen's attention.

"Aye, there's Captain Paddy coming over."

As the boat angled toward the pier, the men glimpsed Paddy's dark eyes beneath his cap.

"What kind of mood ye think he's in today?" one of the dorymen joked.

"No telling with Captain Paddy, he can turn like the wind, but one thing is certain: The skipper will be happier once he gets out to sea."

"Aye, he's had a rough go this year not getting that commissioned boat."

The dorymen remembered the talk around the north and south sides of Marystown at Paddy's fury over the lost government-built vessel. He had been promised shares in the schooner. A seventy-footer, she would have carried six dories and sixteen men. The vessel could have handled the monthlong trips to the Grand Banks and beyond, but after gathering a crew, Paddy learned that the government ran out of money before his boat could be completed.

"You'd of thought he was going to beat someone bloody over that one," a veteran doryman nodded as his calloused hands scrubbed the hull of his dory clean.

After promising his smaller schooner *Mary Bernice* to his son James, Paddy was left without a boat to sail as the March ice thawed.

"Do you remember Paddy's face after his brother Ernest arrived with his first catch this spring?"

"Aye, Ernest had thirty quintals of fish on deck, and here Paddy is wit' nothin'."

"Paddy 'twasn't happy about that one. Him usually being the big fish-killer and his brother home with more than three thousand pounds of fish before Paddy's even got a boat beneath 'im."

Eager to haul home more fish than his brother, Paddy quickly found himself another boat, buying shares in *Annie Anita,* a small schooner owned by the merchant James Baird. Other captains might have struggled to find another boat so quickly, but Paddy had told his crew they'd sail in March, and the skipper never went back on his word, especially when it came to fishing.

"He's like a dog to fish," a gray-haired doryman agreed. "Gad himself would have to strike Paddy dead to stop the skipper from setting out."

The fishermen nodded to one another. They had witnessed Paddy's resolve in years past when his newly built schooner *Lillian* had got stuck in the spring ice.

Built up in Creston on the upper reaches of Marystown's Mortier Bay, Paddy had been eager to sail the new schooner that he had proudly named after his wife. But the March winds had blown bitterly cold, and the bay was still frozen over when it came time to ease the thirty-ton boat off its cradle.

Still, the ice did not stop the skipper from launching his schooner. From the north and south shores of Marystown,

Paddy's shouts could be heard: "Free rum to any man who will help haul a schooner over the ice!"

Paddy hollered to the land from his horse and cart as he dragged a barrel of rum along the frozen bay. By the day's end, one hundred men had lined up along the ropes tethered to the *Lillian's* bow. They pulled the fifty-foot schooner a mile and a half over the ice until it broke free and slipped into the open water.

"Jaysus, that was some sight," laughed one of the dorymen. "Paddy ladling out rum from his horse and an army hauling the boat for 'im."

The sound of a dory scraping rocks pulled the fishermen back to the August morning. As the ferry master dragged his boat to land, Paddy stepped out onto the sand. The dorymen quickly shed their grins and put their thoughts aside; they knew better than to smirk in front of the skipper.

"Morning, Capt'n," they offered, tipping their caps.

"Morning, fellas," Paddy replied, his eyes taking in the men's worn clothing and tattered leather boots.

"How's the crew shaping up for yur upcoming trip, Skipper?"

"Fine, boys. Got a good crew for James and myself."

"If yur needing another doryman, I'm available, sir," offered a young, red-haired fisherman.

"Thanks lad, but I'm set for now. Yur turn will come soon enough."

The dorymen's eyes followed Paddy as he walked toward Baird's store. Paddy could feel their gaze as the conversation continued behind him. He knew the men were hungry for a spot on a schooner. A lot of lads were having a tough go this season. Not enough work to go around when skippers had trouble financing a boat. The merchants and boatbuilding firms had cut back on hiring captains to sail their schooners. Poor prices for the fish produced fewer profits for the merchants, who were holding tight to what cash trickled into their coffers. While the lower prices meant Paddy himself earned less for his catch, the strain on the fishery offered the captain his pick of skilled dorymen. He took comfort knowing he had lined up some experienced hands for James on his first journey as skipper.

Paddy went over their names in his mind: Dennis Long, Michael Farrell, Billy Reid, and Richard Hanrahan. Hanrahan had not committed to Paddy yet, but the skipper was hoping he could convince the seasoned fisherman to accompany James. Like most of the dorymen, Hanrahan had been fishing since he was a small boy. The same age as Paddy, Hanrahan had weathered his share of narrow escapes and understood the subtle changes in the sea. If James turned ill on the trip or a storm blew in, Paddy knew Hanrahan could sail the schooner home. But the doryman had spent the spring and summer starting his own fish-drying business, and Hanrahan was not keen on returning to the sea.

"I'm trying to keep me boots on the land," Hanrahan had told Paddy a few days earlier. "Want to be home with me children and wife."

Paddy understood Hanrahan's desire to be with his family, but he pressed the fisherman. "Just one more journey to help me and James out. It would ease my wife Lillian's mind if you'd be there to watch over her son."

Hanrahan told Paddy he'd give it some thought. The captain pushed open Baird's wooden doors and reminded himself to visit Hanrahan later in the day. Inside the darkened shop, kerosene lanterns hung from the walls. Paddy adjusted his eyes to the dim light and walked past the barrels of sugar and tea. From the rafters, new oilskins hung, the stiff-coated garments stirring like spirits when the shop door swung open. Paddy eyed the glossy and new garments, goods he knew that few dorymen could afford. Most of the fishermen reapplied layer after layer of linseed oil to their own pants and coats, oilskins that continually cracked and split, weathered by the unrelenting wind and salt of the sea.

Making his way past cases of fishhooks and coils of rope, Paddy walked toward the center of the store. A couple of retired fishermen sat by the potbellied stove, their thin fingers whittling small sticks. Paddy breathed in the scent of the wood fire that mingled with the sweet smell of the molasses dripping from a nearby barrel.

"Fine day, Mr. Paddy," one of the men offered. "Water is c'am. Be good day to set out."

"Aye t'would be," Paddy replied. "We'll be off soon enough."

Paddy nodded to the gray-haired fishermen and walked toward the back of the shop. From the shelves, tins of canned vegetables glinted in the dim light, stirring Paddy's memory of a winter morning five years past. He remembered the women's voices, desperate and high-pitched, on the verge of tears, begging the merchant's clerk to give them a bit of food to feed their children. When he saw the clerk shake his head at the women, angrily waving them away, Paddy stormed past the young man and climbed the ladder that leaned against the shelves. Grabbing tins of food, he tossed them down to the gaunt faces that stared up at him.

"What do ye think you're doing?" the clerk had sputtered, his eyes startled and wide.

"Just write it all down in yur damned ledger," Paddy hollered.

"But their credit is no good, Mr. Paddy," the clerk stammered.

"Well put it down on my credit then, boy!"

This winter, Paddy knew, would test more of Marystown's families. There would be more burials and more weeping mothers, children lost over some foolish disease their weakened bodies could not fight. The raised voice of a man at the shop counter drew Paddy's attention.

"What are ye talking about?" the fisherman yelled.

Paddy recognized the man's broad shoulders and blocky build. From the back, the fisherman could have been Paddy's twin.

"Don't let them rob ye, Reid!" Paddy shouted.

Paddy's second hand did not have to turn around to put a name to the loud voice. Tom Reid had heard the old man holler more times than he'd care to remember. *Jaysus, if ye dared slack off at sea, his shouts and curses would cure ye of ever taking a moment's rest again.* Though he never challenged the captain when they sailed, Reid gave Paddy his due when they were back on land, where the two friends had gotten into a few rows now and again. Usually the brawls started after they had drunk several jars from the liquor still they'd hidden in the woods. Drunk or sober, the two of them were as stubborn as the day was long. They could argue over just about anything, how to mend trawl, tie a knot, or fell a tree. Still, Reid wouldn't crew for any other skipper. Paddy's gift of finding the fish was almost frightening. It was as if the captain could sense the cod beneath the sea. "There!" he'd holler, pointing to a patch of dark water, like God or some spirit had secretly guided the skipper to the heartiest fishing grounds. "Put the anchor down, boys. There's plenty of fish below."

The soles of Paddy's leather jackboots echoed in Baird's cavernous shop, stirring Reid from his memories; he turned to face Paddy.

"Morning, Skipper."

"How are ye getting on with the grub?" Paddy asked.

"Seems the merchant could use some persuasion," Reid said. "They're wanting to give us one sack of flour instead of two, and they're cutting back on the molasses and salt pork besides."

Paddy eyed the young clerk who stood behind the counter. The dark-haired boy was no more than seventeen years old. The captain smiled and reached into one of the glass candy jars that lined the shelves. Tossing a peppermint knob into his mouth, Paddy leaned forward on the counter and asked in a voice, soft and low, "You're not going to give us any trouble are ye, son?"

The skipper's voice rose as he continued, "We've got two boats to outfit with twelve men and two boys. Are ye telling me my credit is no good?"

"No sir, I mean, Mr. Paddy, sir," the clerk stuttered. The boy had often heard Paddy roar at the weigh masters when they took stock of Paddy's catch, deciding the cod's worth. The top-quality and high-paying fish went to Portugal and Spain. The poor, broken-up fish were marked for the West Indies and paid bottom dollar.

"Gimme the highest price," Paddy often bellowed to the weigh masters. "Or I'll kill ye!"

The boy wasn't sure if Paddy had ever laid a hand on the weigh master to prove his point, but he wasn't about to test the skipper on this August morning.

"Sure thing, Mr. Paddy," the clerk replied, his eyes falling to the shop floor. "We'll get ye fixed up right."

"That's better, lad."

Reid shook his head as the clerk took quick steps toward the back of the store. "Now why is it he is so eager to help ye and not the likes of me'self?"

Paddy grinned. "Might be because of yur ugly mug."

Reid laughed at the skipper's remark, relieved Paddy was in a fine mood this morning.

"Has Hanrahan agreed to go along with James?" Reid asked.

"I'm off to pay him another visit now," Paddy said turning toward the door. "See if ye can finish getting the grub without a problem now."

Reid waved Paddy off. The skipper had been a bit queer lately, quiet with an odd, faraway look to his eyes. Paddy, Reid knew, like the rest of his crew, had worries on his mind. No matter how many quintals of fish the captain brought home, the price didn't seem to add up to the cost of the backbreaking work.

Reid could hear Paddy now, commanding in the predawn hours aboard *Annie Anita:* "Bait up, boys!"

The work would begin at 2:00 a.m. in the blackest part of the night. The dorymates would bait two thousand hooks on their mile and a half of trawl lines. Their fingers cut and bleeding, they'd load their dories with the four trawl tubs, oars, and gaffs. One by one, the fishermen would step into the small boats, where they would be hoisted up over the schooner rail, swung out, and lowered away.

In the dark with nothin' but the light of their torch to see by, it was fearful enough, but add the wind and a strong sea and the send-off could be terrifying. Reid knew many a man who shut his eyes and prayed as the dories swung over the rail. There were plenty of stories about boats that hit the water cockeyed and capsized their men into the sea. Sometimes they were saved, grabbed by the collar of their oilskins or pulled up with the gaff, but other times the men weren't so lucky. With their heavy leather jackboots that came halfway up their calves and the oilskin pants that quickly filled with water, the flailing dorymen might as well have cement shoes on their feet. *'Twasn't more than a few minutes and the poor lads disappeared in the cold sea. Gone before anyone could save them.*

Most of the time the dory send-offs went smoothly, and they'd be off with their assigned courses from the skipper. Reid and his dorymate always took care to note the schooner's mooring on their compass before they left the boat. To ensure their return, they counted each stroke as they pulled the oars, knowing how many hundred pulls would place them back to the mother ship. A half mile out, they'd drop their first anchor and buoy, tossing out their baited hooks. End to end, they'd tie their twenty-four lines that stretched along seven thousand feet of the sea floor.

Two hours later, their trawl tubs would be empty, and they would be famished and dog-tired, stiff from stooping over the rails of their boat and setting trawl. When they got back on board, they'd have a bit of grub belowdecks, and then it was back in the dory, rowing back out to their buoy marker to check their lines. If luck was with the dorymen, they would haul one fish for every ten of their two thousand hooks, flipping the gray-green cod one after another into the bottom of their boat. When the dory was loaded up, they would row back to the schooner, fork their fish onto the deck, and then head back out for another set.

If the catch was good, there would be no slacking back. Ye'd make four hauls, working day and night. "Back out, boys!" Paddy would holler. *Ye'd be so tired ye could barely stand on yur feet.* Reid had seen men fall face-first into their grub or pass out in the hold as they forked their fish into a pile. Sometimes they'd work seventy-two hours straight without a break. "Fish are running, boys," Paddy would shout. "Put the dories o'er!"

When they could finally turn in, they'd collapse in their bunks stinking of the sea and fish guts. And then there was the weather, the cursed fog that blanketed the seas in summer. *Be black, thick with fog and ye could barely see yur dorymate at the other end of the boat.* Reid himself had gone astray in such weather. *Despite the compass and the course ye'd chart from the schooner, there were plenty of times ye got turned around. Ye'd try to keep yur senses, listen for the schooner's horn, but the fog played tricks on yur ears.* The sounds grew muted, muffled. There were times Reid and his dorymate would go astray for days, their fingers blistered and blood running from their palms as they pulled the oars. *In between sipping water from yur jug and taking bites of hardtack, ye'd do plenty of praying, holding tight onto yur miraculous medal, asking Our Lady to see ye home.*

Unlike some rough and coldhearted skippers, Paddy never gave up on his men if they were lost. The captain stayed out searching for his dories in the night and day, sending men up to crosstrees to scout for the lost boats and cranking the schooner foghorn for hours on end. *Course, when he finally located ye, there'd be hell to pay.* "Did you lose your damn compass and your senses?" he'd holler, his face turning red with rage.

Besides the fog, there was the dirty weather, the wind and big seas that would come out of nowhere. *The fuller the dory, the more ye had to fight to keep the boat steady.* Reid knew many a man had drowned, lost to a watery grave, because the dory had been weighted down with fifteen hundred pounds of fish, the gunnels a few inches above the sea. *If the breakers came in the boat then and swamped the dory, ye had little time to clean her out. Ye'd be throwing the fish overboard then as fast as ye could, bailing the boat and praying ye'd get her cleared before the next wave hit.*

Reid himself had plenty of scares over the past thirty years. *Sometimes ye'd think this is it, the end is coming. I'll never see me family or me wife again. But ye'd keep bailing, keep praying, and somehow ye'd pull through. And the fear that rose up in yur throat would be gone until the next time—when the wind and waves would rise.*

Dory fishing was miserable old work on a good day, Reid thought, *but when the weather was foul and the fog thick, it could be a God-fearing experience. It was a darn rough, rough way to make a living, always shivering cold and wet, knowing yur life could be over at any minute.* Many years past, an old fisherman told Reid, "Anyone who would go dory fishing for a living would go to hell for a pastime."

Aye, 'tis nothin' truer than that, Reid thought as he waited for the clerk at Baird's to return to the counter.

Outside in the thick morning air, Paddy walked the dirt path along the bay, his mind working over how he'd convince Hanrahan to accompany James on his upcoming journey. A raspy cough disturbed his thoughts and Paddy knew McGettigan couldn't be far behind. The priest's perpetual hacking announced his presence long before anyone spied his black robes. Terrified of McGettigan's booming voice and stern gaze, children ran into the woods as soon as they heard the priest's cough.

"Morning, Father," Paddy offered at the sight of the stocky priest coming over the crest of the knoll.

"Morning, Skipper," McGettigan answered before drawing on his cigarette.

"When ye going to give up those terrible things, Father?"

"As soon as you do, Paddy."

"Aye, when the Labrador Current warms up like the Florida sea, I'll give it some thought, Father."

McGettigan laughed and tossed his cigarette to the ground.

"What are you doing taking a leisurely stroll? I'd have thought you'd be busy barking orders at your crew, getting them ready for the journey."

"Still gathering the crew. In fact, I was hoping ye'd give a poor ole skipper a ride to Little Bay in your skiff."

"You may be old, Paddy, but poor you're not. I could show you some poor people."

"Save yur preaching for Sunday, Father. Will ye give me the lift or not? I've got to have one more talk with Dick Hanrahan. See if he'll go along with James's crew."

McGettigan caught a glimpse of worry in the skipper's eyes before Paddy looked away. Paddy was proud of his eldest son, James, but McGettigan also knew that the upcoming journey as captain would test the young man. While Paddy had little fear of death or anything else, James did not share his father's confidence. Though he never voiced his concerns over his son, Paddy had asked McGettigan to say a few extra prayers over *Mary Bernice* as he blessed her this spring past. The priest remembered the look of concern on Paddy's face as he sprinkled the holy water on the boat's bow. McGettigan had heard the older fellers talk about *Mary Bernice*. "She sits high in the water now doesn't she? Even when she has a load of fish in her. She's a'needing more ballast in 'er."

Still, Paddy had fished off *Mary Bernice* without a problem. The priest reckoned James could do the same. As the skiff pushed off from McGettigan's pier, Paddy took in the view of his three-story home on the southern shores of Marystown. With its white picket fence and its thick double front door and twin chimneys, the house stood out among the smaller cottages. First built as the Molloy Hotel, the home rivaled the town's wealthy merchant houses with its mahogany ceilings, scrolled banisters, and stained-glass windows. Paddy had bought the old hotel for his wife soon after he married Lil, knowing she had admired the grand structure since she was a young girl.

During a recent game of cards, Paddy had confided to McGettigan that the merchants wanted his home to pay off the mounting debt the skipper owed for fishing gear and supplies. As he steered past Paddy's wharf, McGettigan watched Paddy's lips tighten as if he wanted to strike something.

"The creditors still after your home, Paddy?"

"The bastards would like to get a hold of it, but they won't be getting their hands on it. I put the house in Lil's name. They'll have to look elsewhere for their damn money. They want to come through my door, they're going to have to kill me first."

"Well then, I'd have to bury you and say kind things about you at the altar, and you know how I hate to lie, Paddy."

Paddy turned to the priest and laughed. *Things could be a lot worse for me and me family,* he thought. His family wasn't on the dole like a third of the country, relying on government relief and its paltry six cents a day. And his seven children weren't eating blackbird soup or begging for vegetables door to door.

The two men fell quiet as the green hills of Little Bay came into view. Paddy always enjoyed the sight of the small village, one of the last outports he saw before venturing out to sea. McGettigan steered toward a small wharf and cut the throttle. Paddy grabbed the rope and tossed it to a young lad standing on the wooden pier.

"Thanks for the lift, Father. Save a bit of yur St. Pierre rum for me when I return from the Cape."

"Aye, Paddy. I might save a drop for you."

Paddy nodded and turned toward the hill that led to Richard Hanrahan's home. Before he made it halfway up the path, Hanrahan stepped out his door and began walking toward the skipper. Paddy noticed the doryman's gait was slow and unsure, his head bent low as if just he'd lost a battle.

"Morning, Richard."

"Morning, Capt'n."

"Give any thought to going along with James?"

The fisherman fell quiet and rubbed the middle finger on his right hand. Paddy knew Hanrahan had broken the finger years ago when a block of ice crushed it in the fish hold. The finger remained crooked and bent, a constant reminder to the doryman of the dangers he faced at sea.

"Aye," Hanrahan said, lifting his gaze to meet Paddy's eyes. "I'll go."

Paddy shook Hanrahan's hand and patted his back.

"Lillian will be beside herself with relief."

"My wife Angela's not so happy with my decision, Skipper," Hanrahan said, his voice low and flat. "She doesn't want me to chance the sea any longer. But our cupboards barely have a crust of bread in 'em, and the children are getting little more than vegetables and broth for dinner."

Hanrahan turned to the sound of his daughter laughing in the field behind his home. Barefoot, the girl's spindly legs raced toward her father.

"'Tis no way to raise a family," Hanrahan said quietly. "Me salt-fishing business isn't doing as well as I'd liked. There's no hope of making do except in me dory hauling trawl."

Paddy took in the sight of Hanrahan's modest home. Clothes snapped on a rope line, and rows of plants peeked from beneath the black soil. From the kitchen window, a curtain fluttered, and a shadow disappeared beyond the thin cloth.

"I'll make sure yur treated well on this trip, Richard," Paddy assured the fisherman. "It'll be worth ye going. Yur cupboards won't be bare for long."

Hanrahan nodded, knowing he had no choice but to believe Paddy's words. His shoulders bent forward, the doryman turned and headed back up the hill where he knew his angry wife waited.

CHAPTER 8

THE SISTERS GATHER—NEWBURYPORT, MASS., MAY 2003

Deep into the night, after the dinner plates have been cleared and the margarita pitchers emptied, I slip Ambrose's name into the conversation. At the mention of our grandfather, my sisters fall quiet, the laughter and loud conversation halts. Their faces grow solemn, serious, as if I have informed them of a relative's sudden death.

"He was a bastard," my older sister Diane says, her voice flat and factual. "He never gave Dad, Uncle Bill, or Nana a nickel. He abandoned them, and that was it."

Pragmatic and unflinchingly honest, Diane, or Dede as she is known in our familial circle, is never shy in offering her opinion. The other sisters silently ponder her words. We sit, the six of us, around a dining room table littered with salt-rimmed glasses and bags of pretzels and potato chips. A cold rain lashes the windows, and bells from the nearby Immaculate Conception Church toll multiple times, reminding us that it will soon be midnight. Before I mentioned Ambrose, conversation spilled from three different directions, our voices and laughter drowning out the music from the living room speakers.

Gathered for an overnight at my sister Janice's Newburyport home in Massachusetts, we are together for what we fondly call "a sistas weekend," twenty-four hours with no children or husbands. Traveling from our various homes in Maine, Massachusetts, and New Hampshire, each of us had arrived earlier

that afternoon. We feasted on mussels, chicken stir-fry, aspar-
agus, salad, and homemade bread. The evening hours passed
like minutes as we swapped stories about husbands, boyfriends,
kids, jobs, and our parents. In the past, during other weekends
together, we had often gone out for drinks or to dance, but as
we've grown older, we realized there is no need to leave my
sister's dining room table, where we can laugh and cry and tell
each other things we will not or cannot tell anyone else.

Known as the "Walsh girls" in the small town of Pelham,
New Hampshire, where we grew up, we were mostly birthed
within tidy, two-year intervals with nine years separating the oldest from the youngest. Born in 1966, the twins, Janice and Joan,
brought up the tail end of the family; two sisters, Jacqueline and
Laura, held up the middle; and my older sister Diane and I (Irish
twins born eleven months apart) shaped the older end. The six
of us look alike (dark hair, freckled skin) and have similar mannerisms (talking with our hands, hugging often, and punching
people as a form of saying hello). Many of our characteristics,
we have come to realize, mimic those of our Great-Uncle Paddy
and our grandfather, Ambrose. "We can be," I told one sister,
"vicious on a good day." We have quick tempers, sharp tongues,
and are competitive with everyone else and each other, a trait
which prompted my twin sisters to brawl on the basketball court
during one high school home game and spurred two other sisters to nearly kill themselves trying to beat each other in a local
road race.

Our own Irish clan, we are stubborn, fiercely loyal, and protective of one another and our parents. An insult or hurt to one
is a wound to all. Family gatherings, birthday parties, holiday
dinners are frequent affairs, and there is nothing that makes any
one of us happier than to be together, in each other's company.
"Blood is thicker than water," my father often told us when we
were younger, and I felt this so deeply that I was terrified when

my sister Jackie announced in 1985, "I'm getting married." I cried when she told me. I left her multiple notes in her Volkswagen Beetle: "Don't do it," I begged. My feelings had nothing to do with her fiancé, whom I liked; it was more that I saw her marriage, the first among the sisters, as an unnatural separation, a fracturing of our family. My irrational fears proved unfounded; decades later, as four out of the six sisters raise their own families, we remain so close, so adamantly faithful, that our friends often remark, "You guys are like the Mafia; you're lucky to have such a strong family bond."

So it comes as no surprise on this rainy May evening that the mention of Ambrose stirs a flurry of deep and raw emotions in each of my sisters.

"I don't care about him," Jackie says, her eyes focused on the napkin she folds into small squares. "I never knew him. I don't have any emotion toward him. I don't want to care about him. He didn't care about Dad, Nana, or Uncle Bill."

The resentment in my sister's voice surprises me. A middle sister, Jackie is often the first to defuse anger, to forgive. It is rare for her to speak ill of anyone; she is the peacemaker, quick to encourage her sisters to "be nice," to brush off ill-tempered or unintentional slights. Yet, she is not willing to do this for our grandfather.

After listening to my father recount what happened in San Francisco, I have my own strong feelings about Ambrose. I want to ask my grandfather, "Why? How could you leave your family, abandon them twice? How could you live with yourself?" My grandfather has been dead now for thirteen years, succumbing to colon cancer in June of 1990. In the years before his death, his daughters Donnie and Kathy grew closer to him. They came to understand and appreciate their dad despite his flaws. I consider Donnie's words in her first e-mail to my father, her conflicted feelings about Ambrose: "I know when Dad died he had a lot of regrets, and that's something he had to work out with himself. Dad was not perfect in any way, a bit spoiled, no, he was downright spoiled. We butted heads a lot as I got older; but I could always call him and he would be there for me; that is what I will remember about him, of the good he did and not what he did in the past."

Ambrose's daughters loved their dad unconditionally, like my sisters and I love our father. Throughout their childhood and adult lives, Donnie and Kathy witnessed their father's loyalty. They had no fear that Ambrose would repeat his past, leaving them as he did his first two sons. There had to have been good in him, I tell myself. He embodied more than his worst mistakes. But his mistakes, his abandonment of his children—my father—were so wrong I cannot see past them. I know my emotions taint my grandfather's image; I can only see the dark side of his character. Yet, I know there is more to him.

"No one person, no story is ever black and white," a veteran newspaper editor once told me. "There are always many shades of gray." It was a lesson I heeded over my thirty years as a reporter. My editor's words echo in my ears on this cold spring night as I halfheartedly pitch Ambrose's positive attributes to my sisters, characteristics that I know will not be well received.

"Some people believe Ambrose was a good man," I offer. "A lot of people, his ship-rigging employees liked and respected him."

My sisters cut me off before I can continue. A few of them shake their heads in disgust.

"So what if he did some good things, think of what he did to Dad," Janice says, her voice rising with disbelief and rage. "How could he be so heartless?"

"But he's our *grandfather*," Janice's twin, Joanie, argues. "He's our blood, our stock; he is what we're made of. Dad isn't just all Nana. Ambrose is a part of who we are. We're all intuitive, good with people. Dad had the knack to motivate people who worked for him, and that's from Ambrose."

Emotions and words arc back and forth between the twins. Tapping her chest, Joanie argues that Ambrose is in each of us, in our "genes." Janice shakes her head refusing to consider Ambrose's blood, his DNA that tethers us to him. Like my father, she is repelled by his decisions, his betrayals.

The twins' voices rise as they argue, their passion drawing raised eyebrows from Laura, who sits between them. Four years older than Janice and Joan, Laura is hesitant to voice her thoughts on Ambrose. Like Jackie, the other "middle sister" Laura is not likely to jump into a conflict or argument, preferring instead to shrug her shoulders and utter "whatever." On this evening, she sits quietly as her green eyes follow the conversation that escalates around her.

"He was so selfish," Janice says.

"We don't know what was in his mind," Joanie admonishes. "You can't judge him."

"After what he did, why the hell shouldn't we be able to judge him?" Janice hollers back.

Knowing that if the twins continue to argue, they may leap across the table and throttle each other, Dede, the eldest, intercedes. "Joanie's right," she agrees, her voice low and calm. "Like it or not, Ambrose is part of our family, our history."

"He may be our family," Janice says, "but we don't have to forgive what he did."

After so many years of not knowing, of not thinking of our grandfather, it is odd to hear my sisters debate his morals, his decisions, with such fervor. Derived from the Greek *Ambrosios,* Ambrose's name means "immortal, undying," Strangely, though we have never met our grandfather, his deeds and his decisions live on in each of us.

Regardless of their feelings, my sisters are thrilled with the news that my father has decided to travel to Newfoundland. The conversation shifts toward this less contentious topic and the unlikely trip that he will make in June.

"I can't believe he is going," Joanie says.

It was Joanie who had called our parents' home several weeks ago and told our father, "I want to go to Newfoundland."

My father did not hesitate in his reply: "Have a nice trip." He had no desire to visit Marystown, to see Ambrose's birthplace, or to acquaint himself with relatives he had never met. What was the point? Ambrose had died more than a decade ago.

But Joanie persisted. "I want to know more about where we're from."

Knowing Joanie was not going to relent, I agreed to go with her, but I did not care to learn more about Ambrose. I wanted to discover more about my Great-Uncle Paddy Walsh and the August Gale. Chasing a killer storm was easier than trying to figure out my grandfather and his heartless choices. When my father learned we both planned to journey to Marystown, he reluctantly agreed to come along. "Alright," he sighed. "I'll go with you."

As the church bell rings tolling midnight, my sisters and I begin to clear the empty glasses and cocktail napkins from the table. "It's good he's going to Newfoundland," Dede says, before retiring to bed. "It's good you're getting him to talk about all this."

I nod, but I am unsure of whether it's good or not. Since I have begun asking my father about Ambrose, both of us have lost sleep. My father has lain awake thinking of his childhood, his anger, the hurt his mother endured. I lose sleep wondering: *Why am I stirring up bad memories?* This is not a newspaper story that I can distance myself from. This is my father's story, and I am not sure where it will take us. I only know that I do not want to harm my father, to cause him more pain.

That night, I lie awake in one of my sister Janice's spare bedrooms, eyeing the sliver of street light that falls on the comforter. From across the nearby parking lot, the Immaculate Conception Church bell tolls once, and I know that I will hear it several more times as it rings at 2:00, 3:00, and 4:00 in the morning. Across the bed, Dede punches her pillow, unable to fall asleep herself.

"Nana used to tell me stories about Ambrose sometimes," she tells me.

"What stories?" I want to know.

"She used to talk about how he had another family in California," she says. "She'd bring him up sometimes when I'd drive her home to Watertown."

The Boston suburb of Watertown had offered Nana a new start when she returned from San Francisco heartbroken, shamed, and penniless in 1949. Unable to pay rent or buy food, Nana relied on the generosity of her sisters and brothers.

"She was very quiet when she came back," Nana's sister Eleanor remembered. "She just felt bad. It was a miserable time for her, and a miserable time for the kids."

Bounced from one house to the next, my father felt like a gypsy, a beggar. It was then, at the age of fourteen, that his bitterness against Ambrose took seed. "I'm through with him," he told himself. "I don't ever want to hear his name mentioned."

The new kid at Watertown High, Ambrose's son had two strikes against him. He was from a broken home in 1949—a time when few families dared to even talk about divorce—and he was also poor, living in an affluent town. Angry, he used his fists to quiet anyone who dared tease him.

Without money to buy winter coats, his mother stayed up till dawn knitting her sons sweaters so they would have something warm to wear to school in the morning. She also took the only job she could get, washing dishes in a small restaurant.

Her boys ate dinner at the counter for free as they watched their mother in the back kitchen, bent over a sink scrubbing pots and pans. "I hate this," her eldest son thought as he reluctantly ate his food. "Poor Ma."

My father's memories create pictures in my mind as I struggle to sleep in my sister's Newburyport home. The image of my Nana's face, her soft white curls, the scent of her perfumed Cote face powder stir fond remembrances. She was my hero, the grandmother who taught me pig Latin and to play penny poker. A storyteller, she told me and my sisters scary tales as we took walks over dark bridges or along dirt roads. Mounds of dirt became castles, tree branches transformed into the fingers of unseen ghosts. When we visited her Watertown home, she tickled us until we cried, fed us as much candy as we liked, and when it came time to leave, she could never bid us good-bye. "See you in the funny sheets," she'd tell us. Saying good-bye brought back the memory of her mother's death. She was four as she stood by her mother Bridget's bed, silent and scared. "Good-bye," her mother said with her last breath.

After her mother passed, Patricia's father married a feisty Irish woman from County Galway, a woman who was not afraid of standing up to her husband. The last of seven children born to Tom O'Connell's first wife, Patricia often retreated to the porch steps as her stepmother and father bickered and hollered.

"She got nervous when they shouted," Patricia's sister Eleanor recalled. "She was a soft, soft individual. If you'd ask her for something a second time, she'd give it. If anything went wrong, you could always go to her."

It also was not Patricia's nature to complain, and despite the sorrow Ambrose inflicted upon her, she never spoke a bad word about him. Yet a few months after she returned from San Francisco, she confided to Eleanor: "If there is such a place as hell, I hope he ends up there."

"He'd probably talk his way out of it," Eleanor quipped.

The two sisters shared a laugh over Ambrose's ability to talk at length about any given subject.

More than fifty years later, laughter is not on my mind as I think of my grandfather and the pain he wrought on a woman who spent her life caring for others. My older sister's words spoken hours earlier on this night return to me in the dark.

He was a bastard.

CHAPTER 9

FATHER MCGETTIGAN'S TORMENT— MARYSTOWN, LATE AUGUST 1935

Lizzie Drake started at the slam of the kitchen door.

The young woman kept her eyes focused on the potatoes in the sink as Father McGettigan pushed a chair from his path. *Aye, he's in a fine mood this evening,* Lizzie muttered to herself. As the August days waned, she had noticed the priest's demeanor growing increasingly sour. Just the other night, he'd kicked her bucket of suds over upon his return from counseling a family, parents who had lost their beloved baby to pneumonia. Lizzie had been kneeling there on the kitchen floor, scrubbing his own holy footprints, when he stormed in and upturned the water in front of her. Not a word he said to her then, nor now. Not that twenty-year-old Lizzie wanted the reverend to speak to her; she had little to say to the gruff priest. *'Tis better off there be few words among us,* she thought. And with these desperate times, she knew she was lucky enough to have a bed in the parsonage attic and a bit of beef on her plate. The four dollars a month wage she received for her housekeeping and cooking duties was a bonus that she was grateful for.

Still, the priest's presence kept the maid jittery as a boiling teakettle. She wondered if the absence of McGettigan's dog, Jocko, had anything to do with the reverend's foul moods. If he regretted the dog's passing, he was likely the only one in Marystown to harbor remorse. The creature, big and black, taller than

Lizzie herself when it stood on its hind paws, was worse than the devil himself, terrifying everyone that walked past the parsonage. He had attacked the poor and rich alike; tearing the coat off a well-to-do missus from the north side—a coat that the priest later paid a pretty penny to repair. And then there was the unfortunate soul, the fisherman passing by the priest's home on his horse and cart. Jocko charged the horse, so frightening the large animal that it tumbled in the dirt, tipping the cart and tossing his master to the ground. The fisherman never recovered from his head injuries, his sufferings severe enough to render him a cripple, no longer fit to earn his living by the sea. And the worst incident of all, to be sure, involved poor Tommy Flanagan. Cornered by Jocko as he ambled past the priest's home, the simpleminded lad grabbed a broken piece of picket fence to defend himself. His teeth bared, Jocko leaped toward Tommy's face. Terrified, the boy struck the dog with the sharp end of the picket, unintentionally poking the animal's eye out.

The sight of his bleeding and injured pet had outraged McGettigan, who demanded swift retribution from the local constable. "Give the boy whatever punishment the law can!" he ordered. A few days later, Lizzie and the local women watched from their kitchen windows as the sixteen-year-old youth huddled in the back of the constable's horse cart, destined, the poor lad, for the nearby jail in Burin town. Lizzie whispered prayers as Tommy shivered in his oilskins, his only shield from the winter wind. Confused and cold, the boy would serve his two-month sentence without a clue of what prompted his confinement.

Aye, Jocko could terrorize whomever he liked, Lizzie knew, until the dog turned on the priest. Not long after Tommy served his jail time, Lizzie remembered McGettigan's eyes, black with rage, as he dragged Jocko outside and shouted: "I want this dog drowned tonight!" She ran through the woods to fetch the priest's handyman in the winter cold. Her heart pounding and her breath visible before her, she knocked on Billy Baker's door. In short gasps, she explained how Jocko had bit McGettigan's ankle after the priest tried to kick the dog's bone from its mouth.

A longtime caretaker for the parsonage, Baker knew there was no sense in trying to convince the priest that Jocko's demise could wait till daylight. When McGettigan made up his mind, no one but the Lord himself could change it. The handyman nodded to Lizzie and turned to grab his coat. From her attic window, Lizzie watched as the priest and Baker motored into the middle of the bay. Jocko, a water dog always eager for a boat ride, sat in the bow with a rope around his neck, the far end of the line wound around a large rock. McGettigan held Jocko's bone in his hand and Baker would later recount the priest's words as the reverend tossed the dog's treat into the deepest waters of the harbor: "Go fetch it, Jocko!"

No, the unruly animal didn't terrorize anyone after that night, Lizzie thought. As she continued scrubbing dirt from the sink full of potatoes, the summer sun blazed red in the sky. A fine night it 'twas. *Too bad his holiness was not enjoying the brilliant sunset. Himself always talking appreciating the gifts from the Lord, yet the priest was all but blind to the smell of the sea and the glimmer on the harbor bay.* Lizzie knew the priest had settled in the parlor to begin his nightly bout of brooding. She heard the consistent creak of the rocking chair, a certain clue as to how the evening would play out. *He's in there alone again with his dark thoughts.* Soon he would be pouring himself a glass of rum, and then she knew the night would slip away from him in a haze of liquor and smoke. Perhaps he would write some of his poetry for a bit, or read one of his books penned by that Shakespeare character he rambled on about. Lizzie knew he pined for his high-society crowd, his family, and the friends he had left behind in St. John's. There were certainly no fine restaurants, bookstores, or high-browed plays for McGettigan to attend in Marystown.

The best he could count on were the local school performances and the ceili dances at St. Gabriel's Hall. Still, the local fishermen had little to say to the priest besides "How ye getting on, Father?" There were few folk educated past sixth grade aside from some of the local merchants, Dr. Harris, and the constable.

Of course, then there was Capt'n Paddy, whom the priest had grown close to. The pair of them got on famously despite Mr. Paddy's scant years of school learning. But whatever the skipper lacked in books smarts, he made up for with his brawn and fearsome talent at sea. McGettigan dined at Paddy's grand home many Sundays, but the skipper was often on his schooner more than he was on land, leaving the priest alone to stew in his morose moods. Yet, on those lonesome nights, there had always been Jocko to comfort the reverend. The two of them had sat there before the roaring fire for hours, McGettigan rocking in his chair with a glass of rum by his side and the dog stretched out before him on the rug. *Surely the old fellow missed his scoundrel of a dog. Did the reverend feel a twinge of guilt for drowning his loyal companion? Sure now, even if he harbored remorse, the priest could absolve himself for killing the animal. He could offer himself absolution for just about anything now couldn't he?*

Lizzie heard the chair stop rocking and quickly pushed her musings from her mind. She listened closely for more hints to the priest's intentions. *God forbid his holiness's dinner was late.*

In the parlor, McGettigan stood and reached for the glass decanter on the table before him. He poured himself a generous amount of the amber-colored rum and sat back down in his rocker. Taking a sip from his glass, he drew in the scent of the sweet liquor he purchased from the nearby French island of St. Pierre. *'Tis at least one benefit to living in this isolated outpost,* the priest thought. Rubbing his temples, McGettigan sighed. Dusk had not settled in on the shores outside, yet he could easily retire to bed for the night. Over the last few months, a deepening fatigue had overcome the middle-aged priest, a leaden feeling he could not seem to shake. *Was it the summer heat,* McGettigan wondered, *or thoughts of the long winter ahead?* No, the priest knew it was more than the frigid temperatures that froze the bay over into thick sheets of ice. On Sunday mornings, he could hardly bear to look down upon Marystown's families as he preached from the pulpit. They sat, the men, women, and children, in the wooden benches looking to him for hope, for guidance from God, for a sign that soon things would get better; that they would have something more than turnips and potatoes for dinner, that soon the fish prices would rise again like they had before these miserable times had emptied their cupboards and forced them to live like their ancestors in Ireland: desperate and hungry, with no chance of a future, no belief of a better tomorrow.

Ah, how could he expect anyone to listen to his sermons, about the love of God, the fear of the Almighty, when their stomachs rumbled and ached from the emptiness? He saw it in the fishermen's eyes, their defiant glares, the anger and resentment of working so hard for so little. Even his good friend Paddy, who was never troubled by anything a'tall, appeared worn down, burdened by his mounting debt. McGettigan had done his best over the past nine years to bolster the spirits of his parish and to grow the community as well as the economics allowed. He had brought in the Sisters of Mercy to better school the children; he had built a new parish hall and a new school. He had counseled and chastened Marystown's wayward sinners, broken up more fights than he cared to count, married young and naïve couples, and baptized innumerable babies. In return, the village men and women offered him what they could: spare vegetables, an odd chicken or two, a bucket of milk, a few pennies in the collection box. From the start of his appointment at Sacred Heart Church in 1926, McGettigan had admired the determination of Marystown's men and women, how they made do with so little, how they kept their pride despite their tattered clothes and humble homes. But by the mid-1930s, the will and fortitude of the fishing community slipped away like the tide; despair and death shrouded the outport like the smell of fish that hovered incessantly in the parsonage meadow.

In recent years, he anointed holy oil on the foreheads of far too many of Marystown's young and old, parents and children, their malnourished bodies succumbing to epidemics of tuberculosis and pneumonia, typhoid and diphtheria; diseases that routed the small village like a blighted crop. McGettigan murmured the prayers of the Extreme Unction over their bodies in their final hours. The scent of the sweet balsam oil and the voices of weeping mothers returned to him now as he uttered the Latin words that had become so familiar to him: "*Per istam sanctam unctionem et suam piissimam misericordiam, indulgeat tibi Dominus quidquid deliquisti. Through this Holy Unction and through the great goodness of His mercy, may God pardon thee whatever sins thou hast committed.*"

There was nothing more horrible than counseling the mothers who lost their babies to the illnesses that killed the tiny souls with swift vengeance. He would rather fend off the Black and Tans, as he did in Dublin during his seminary days at All Hallows, than listen to the wails of the grieving mothers. Their shrieks haunted him at night when he tried to sleep; he tossed and turned, willing himself to forget their screams, to conjure instead the shouts of the Black and Tans, the British auxiliary soldiers who had marched onto the fields surrounding the Irish seminary. *Aye, he'd fight a dozen of the Black and Tans again on the soil of Drumconda, rather than meet the eyes of a child who understood he would never grow old.*

Across the narrow swath of bay, children's voices cut through the quiet night air, echoing across the water; their singsong words and joyful cries carried through the meadow and into the open parlor window, pulling the priest from his grim thoughts. McGettigan stood and turned to the thick panes of glass and focused his gaze on Paddy's wharf. Across the inlet, the skipper's young sons, Frankie and Jerome, ran toward the deck of *Annie Anita*. Their small duffle bags dwarfed their thin frames as they climbed on board with their gear. Further along the pier, McGettigan spied Paddy's broad silhouette as the skipper walked to his sons.

The priest knew the skipper planned to depart not long after midnight this evening. McGettigan took in the sight of Frankie's slight frame. The boy now stood quietly, perhaps fretting over his seasickness and his fear of the water. *Ah,* the priest thought, *the lad would gladly stay on land for the rest of his life, if it was not for the shame of being a sissy, a lass who could not weather the sea like his father and grandfather before him.*

McGettigan watched as Paddy's eldest son, James, stepped on board the *Annie Anita,* joining his family on deck. The slender young man squared his shoulders as he looked up to his father's eyes. Paddy placed an arm around James's shoulder and drew him close, offering him words, advice the priest figured, guidance about the sea and the fish to be caught beneath the shoal water. McGettigan knew this journey, James's first as a captain, would set the course for the young man's future, and there was no son more eager to prove himself and earn his father's pride. *But what a father to live up to,* McGettigan thought. *How does a son measure up to a fearsome legend like Paddy? Big boots to fill, my son,* McGettigan whispered. *Big boots, indeed. May God watch after you all. Fair winds to ye.*

From the kitchen table, Lizzie peeked through the parlor door. She glimpsed the priest's profile in the window, the serious look beneath his spectacles. She could hear Paddy's laughter across the bay, and she knew that it was the skipper who had captured the priest's attention. *Aye, the captain would soon be off, and then the priest would miss his weekly card game and laughter with Paddy. 'Twould be no one around to distract the reverend from his gloomy thoughts. She'd make herself scarce this week, she would. She didn't want to have another bucket of suds upturned on her. No, indeed. She'd leave the priest alone with his moods and his fierce temper. No telling what he'd do in the next fortnight if he had to bury more of Marystown's young and old. No,* McGettigan, she knew, *could not bear to counsel another woman keening over a dead child or a lost spouse.*

Another tragedy, Lizzie reckoned, would drive him mad.

CHAPTER 10

PICTURES OF THE PAST—MAINE, JUNE 2003

I had never seen my grandfather's eyes. Never glimpsed his face. I had never even considered what Ambrose looked like. Now on this summer morning, I stare at a photograph of my grandfather, mesmerized. For several long minutes, I take in every detail: his tanned skin, thick brows, his dark eyes, broad smile. *This is Ambrose. This is my grandfather.*

The photograph is one of three that I receive in an e-mail from my father. In the electronic note, he does not comment or share his opinion about the pictures; he simply passes them along with a message from Jerome Walsh, my father's second cousin who lives in Marystown, a relative we will meet when we travel to Newfoundland in a few weeks.

The former mayor of Marystown and a genealogy buff, Jerome has researched the family back to the early 1700s, accumulating hundreds of photographs, including these three he has sent my father. The first picture I pull up on my computer screen is a black-and-white image of my grandfather; he stands between his two brothers, Leo and Ernest. All three men are smiling, their arms wrapped around each other. The youngest of the brothers, Ambrose's hair is jet-black though bits of gray peek from his sideburns and his mustache. His head is cocked slightly to the right; his smile is natural, confident. He appears happy to be among his brothers.

He wears a T-shirt that shows his muscled and trim physique. He is strikingly handsome, his features reminiscent of Clark Gable. His older brothers appear to be in their seventies and eighties; Ambrose is perhaps in his late sixties.

While Leo and Ernest are light-skinned, pale, Ambrose's face is tanned from the warm Californian climate of his home. His gaze meets the camera straight on, and I magnify the photo several times, until Ambrose's eyes and his thick brows fill my screen. I search for guilt, remorse, recognition of wronging his first two sons, and his wife Patricia. But there is no malevolence or sorrow, only softness, an impish glint in his brown eyes, eyes that remind me of my father.

The second picture portrays Ambrose many years earlier. He and his brother Leo stand in a garden in front of Leo's Staten Island home. The summer flowers are in bloom; carnations and petunias frame the picket fence that rises up behind the two men. In his thirties, Ambrose wears a short-sleeve, buttoned-down shirt, trousers, and a tie that is loosened around his neck. While Leo smiles and stares at whoever is taking the photograph, Ambrose's gaze is unfocused, haunted as if he had just learned of some terrible news. His left hand is clenched, ready to strike something or someone. His shoulders slump forward, his mouth remains slightly ajar, like he had been suddenly sucker punched. I wonder what troubles my grandfather in this frozen moment of time. Was the photograph taken in August 1935? Snapped days or weeks after Ambrose had learned about the August Gale that tore up Newfoundland's coast? Was it the killer hurricane that preoccupied my grandfather?

Except for the wedding band on my grandfather's left hand, there is no hint of my Nana in the photograph. Was she standing in front of Ambrose and Leo? Did she take the picture? Or was she inside her home, cradling her newborn son, Ronnie, holding a warm milk bottle to his mouth.

Unlike the other picture in which my grandfather poses for the camera lens and flashes an easy smile, this image captures him unguarded, off kilter. He is vulnerable, lost, and I wish I could step into the photograph, step back in time to learn what has disturbed him, left him with the punch-drunk gaze.

I open up the third and final picture of my grandfather and a wave of anger washes over me. In this snapshot, Ambrose is in his late sixties or early seventies. He and his second wife, Arlene, sit at a table. Their heads tilt toward each other, touching. Arlene's honey-colored hair is swept back in a chignon. She wears a dress and a dark cardigan; her thin lips blush with color and press together with a hint of a smile. Her eyes are almond-shaped, her cheekbones high, chiseled; she is a beautiful woman.

Ambrose rests his forearm on the table, his mouth is open, forming a word, as if he were telling the photographer: "Hurry up and take the goddamn picture!"—a phrase my father often utters when anyone takes too long to snap the shutter button.

There are white crumbs scattered on the table before Ambrose and Arlene and the edge of what looks like a sheet cake on the photograph's border. Were they celebrating an anniversary? Marking the decades they had been together? They seem comfortable, at ease with one another and their opposite personalities—my grandfather: blustery, full of himself, a charismatic character; Arlene: reserved, shy, and unsure.

Just as I never imagined my grandfather's face, I never considered Arlene's likeness. Scrutinizing her portrait, I realize that I do not have any strong feelings against her. Oddly, I do not harbor anger for this woman who allowed my Nana to care for her firstborn, who shared tea with my grandmother in a small San Francisco apartment, and who ultimately won Ambrose

Portrait of William Patrick "Paddy" Walsh circa 1910 as a doryman sailing out of Boston, Mass.

Portrait of Lillian Ducey Walsh shortly before her January 1912 marriage to Paddy Walsh.

Patricia O'Connell Walsh (on the left) and Ambrose Walsh soon after their April 1929 wedding.

Paddy Walsh with Jerome (center), Frankie, and Lillian in their garden circa 1928.

Paddy Walsh and his children,
Paddy Jr. and Lillian, circa 1933.

COURTESY OF WILLIAM PATRICK WALSH JR.

Paddy, Lillian Walsh (center), and unknown woman standing by the Ford Model T
Paddy owned with another Marystown businessman.

COURTESY OF WILLIAM PATRICK WALSH JR.

Frankie (center) and Jerome Walsh with their Uncle Philip Walsh circa 1927.

COURTESY OF
WILLIAM PATRICK WALSH JR.

Frankie and Jerome Walsh in a boat circa 1927.

COURTESY OF
WILLIAM PATRICK WALSH JR.

*Captain James Walsh
circa 1931.*

Father John McGettigan, Marystown priest, 1926–1936.

*Captain Paddy Walsh's house,
the old "Molloy Hotel," was
one of the largest homes in
Marystown circa 1930.*

Schooner similar to the
Mary Bernice.

Schooner similar to the
Annie Anita.

Annie Anita *doryman*
George Mitchell.

Annie Anita *doryman*
Dominic Walsh.

Mary Bernice *doryman*
Richard Hanrahan.

back. My hostility is reserved for my grandfather, the married man who strayed with a woman ten years his junior.

I shut off the computer, erasing Ambrose and Arlene's faces from my screen. Still, the image of my grandfather lingers in my mind, resurrecting my father's stories about San Francisco and the difficult years that followed. These photographs give form and flesh to my grandfather. He is suddenly real to me, no longer faceless, vague, undefined. My memory now can conjure Ambrose's eyes, his muscular build, and thick forearms—characteristics that live on in my father.

From my own scrapbook, I pull photographs of my grandmother. There are three sepia-colored prints. Two of them depict my Nana when she is seven or eight. In one image, she stands with four younger children, her half brothers and sisters from her father's second wife. My Nana, Patricia Mary O'Connell, wears a white dress with a sailor's collar accentuated with a broad dark tie. Her blonde hair is cut in a pageboy, and several strands are pulled back in a bow. There is a smile, pure and innocent, on her face. She is pretty, and at this moment, the future of the successful Irish builder's daughter holds only promise and prosperity.

A picture taken ten years later shows my Nana sitting on the front steps of her Staten Island home, her arm wrapped around Eleanor's back. There is another younger girl, perhaps another sister, in the photograph, too. Nana and Eleanor both wear dresses, nylons. While Eleanor wears high heels, her older sister Patricia presses flat, laced, commonsense shoes against the stair riser. The summer sun is bright, casting dark shadows on the large window shutters that fill the corners of the porch. A vine creeps up one side of the house, and bushes rise up the other.

Patricia is perhaps sixteen or seventeen. She is tall, big-boned, and her hair is now cut in a bob. She is a striking young girl, who stares at the camera with only a hint of a smile. Had she met Ambrose yet, I wonder? Has the son of Newfoundland fishermen asked her out? Has she fallen for the dark-eyed young man whom she will forever love?

The last image in my scrapbook shows Nana again with her older sister, Ruth McCormack. Ruth and her family had taken in my Nana, dad, and uncle when they returned from San Francisco and had nowhere else to live. In the picture, the two of them stand by a 1940s car. The passenger door is open. Ruth rests a white-gloved hand on the back door. She is dressed fashionably with a long skirt and matching bolero coat. Nana wears a long, dark skirt and a white short-sleeve blouse adorned with a flower corsage. Perhaps it is Easter Sunday, and they are either coming or going to church. While Ruth gazes toward the inside of the car, her younger sister glances down toward the sidewalk. Nana's brow is furrowed. Her lips are pressed together. Her arms hang limply by her sides, and she appears sad, worn.

Triple-decker homes line the streets in the background. How soon after the California trip was the picture taken, I wonder? How many years have passed since she arrived in Dorchester and Watertown, penniless and shamed, forced to ask her sisters and brother for help?

Another photograph shows my father and Uncle Bill with one of Ruth's sons, their cousin David McCormack. The picture was taken, I presume, on the same Easter day. My father and uncle wear suits and pose in the McCormacks' backyard. Handsome in his Sunday clothes, my dad's stance is nonchalant, cocky, as if nothing or no one could faze him. He is fifteen or sixteen, a few years away from joining the Navy, a young man who has washed his hands of his father and looks, instead toward his own future, pushing away the past like a bad dream.

CHAPTER 11

A PREMONITION AND A DARK CLOUD— MARYSTOWN, AUGUST 1935

Lillian placed the teakettle on the cookstove and rubbed her palms together for warmth. She pulled her shawl tighter and peered out the window. The sky to the east was clear, the wind still. A good omen, she thought. There were no signs of gales, no dark clouds.

Paddy and her sons would be off in a few hours, their schooners sailing in the blackest part of night. The thought of it—all of them—leaving together, stirred a chill deep inside her bones. They would sail forty miles southeast to Cape St. Mary's, then on to Cape Pine. Sure now, there were plenty of sunkers, jagged rocks there in the capes, but Lillian took comfort knowing her sons would not journey as far as the Grand Banks or near the treacherous Sable Island. Paddy promised her they would sail no farther than five miles from shore. There the shoal water measured twenty and thirty fathoms deep—not deep enough for a body to disappear. What could happen so close to land, so close to safe harbors? *Things will be fine,* Lillian whispered. *Please the Lord, things will be fine.*

The kettle rattled on the stove drawing her thoughts back inside. Steam rose from the spout, prompting Lillian to shake her head at the memory of Paddy weeks past, coming home hungry after having one too many jars of rum. "Where's me dinner?" he shouted to the maid after he stumbled through the kitchen door.

"'Tis not ready yet, sir," the young woman replied, her voice quavering. "But your food will be on the table shortly now."

Not happy with her response, Paddy pounded the kettle with his fist, slamming the spout clean into its metal innards. Shouting and muttering to himself, he retreated to the kitchen settee, put his head down, and took a nap, his hand no worse for the smashing he had given the teapot. *Did not seem to hurt him a'tall,* Lillian thought. *He was tougher than a rock and just as thick. She wished she had a penny for every time he had broken up a piece of furniture in a fit of rage or drunken foolishness.*

But then there was the gentler side of Paddy, the side few but Lillian and her children witnessed. She cherished those moments: The proud look in his eyes when he read the school report cards of his sons and daughters, and his long, hearty whistle over the high marks that each of them had earned. The faraway sound to his voice when he took in the sight of his seven children, walking along the footpath to Sunday Mass. "We are some lucky," he told her. "Grand kids they are, every one of them." The smile on his lips when he boasted of James at the helm. "Aye, ye should have seen him, Lil. A right smart skipper he is. Plotting the course to the Banks, like he'd been doing it all his life. Me son will make a fair captain, he will."

The back door swung open, and Paddy's heavy leather jack-boots slapped the floor. Lillian straightened herself, preparing for the ritual that was inevitable as the rising sun. He had said good-bye to her and the children hundreds of times, yet her nagging fear, her relentless angst never wavered. Forcing her tears aside, she pulled two cups and the tin of tea from the cupboard.

"Fine evening, Lil," he told her, his voice booming across the kitchen.

Before she could answer, footsteps echoed down the stairs, growing louder as they raced through the hall and into the kitchen.

"Da!" their youngest daughter, Little Lillian squealed as she ran to her father. "Da, why can't I go along with ye and the boys?"

"Ah, Lillian, you're a bit young yet for these journeys, and ye do know that the dorymen are a superstitious lot. A woman on a boat is bad luck to them now, me girl."

Lillian frowned and tugged on the sleeve of her dress. Seven years old, she took to fishing like a cat to milk, more at ease with a rod and hooks than the dolls and books that lined her bedroom shelves. "Why is it ye won't take me on yur sails?" she often asked. "I don't want to be left behind, Da."

To console her wounded feelings, Paddy frequently took his daughter fishing by the small creek near their home. The two of them had spent many hours there with their rods, hauling trout from the cold waters.

"I'll take ye fishin' when I return. We'll pack a picnic and hike into the woods for our own adventure."

Lillian hugged her father and kissed his cheek.

"I'll miss ye, Da," she told him.

Paddy watched his daughter turn on her heels and run from the kitchen. He knew Lillian's tears would be streaming down her face before she cloistered herself in her bedroom, angry and hurt. How he cursed these good-byes. He despised the lot of it: the weeping, the worried faces, the look in his family's eyes, the unspoken question: *What if we never see ye again?*

The smell of tea brewing pulled Paddy's gaze to the table, where his wife sat. She spoke to him softly, her voice distracted, "Come and have a cup of tea now, Paddy."

He pushed the kitchen chair aside and sat down. Lillian's gaze focused out the window, toward the darkening sky. Paddy studied her profile, her lips pressed tightly together. After twenty-three years of marriage, he knew her thoughts as well as his own, the fearsome images she conjured in her mind: the rough seas, sudden winds, and mountainous waves.

"C'am waters this evening, Lil," he told her. "Still and steady."

"Yes, but the weather can turn can't it, Paddy? Turn quicker than a flash of lightning."

"I've always come home, haven't I, Lil?"

She nodded and turned away at the sound of small feet shuffling along the wooden floor.

"Here's me boy," Paddy called to his son, Paddy Junior.

The four-year-old climbed up on his father's lap, his small fingers tugging on his Paddy's hand. "Play, Dada?"

"Not tonight, lad. When I come home, there will be plenty of time to play. Plenty of time."

Intrigued by the family cat, the boy slid off his father's lap to chase the pet as it ran into the parlor.

"Where are me girls, Lottie and Tessie?" Paddy asked of his older daughters.

"Tessie is off saying good-bye to Billy Reid, and Lottie is putting in extra hours tending the till at the store," Lillian explained. "They'll find you before you go. They know your plans to leave at midnight."

Paddy knew Tessie, like her mother, was none too happy about this journey. She was engaged to Billy Reid, a member of James's crew on the *Mary Bernice*. A schoolteacher, Tessie doted on her students as if they were her own. The girl pined for a wedding and children she could coddle from morn to night. Paddy remembered how Lillian had wanted the same. A thin wisp of a woman, Lillian Ducey had lived on the north side of Marystown. One look at her and Paddy had been smitten, drawn in by the sight of her dark hair, bright eyes, and the way she carried herself, regal and proper like she was the Queen of England.

They courted for a few years, and Paddy proposed to Lillian in the fall of 1911. The two of them were married when Paddy was sure to be on land and not at sea. As the winter wind tore across the bay and the January snows fell, the couple stood before a priest and received the sacrament of matrimony on a Saturday in 1912. Over the next four years, Lillian birthed James, Loretta, and Theresa, guarding each of the babies against the rampant diseases that tore through the small outport. The three children thrived, and Lillian's prayers and good fortune held until she birthed Cornelius in 1917; the infant died of pneumonia three months later. A year after his death, Lillian held another newborn, Mary Bernice in her arms, only to lose the girl five months later to the same wretched illness that claimed Cornelius.

How Paddy had cursed the Lord then, cursed God Almighty for taking their two infants. Paddy could still hear Lillian's wails, the sobs that tormented their home for months on end. He had worried his wife would never recover from her grief, but then their luck turned. Lillian birthed four more children who thrived and filled their home with a constant laughter. Still, Lillian never forgot the loss, the two infants buried in the ground. She fretted over each of her surviving sons and daughters, fearful of their ragged coughs, their fevered brows. She lived in dread of burying another child, losing them to disease or the cold, deep sea.

Paddy took in the sight of her now as she peered out the window, her gaze focused on the hills of Little Bay and the water that led to the fishing grounds.

Lillian turned to meet her husband's eyes, "Paddy," she started, the beginning of a plea, but before the words tumbled from her lips, a sudden gust of wind silenced her. A queer breeze had stirred up the meadow outside, pelting sand and grass against the window.

"Dear Lord!" Lillian screamed. Startled, her eyes scanned the horizon for an oncoming storm. "Where did such a wind come from on such a still night?"

Paddy shook his head and reached across the table for his wife's hand.

"It's just a whirlwind, m'dear. Nothing to worry yurself over."

Paddy stood and placed his cap on his head.

"I've delayed it long enough, Lil. I best be off 'n have another look on board the schooner before we set out."

Lillian followed her husband through the hall, her long skirt dragging along the pine boards beneath her. The smell of salt-water and freshly cut hay drifted into the parlor as Paddy pushed open the front door. Lillian stepped outside onto the porch and turned to the sky. In the east, a single cloud, black as tar, loomed in the otherwise clear night.

Lillian shook off a chill and remembered the date: August 20, the day her daughter Mary Bernice died of pneumonia. Dread and fear struck her heart. *Surely, the sudden whirlwind, the dark cloud portended death, disaster.* And in just a few hours, her eldest son, James, would sail off on *Mary Bernice,* trailing Paddy's schooner.

"Paddy, please do not sail tonight," she begged, pointing to the large, ominous cloud.

Paddy looked into his wife's eyes, saddened by her sudden fit of terror. He pulled her close and tucked her head against his shoulder.

"If it will comfort ye, we will sleep on board tonight; we will not sail until daylight."

Lillian nodded and whispered in her husband's ear. "Look after them, Paddy. Bring my sons home, safe ashore."

She watched him go, a shadow in the dark, his figure growing smaller as he disappeared beyond their white picket fence to the footpath that led to the wharf.

On the southern shores of Marystown, lamps cast shadows on the faces of other fathers, husbands, and sons who bid their own families farewell. In the small, modest homes nestled along the bay, the crew of *Mary Bernice* and *Annie Anita* packed their seabags. Spare woolen socks, extra jumpers and pants, sou'wester hats, oilskins, tins of tobacco, boxes of matches, and pictures of their families—daughters, mothers, and their betrothed—pictures they would hang in their bunks or keep in pockets pressed against their hearts.

In their small drawstring bags, they placed their religious tokens: palm-size crosses, Blessed Virgin medals, tiny bottles of holy water, and bits of burned Ash Wednesday palms. If the waves grew to mountains and the wind roared, they held the crosses and medals, and they prayed; they sprinkled holy water and ashes into the angry sea, beseeching Mary the Mother of God to calm the waters, to guide them home.

It was never easy for the fishermen to bid their families farewell, but an August journey conjured more than the usual discontent among the dorymen. Still, their tongues did not speak of the gales, their voices did not utter apprehension about the violent storms that struck suddenly, stirring a silent sea into a roiling devil. No, it was no good talking about such worries, but each of them—the fishermen and their wives—felt the fear as if it were a living, breathing being that walked among them.

Odd misgivings gripped Dominic Walsh as he paced the floor of his family's kitchen. Paddy's nephew, Dominic had a berth as a doryman on board *Annie Anita*. Rattled about his unease, Dominic turned to his mother, who sat before the fire cradling a cup of tea. "Should I go, Ma? Should I leave? I've a peculiar feeling about this trip."

His mother Margaret understood her boy's angst. Soon to be married, Dominic did not want to leave his betrothed behind. But she also harbored misgivings about this August journey. She feared the storms that had no mercy for the lives of fathers and sons.

"Don't go, Dominic," she told him. "I have me own worries about this trip."

"But how will I be paying for the house I'm building for meself and me bride? I can't be slackin' off now."

Dominic hoisted his duffle and hugged his mother goodbye. "I'll see ye in a week or so," he told her. She watched his thin frame retreat down the hill. "Safe seas to ye, son," she whispered, pushing back her tears. "Safe seas, please God."

Past the hills leading to Little Bay, Bride Hanrahan watched her father pack for his journey. The fifteen-year-old girl relished time with her father when he was ashore. She had hoped her da would treat her and her siblings to some singing, dancing, in the kitchen before his journey, but her father's mouth organ had remained untouched in its place by the mantel.

Bride had noticed her father's sullen spirits over the past few days. She knew he regretted his decision to accompany James Walsh on board *Mary Bernice*. Sure now, her father was quiet on a good day, but she could barely stand his sorrow on this evening. She hated to see him go with such a heavy heart. Though he had spent much of her childhood away at sea, her da always had time for her when he was home. Bride chased him from morn to night then, shadowing his every move. She followed him into the forest to cut wood and helped him haul the kindling into the horse cart. She would do anything to be near his side; chores never bothered her a bit, as long as her father returned her efforts with a soft smile.

She blinked back her tears as her father lifted his head to her now.

"Good-bye, Da," she told him as he held her close.

He nodded and tossed his burlap bag over his shoulder. Bride watched as her father stepped out the door and down the small hill to the harbor. She held her eyes steady on his silhouette as he flung his duffle in the dory and seated himself inside the boat. Setting the oars in the tholepins, his thick arms rowed slow, steady strokes, rippling the waters as he pointed the bow toward Marystown and the schooner that waited for him. Bride knew he would not turn to look at her, would not turn to wave for fear of summoning ill luck. She closed her eyes and said a silent prayer for her father's safe return.

"Love you, Da," she whispered in the chill night air.

As Richard Hanrahan pulled on the dory oars in the dark, thousands of miles to the south, a small storm brewed in the warm Caribbean waters. Just northwest of the Turks Islands, the tempest continued to gather strength as it whirled past the Bahamas and headed north.

CHAPTER 12

HEADING INTO THE STORM—NEWFOUNDLAND, JUNE 2003

I reach for my father's hand as the jagged coast of Newfoundland appears.

The barren landscape rises up from below: unforgiving patches of boulders, soaring cliffs, and scrub brush. Fishing boats provide the only sign of life, their wakes white feathery trails, stark against the dark ocean.

Three thousand feet above the sea, my father, sister, and I sit in a small plane that carries us north toward the land where our Irish ancestors immigrated more than a century ago. We have remained quiet during most of our early morning flight, lulled into silence by the rhythmic drone of the propeller that whirs loudly outside our window.

Two hours into our journey, the province known as "The Rock," for its rugged, glacier-ravaged terrain, comes into view. The sight of this island, the sight of Newfoundland, the realization that we are actually nearing my grandfather's homeland— jars me awake. I breathe deeply, trying to contain the rush of emotions this country stirs.

From his aisle seat, my father leans toward the window. His brown eyes take in the coast of Newfoundland as it grows larger, closer. The knowledge that we are almost there, nearing Ambrose's birthplace prompts him to sigh, a breath that is long and deep. For much of the flight from Boston, he has exhaled often, as if trying to release the worries that bubble up inside him. He has had many second thoughts since he agreed to accompany my sister Joanie and me to Marystown. A few days before our journey, my younger sister Laura spoke with him on the phone. "So," she asked, "are you excited about your trip?"

"How the hell do you think I feel?" he erupted. "I don't know these people or what they're going to say about my father."

The night before we left, he sipped from his red wine glass as Joanie, my mother, and I sat in the living room of my parents' home. Our suitcases sprawled out on the floor, Joanie and I tried to repack our clothes, eliminating extra baggage for our early morning journey.

My father, who hated to be late—especially if it involved a flight, church obligation, social event, or a golf tee time—had already packed his small duffle and watched as his daughters folded and refolded piles of clothes.

"You know, if you two weren't going, I'd be changing my mind right now," he told us.

I, too, worried that maybe this trip was a bad idea. Though I was excited to learn more about the August Gale and my Great Uncle Paddy, I was not so eager to hear stories about Ambrose, stories that would rekindle my father's childhood pain and anger. Neither my dad nor I slept well the night before our flight. Both of us fret before long-distance travel, and this particular journey presented more than the usual "will I make the plane, will there be delays?" angst. The following morning, we rose at five a.m. with dark circles beneath our eyes. After quick cups of coffee and a forty-minute ride south to Boston's Logan Airport, we dragged our suitcases and carry-on bags from the car. My mother hugged and kissed each of us good-bye, and as I drew her close, I noticed her eyes were shiny with tears. I hugged her one more time as she told me, "I wish I was going with you."

My mother, Patricia Enis Walsh, loved travel and adventure. At a young age, she acquired her father Daniel's curiosity and a yearning to explore. On Sunday mornings, Daniel Enis packed his five kids and wife in the sedan and set off determined to find new vistas. Carrying on her father's wanderlust, my mother has traveled to Portugal, England, Ireland, and New York City with my sisters and me, trips she savored more than all of us put together. And though she knew this excursion to Newfoundland would be memorable, she decided that it was best experienced without her, a journey to be made by two daughters and their father. At the airport curb, she stuffed her homemade granola bars into my pocketbook and waved good-bye before retreating to the car.

Hours later in the small Air Canada plane, I stare at the dark blue sea and consider the *Titanic,* which lies somewhere deep in the dark caverns below. Though it is the one of the most memorable ships to have sunk off Newfoundland's coast, it is but one of the ten thousand or more vessels that have shipwrecked or disappeared in these waters since the sixteenth century. North of the forty-degree latitude, sailors contend with more than a wild and unpredictable sea. Year-round, icebergs drift south from Greenland and along Newfoundland's east coast. Monster mountains of ice, they can tear a ship in two. In the summer months, the collision of the warm Gulf Stream and the cold Labrador Current creates curtains of fog, relentless and thick banks that shroud fishermen and boats for days, leaving them lost and at risk of deadly collisions with other vessels. And then there are the rogue waves, freaks of nature that tower seventy, eighty, and sometimes even ninety feet high, carrying a lethal force capable of capsizing and destroying cruise liners, tankers, and three-hundred-foot-high oil platforms.

Ever present along the island's six thousand miles of coastline in good weather and bad, there are numerous sunkers, deadly reefs hidden below the ocean's surface. Thousands of years ago, glaciers stripped Newfoundland's soil and cast the deposits into the sea, creating the underwater ledges that threaten unwary captains and ships tossed about by storms and violent hurricane winds. I picture Paddy in these fierce and unforgiving waters, a skipper who had shipwrecked in heavy seas, sailed through blinding fog, and remained trapped for weeks in winter ice floes. With nothing more than his compass, charts, and the "glass"—the barometer that foretold foul weather—he sailed these seas for much of his life. I imagine him on his schooner, *Annie Anita*, on his August journey, a careful eye trained on the sky and the sea, searching for a change in the current, a shift in the wind, a gale that might descend without warning.

And like many other August gales, the 1935 hurricane roared up the North Atlantic coast with a vengeance. In our research, my father and I have recreated bits and pieces of the gale. We have collected newspaper stories, talked with dozens of relatives, and have read firsthand accounts about the hurricanes that have plagued Newfoundland's coast for centuries. For much of our flight, my father has dutifully reviewed our material. He has studied notes from my interviews and reread the Marystown census names. He has pulled papers from his leather zippered briefcase, methodically reading each page. From my own files, I have scanned notes from my phone conversations with Marystown residents. I am eager to see their faces, these children who lost fathers, grandfathers, uncles, and brothers to the gale. I am anxious to glean more details from their memories, to hear them talk about the storm that forever changed their lives and their small rural outport.

I am curious, too, about our relatives, the Brentons, who invited us to use their summer cabin during our stay. A month or so before our trip, my father contacted his cousin, Alan Brenton, to let him know we would be coming. Brenton's mother, Donalda, was Ambrose's older sister. My Nana wrote her several letters and developed a long-distance friendship with Donalda through their correspondence. Alan Brenton, like most of his Newfoundland relatives, had been fond of his Uncle Ambrose, and he looked forward to meeting my father. Nine years earlier, Brenton had met my Uncle Bill when he made an unexpected trip to Newfoundland. Wanting to know more about his namesake, William Patrick "Paddy" Walsh, my uncle surprised Brenton with a phone call.

"I'm William Patrick Walsh, Ambrose's son," my uncle told Brenton. "I'm in Newfoundland. I'll be in Marystown in a few days."

Brenton invited my uncle and his family to stay with him, and one evening over dinner and drinks Brenton asked, "Do you think your brother Ron would ever come to Marystown?"

My uncle shook his head, knowing my father's feelings about travel and Ambrose. "It may come to the point sometime in my life where I could forgive my father," my uncle explained, "but I don't think my brother Ron would ever forgive him."

Now, thirteen years later, I sit next to my father on a small plane headed for Newfoundland. I turn to him, eyeing the gray hair that peeks beneath his Navy baseball cap. Dressed in khakis and a blue sweatshirt adorned with large yellow letters that also proclaim NAVY, he is a few months shy of celebrating his sixty-eighth birthday. I hope this trip will be an early gift for him; a chance to understand, to know his father better. A chance to consider forgiveness.

As the pilot pulls back on the throttle, slowing the plane's engines, the red light over our seats pings, warning us to buckle our seat belts and prepare for landing. I pull my belt tighter and wonder what Brenton and others will say to my father about Ambrose and what my dad will say in return?

My father glances out the window at the massive island that is now beneath us. He shifts his weight and sighs, knowing we will soon be among Ambrose's relatives, people who are fond of the man who remains a mystery to me and provokes a long-standing bitterness in my father's heart. Would my dad turn this plane around if he could? Would he abandon this trip now if Joanie and I were not with him?

Hoping to offer him reassurance, I reach for my dad's hand. His eyes meet mine, and I ask: "Did you ever think you'd be coming to Newfoundland?"

Though he does not have to think about his answer, my father speaks slowly: "Not . . . in . . . a . . . million . . . years."

We both fall silent again, and I turn to the window so he will not see my tears. Wiping the drops from my cheeks, I look across the aisle toward the back of the plane, searching for Joanie. She is seated a few rows behind us and is the picture of calm; she harbors no worries about this trip. She is eager to meet our New-foundland relatives and to connect with our past. Noting my concerned face, she offers a smile. I smile, too, but my heart is far from at ease. I pull my seat belt tighter as the plane's wheels kick open with a thud, preparing for its arrival in St. John's, Newfoundland's capital city. I close my eyes and whisper a silent prayer, bracing for the landing and an uncertain journey to my grandfather's homeland.

CHAPTER 13

MUSTERING COURAGE ON BOARD
ANNIE ANITA AND *MARY BERNICE*—AUGUST 21, 1935

The sails clapped like thunder in the wind.

"Hoist the main!" Paddy shouted to his crew.

Frankie Walsh cast his eyes heavenward following the canvas sail as it soared up the sixty-foot mast. Two of the crew groaned as they tugged on the halyards, securing the sheet. The southeast wind at their backs, the sails held taut against the breeze. Waves slapped the bow, sending sea spray onto the deck as *Annie Anita* glided through the bay.

"We're underway, boys!" Paddy hollered to Frankie and Jerome.

Jerome ran to his father, eager to stand at the helm; Frankie kept his place. He leaned against the stacked dories mindful of the crew that scurried about him. He did not want to get tangled up in a line or trip up the men. The twelve-year-old boy drew a deep breath to calm the worries that bubbled up inside him. Searching for a distraction, he looked toward the stern where his father stood, his large hands on the wheel, his eyes focused on the schooner's course. Frankie reckoned his da's mind was busy now, thinking on where he'd find the fish, where he'd drop the anchor once they hit Cape St. Mary's. The journey, Frankie knew, would begin slowly at first as the schooner traveled east in the protected inlet that wound its way past Marystown, Little Bay, Beau Bois, and Tides Point before sailing into the vast open sea.

Wanting one last look at his home, Frankie turned west and glimpsed the whitewashed house on the hill as it faded from view. His mother would have risen early, poured herself a cup of tea and gazed out the window, watching for their parting sails. The thought of her without them, the three eldest boys and their father, saddened him, for he knew her heart would be heavy with worry during the week they were gone.

Jerome had tried to comfort her before they left: "We'll be fine, Mum. We'll be home soon enough."

Frankie only offered her a quiet, "So long, Mother," and a quick hug good-bye. She had not wanted to let them go, delaying their departure, packing and repacking their duffles with extra woolens caps, mittens, and their Sunday suits in case they stopped in a church or somewhere proper along their journey. On top of their clothes, she carefully placed their pocket Bibles. "Read the good book before bed and on Sunday, and don't forget your prayers."

"Yes, ma'am," they had told her.

No, Frankie would not forget his prayers. He prayed to the Lord over the past week, pleading for courage. The boy tried to embrace the sea like his father and two older brothers, but he was not fond of how the ocean changed so quickly. It could be calm, safe like the bay outside his home. And then it could be dark, with ragged waves that grew taller than a ship's masts. Last summer's journey with his da had been miserable. The sea swells and the constant motion of the schooner had brought on the queasiness and trips to the bucket at all hours of the day and night. His father tried to comfort him, "Keep yur eyes focused on the horizon, me boy," but the advice did little good. Frankie came home red-faced, shamed. The lads at school had been ruthless with their taunts. "Sissy. Seasick sissy. Are ye sure yur Capt'n Paddy's son? Ye ought to be staying home with yur mama."

Frankie heard their voices in his mind now as the wind rose and cold water sprayed his cheeks. *Stand tall,* Frankie told himself. *Yur Capt'n Paddy's boy. This August journey will be different. This time, I might even have some adventures aboard* Annie Anita. *Perhaps, I will have some stories to tell the fellas back home about the cod I hauled, the dory I rowed.*

"Frankie," Jerome hollered. "There's Tides Point! We're almost to the sea!"

Paddy grinned as his boys raced to port to view the red-and-white-striped lighthouse that rose up from its perch atop a cliff. The sight never ceased to stir Paddy's heart. The last protected cove, Tides Point bordered the sea, heralding the start of the journey, the beginning of the adventure, and a freedom that he could never taste on shore.

Paddy remembered the joy he experienced on his first trip with his own father, Tom Walsh. A boy of twelve, he was awed by the wild and unpredictable sea, the challenge of finding the fish, and the fierce competition among the dorymen and skippers. Oh how he loved standing on board, watching his father race back to Marystown, wanting to be the first to return with a boatload of cod.

His love for fishing and the sea grew with every sail, every journey. "Yur a natural son, a born fish-killer," Paddy's father had told him.

When he returned from Boston, a man in his twenties with a few years' apprenticeship behind him, Paddy was confident and prepared to take on the job of a skipper. And he soon learned: *There was no greater calling than to command a vessel, command a crew. Ye felt like a king, in charge, from dawn to dusk, fighting the sea that could be yur friend or foe.* And no matter the conditions—ca'am waters, gales, fierce wind or t'ick of fog—Paddy always found the fish. His reputation had spread far and wide from Newfoundland's shores. His legend grew with every catch, every return as the "highliner," the captain who always came home with his vessel loaded to the brim, overflowing with fish, rail to rail.

And now he stood at the helm of *Annie Anita,* ready for another go, another challenge. *Aye, but along with the thrill came the responsibility of getting the crew home safely, making sure they made a fair catch, a good haul to feed their families.* He sized up his men now as they finished securing lines. His second hand, Tom Reid, towered over the others. A giant of a man, he always met Paddy's gaze straight on and followed orders without a fight. Reid could be counted on to work hard, keep his wits about him, and take command if needed.

Paddy recited the other crew names in his head: John Brinton, George Mitchell, Dominic Walsh, Charles Hanrahan, and Edward Cheeke. Good men, each had sailed with Paddy many a time. With the exception of Dominic, who was soon to be married, all of the other crew members had children and wives depending on them. Paddy never forgot the men had families at home waiting and worrying, families that prayed for their safe return. He had never lost a man in his years as skipper, and despite the dorymen's unspoken worries about this journey and the August gales, Paddy was not about to lose a member of his crew now.

As the sun rose higher, it colored the dawn like a kaleidoscope with streaks of pink and peach. Paddy searched for oncoming clouds, clouds as gray as mackerel tails, but his eyes spied nothing but swaths of blue.

Aye, a fine day, and a fine stretch of weather ahead, Paddy told himself. *Me boys will have a good trip.*

A few miles behind Paddy's vessel, James Walsh stood at the helm of *Mary Bernice.* James gripped the wheel and tried to contain the joy, the fierce pride that threatened to burst through his chest. In the days before they sailed, his father Paddy had told him, "James, there's no describing it, no telling what it's like to captain a vessel, be yur own man, yur own boss, king of the seas."

For years, James took orders from his father and other skippers, listened to their shouts and curses. But now he was in charge, the one who barked the orders, plotted the course, decided where to fish, and when to lower the dories over the side. Not long after they hoisted the sails that morning, a crew member had called him Capt'n, and James had nodded nonchalantly. But silently he told himself: *I'm a captain!* Since he was a small boy rowing dories in the bay, he dreamed of being a skipper, a highliner like his da, outfishing, outsailing the other schooners. And now James had his chance, his own vessel to master, to command.

Aye, his father was right: 'Twas no feeling like it. Nothing compared. Still, James knew his shoulders bore a tremendous responsibility. He had heeded the advice from his father. "Respect the sea; know its strength, its fearsome power. If ye don't, ye and yur crew won't live very long."

James watched his crew now as they stood on deck, the four men his father had handpicked: Richard Hanrahan, Dennis Long, Michael Farrell, and Billy Reid. Except for Reid who was in his twenties, all of the other men were veteran sailors, dorymen who had seen their share of storms, gales, and had spent many days lost at sea, rowing their dories in fog and dark of night. He hoped to give them all a fair journey, find the fishing grounds that would offer them tubs of cod, a successful trip for his maiden voyage, a grand trip for them all. And of course, James would like nothing more than to beat his father, to fill his hold first. But there was another reason he had hoped to land the cod quick and fast: He knew his wife, Lucy, wept over his absence.

The image of her sobbing tormented him. In the hours before he departed, she sat by the kitchen stove, her feet swollen, her broad belly stretching the seams of her cloth dress. James had knelt at her feet and held her hand.

"It will be alright, Lucy," he told her. "I'll be home in a week's time."

"But what about the baby?" she cried. "It will be here soon. I want ye near."

"I'll be by yur side soon enough. The cold months are comin' and we won't be to sea then. I'll be here with ye through the winter, helping ye care for our wee child."

Lucy wiped her tears, knowing there was little she could do. She knew James had desired to captain his schooner long before he met her. He had talked, dreamed, planned for this trip over the past four years. Now the time had come for James to stand at the helm, and Lucy understood that nothing—not even the birth of their child—could keep him ashore.

She fingered the Rosary beads in her lap and made the sign of the cross upon her forehead as her husband turned to leave. Her words, a plea loud and desperate, followed him out the door: "Mary, Mother of God, bring him safely home to our baby."

CHAPTER 14

"WELCOME HOME"—MARYSTOWN, JUNE 2003

The directions seem simple enough.

"Turn left at Goobies," my cousin Jack Brenton, Alan's son, tells us. "And just keep going straight till you hit Marystown."

"Goobies?" my father, sister, and I ask each other.

After landing at St. John's, renting a car, and traveling one hundred miles west along the Trans-Atlantic Canadian Highway, we arrive in the small village of Goobies. A community of near two hundred, the village is known among travelers as a place to gas up and get grub at the Irving petrol station. The rest stop is also renowned for Morris the Moose, a statue which towers over the parking lot. Ten feet tall, the sculpture was created as a reminder to tourists and Newfoundlanders to keep a careful eye out for the 110,000 moose that roam the province and cause up to nine hundred car accidents a year.

Thankfully, dusk (the preferred time for moose to forage) is three hours away on this June evening as we leave Goobies and head south. My cousin does not tell us much about the two-lane throughway that will take us through the "barrens" and onto Marystown and the Burin Peninsula but we soon learn: It will be a long and lonely ride.

For the next ninety minutes, we will see few cars and minimal signs of civilization. Ten thousand years ago glaciers ravaged this land, scraping the terrain of its topsoil and trees. What remains are the barrens—miles and miles of rocks, boulders, and cliffs—remnants of mountains that were broken up by ancient sheets of gigantic ice. Aside from occasional birds, we see no other evidence of life. The stark landscape stretches south for nearly one hundred miles, testing our eyes after a full day of travel. My father, tired and still uneasy about this trip, utters the first of many "Jesus Christ! Where the hell is Marystown?"

Joanie and I smile and say nothing, figuring we haven't a clue where Marystown is anyway. We take turns driving, and as I focus on the flat stretch of road ahead, I muse that it could be worse. The fog that often shrouds Newfoundland in the summer, endangering fishermen and sailors, would make this ride particularly unpleasant. The sheets of mist would blind us and put us at even more risk of hitting one of the myriad of animals (bears, coyotes, caribou, and moose) that roam the barrens.

I take careful note of the bright yellow road signs that depict a moose and a crushed car. An hour or so into our journey, we are heartened by the sight of villages and harbors. We read markers for Petite Forte, Rushoon, Red Harbour, towns that lie to the east on the shores of Placentia Bay. Settled in the early sixteenth century, the Placentia Bay communities were named by the European fishermen who were drawn to Newfoundland's bountiful waters. Portuguese, French, Irish, English, Spanish, and Basque fishermen sailed along Newfoundland's shores, eager to hunt cod, the bottom-feeding fish that British explorer John Cabot noted were so plentiful that they could be plucked from the sea with a basket weighted down with stone. "The sea is swimming with fish," Cabot reported when he claimed the island in the North Atlantic as "New Found Land" for King Henry VII in 1497.

Four centuries later, I picture Paddy sailing the bays of Placentia and St. Mary's, the hold of his schooner filled with layer upon layer of cod. I see the sails of *Annie Anita* stretched tight against the wind, with Jerome and Frankie on board as the schooner sluices through the water on its August journey. I am eager to reach Marystown and to stand along the bay where Paddy's crew unfurled his sails and heaved the anchor on that warm summer morning. I am excited, too, to see Paddy's home, the old Molloy Hotel bought for his wife Lil. Fortunately the 120-year-old house is still standing and is owned by my cousin, Alan Brenton, who has done little to change the historic building. I am anxious to step inside, to walk along the pine floors where Paddy, Lillian, and their children once stepped.

The summer sun continues to sink lower in the sky, and after traveling nearly two hours along this bleak highway, we are restless to arrive in Marystown, the largest of the five communities on the boot-shaped Burin Peninsula. "Jesus Christ," my father mutters again, exasperated. "I wish I had a beer."

Spotting a roadside shop, we pull over to stretch our legs, get beer, and buy a gift for our relatives. Inside the store, which is actually a garage of sorts, Joanie and I find a sparse collection of groceries—milk, bread, cereal, cigarettes, beer, and liquor. We explain to the woman who presides over the premises that we're looking for a present for our relatives. She quickly suggests Screech, Newfoundland's beloved one-hundred-proof rum. I will later learn the liquor received its name in the early 1900s, after an American commanding officer was offered a shot of the caramel-colored liquid as an after-dinner cordial. Seeing his Newfoundland host toss back the drink, the officer did the same. Not prepared for the scorching sensation as the liquor traveled down his throat, the officer let out a loud and anguished howl. His scream drew the attention of his sergeant, who pounded on the door and asked, "What the cripes was that ungodly screech?" A Newfoundlander replied "The screech? 'Tis the rum, me son."

The setting sun burns the clouds orange and violet as we begin to see houses along the road, signs of an oncoming community; Marystown, we hope. Soon a roadside sign informs us we are indeed in my grandfather's birthplace. "Thank God," we tell each other, relieved that our arduous day of travel is nearly over.

Not long after we enter the town, we find our relatives' business, Brenton Rentals and Sales, which is co-owned by Jack and his father, Alan. We pull up to the large garage doors and yard, where several large tractors and excavators loom. Inside the garage bays, the Brentons are waiting for us. They shake our hands and offer hugs, telling us, "Welcome Home."

Both Alan and Jack are eager to meet Ambrose's firstborn son and his granddaughters. They consider our side of the family a bit of a mystery: the relatives who were never heard from, the family that chose to disavow its Newfoundland roots. Years ago, through Ambrose, the Brentons have heard bits and pieces about our lives. They know that my father was a successful engineer who at one time managed hundreds of employees. They know he has a home in New Hampshire, a wife, Patricia, six daughters, and several grandchildren. And they understand, after phone calls and e-mails with my father, that he is apprehensive about this trip and meeting strangers, relatives who are familiar with far too many details of his life and the life of the man who abandoned him.

After a few minutes of awkward conversation, my father, Joanie, and I realize that the Brentons are sincerely excited that we have traveled to Marystown. While Jack gives us a tour of his offices, Alan silently studies my father, considering the likeness between my dad and Ambrose. He notes their similar build, their tall, muscular frames. Alan also takes a quick liking to my father, whose confident nature and affable manner remind him of his Uncle Ambrose. Still, Alan is careful not to say too much about my grandfather on our first night. An astute businessman adept at reading customers' wants and needs, Alan saves details and conversations about Ambrose for later—some of which will be difficult for my father to hear.

While Alan is more reserved and quiet, his son Jack, a thirty-five-year-old man with a family of his own, is jovial and outgoing. He feels comfortable with us soon after we meet. "It was like I knew ye all my life," he will later tell me. "Ye felt like family pretty fast."

The Brentons' hospitality quickly sets my father at ease. Joanie, too, is surprised at our cousins' friendly nature, and she wonders about their resilience, their ability to thrive in such a struggling community. She sizes up their looks, their features, disappointed that they do not share our family's likeness, our dark hair, our freckled skin.

I am struck by the sound of the Brentons' voices. When Jack and Alan speak, their tone is lyrical, singsong, like the Irish brogue that was first spoken in Marystown and other southeastern outports in the mid-1800s. Their conversation is infused with "aye, right on, and ye," and I am comforted by this connection to our Irish ancestors.

"Right, so why don't we give ye's a quick tour of Marystown before we head out to camp. Aye?" Jack suggests.

We nod and follow the Brentons in their car past Tim Horton's, McDonald's, the town's one traffic light, and over the Canning Bridge which was built in the 1950s to connect Marystown's southern and northern shores. The bay that leads east to the sea is dark and rippled by a slight evening breeze. Here, Paddy's schooners once moored. Here, he unloaded thousands of pounds of cod, his catch drawing a crowd of young and old fishermen, who marveled at his skill in finding the fish. Across the bridge, we turn left and stop before a hill that slopes down the road. A three-story house looms above us. Several of its windows are boarded, the paint is peeling, and the two chimneys are crumbling; still, the sight of my great-uncle's home mesmerizes me. I picture Paddy slamming shut his broad front door and walking along the footpath to his wharf. He would have strolled along on the road where we now stand. I envision young boys carefully doffing their caps and offering, "Evening, Capt'n Paddy, sir." I hear Frankie and Jerome running after their da, hollering as they raced toward the *Annie Anita,* eager to climb the rigging, place their small hands on the helm.

There is a chill in the early June night air, and the sky is black with a sprinkling of stars. Lights flicker in the homes that hug the bay; a century ago, village kerosene lamps cast shadows onto walls, woodstoves warmed small kitchens, and Rosary beads were pulled from pockets for evening prayers.

Knowing we are eager to get inside Paddy's home, Alan promises to give us a tour the following day. Back in the car, we drive over the bridge, past the Sacred Heart Church, past the cemetery, to Jack's nearby summer camp. Not long after we drop our bags in the cottage, we offer our gift to the Brentons. Jack and Alan laugh as they open the bottle of Screech. Jack pours a glass for each of us, and we toast to our unexpected trip to Marystown. I swallow the Screech and wince; the liquor is potent and burns my throat. My father also grimaces. "Wow," he says, "that is strong."

Joanie sips hers with ice and puckers her lips after a swallow. "This isn't bad."

The Brentons have stocked our fridge with bacon, eggs, cheese, milk, coffee, and beer. Their hospitality, we will later discover, has just begun. Noting our tired faces, they bid us goodnight and tell us once more, "Welcome Home."

Exhausted, my father, Joanie, and I quickly claim our beds. My father offers to sleep on the pull-out couch, Joanie chooses the room with bunk beds, and I head to the adjoining bedroom. My father falls asleep quickly, and in the dark I listen to his slow, measured breathing. I cannot hear Joanie from behind her closed bedroom door, and I want to whisper, ask her if she too is awake, but I don't want to roust her or my father. I toss beneath my bedcovers and wonder what the next few days will bring. What stories will we hear about the gale and about my grandfather? How will people treat us, how will they react to Ambrose's son?

In my mind, I hear the Brentons' initial greeting, spontaneous and heartfelt, "Welcome home." Home, they tell us, as if we were missed, long awaited, and are now embraced after decades of absence. Before I drift into sleep, I think of my grandfather and my Nana: What would they have thought of our coming home?

CHAPTER 15

THE TEMPEST ROARS NORTH—NORTH ATLANTIC, 1935

A few days old and whirling north, the hurricane season's first tropical storm caused little concern along the American eastern coast. The National Weather Bureau reported the tempest had blown out to sea with no apparent danger of striking the States—unless it unexpectedly changed course.

While the gale presented little threat to Florida, Georgia, and the Carolinas, weather reports cautioned vessels that the hurricane carried severe winds as it roared up the North Atlantic shipping lanes. Luxury liners and steamers traveling from New York to Bermuda and Puerto Rico on August 23 faced the storm's wrath. The center of the hurricane passed one hundred miles northwest of Bermuda, lashing the island with heavy gusts and waves. The gale battered the twenty-two-thousand-ton *Queen of Bermuda* liner as it rode out the storm five miles off Bermuda's coast. The luxury ship's six hundred passengers, bound for honeymoons and vacations, fought seasickness and injury as the waves and winds tossed the liner like a small boat.

Later on in the afternoon of the twenty-third, the gale continued on a northeasterly path. Weather reports noted that while the storm had lost some of its viciousness, it had gained momentum and speed. Though the hurricane remained six hundred miles east of North Carolina, its powerful winds—which had been blowing steadily on the sea for the past three days—created an ocean swell hundreds of miles north of the storm. Along the New York and New Jersey shores, the surf raged.

At Jones Beach and Fire Island, waves towered more than ten feet high, rumbling like thunder as they crashed along the coast. Few swimmers dared venture into the ocean, and those who did drowned or required rescue. A forty-one-year-old man disappeared at New Jersey's Manasquan beach when a fierce current pulled him under and dragged his body out to sea.

Heavy seas flipped boats and tossed fishermen into the ocean. A series of large waves swamped a thirty-eight-foot boat off Long Island's coast, plunging ten fishermen into the water. Three waves—enormous and unrelenting in their quick succession—battered the boat's cabin to splinters, washed the men overboard, and punched a hole in the vessel causing the boat to sink within minutes.

By midnight August 23, the hurricane continued, as most North Atlantic gales do, on a northeasterly path. Now close to eight hundred miles out to sea, it traveled well east of North Carolina, Virginia, and Maryland, and as the storm spiraled above the cooler waters of the North Atlantic, its intensity began to weaken.

Had it kept on its northeasterly course, the storm would have barely brushed the Grand Banks before extinguishing over the frigid waters of the Labrador Current. But on the morning of August 24, the gale had collided with a massive trough of low pressure that blanketed much of America's East Coast and Nova Scotia. And when the hurricane's warm air mass merged with the trough of cold air, the contrast in temperatures fueled the storm like gas to a fire. Instead of feeding off the ocean's warm water, the gale now fed off the clash of energy, and instead of dying, it was growing bigger. Its ferocity and size magnified, generating violent gusts that blew continuously on the ocean, pushing waves higher and higher until they rose like monsters in the sea. The low pressure front also pulled the gale in a new direction. Hundreds of miles east of Cape Cod's coast, the hurricane dramatically changed course. Instead of continuing on a northeasterly path, it veered directly north, heading straight for Newfoundland.

Hundreds of miles from the hurricane's fierce winds, the waters were calm, and the sun slipped toward the horizon in a clear blue sky. A yellow dory cut through the sea pointed to Lear's Cove, a small beach to the north of Cape St. Mary's fishing grounds. From the boat's bow, Paddy Walsh pulled the oars, his broad shoulders leaning back and forth with each steady, strong stroke. The captain's sons, Frankie and Jerome, sat in the stern of the boat; the boys were eager for the chance to be off the schooner and to stretch their legs on beach sand. Paddy had also reckoned that a quick trip to collect springwater would provide Frankie with some relief from his seasickness. *The poor fella had leaned over the rail and retched for most of the past four days.* The boy also suffered a gash in his palm from a trawl hook while he helped the crew bait the lines. Frankie did not cry while Paddy cleaned the wound, but the skipper knew the boy's hand throbbed from the pain.

Paddy turned to glimpse Frankie's face as he sat in the dory; his cheeks were as white as chalk. *The lad had eaten nothin' but a few crackers for much of the journey.* "Aye, Frankie, we'll be on land soon, me boy."

Frankie smiled at his father and gazed back to the beach where three boys raced along the shore with a couple of black water dogs. "Look, Da!" Frankie shouted. "That one is just like your old dog that shipwrecked with you on Codroy!"

"'Tis a fine likeness of the dog, isn't it?"

For much of his life, Paddy had owned a Labrador water dog. He took the animals on board his schooners; the dogs were known to be good luck, and they were also handy for catching sea ducks to use for bait if the squid and capelin ran scarce. The Labradors were also loyal and had saved many a man from drowning if a dory or schooner capsized. Paddy remembered how his own dog dove into the sea after waves and wind had torn the masts from their vessel on their way home from Prince Edward Island. The dog seemed no worse for wear as he floated to shore on Paddy's sea chest.

The laughter of the three boys on the beach carried across the water as Paddy rowed toward the shore. The dogs barked and raced across the sand, fetching sticks, stones, and anything else they could sink their teeth into.

"They're grand fellas aren't they, Da?" Frankie laughed.

Paddy nodded and before the dory struck the shore, Frankie and Jerome leaped from the boat and ran toward the dogs. Paddy chuckled at the spectacle of flying sand and the blur of black fur. The animals yelped, begging to retrieve, raring for a chance to dive into the sea, chasing bits of bobbing wood.

Dragging the dory onto the beach, Paddy hoisted a barrel that was nearly as big as Frankie. The captain's rubber boots squeaked across the sand as he made his way toward the cliffs that rose up the side of the cove. Cold springwater flowed from the rocks, a treat to bring back to the schooner. As he climbed the cliff, Paddy turned to take in the waning sunlight that lit up the water. The sea reflected the light like a thousand diamonds. The skipper never grew tired of gazing at the water, watching how it changed from dawn to dusk, a kaleidoscope of colors, streaks of violet, red, and blue. *And aye, then there was the Northern Lights. 'Twas nothing like it, standing on deck in the pitch black and quiet, the rainbow lights flashing over yur head, glowing like spirits among the stars.*

But then the sky and the sea could turn ugly, too. The sea she could turn black as night and as fierce as any foe. She was silent, now, c'am, but Paddy knew she could do more. He took in the sight of the *Annie Anita* rocking gently on her anchor. A dozen other schooners moored within a quarter mile of each other. Captains from Newfoundland's southern shore and some from Nova Scotia, they had all fished Cape St. Mary's over the past few days. Paddy's crew had landed more cod than any of the other vessels, but still, the catch was not as good as the skipper had hoped. Paddy wondered if his son James was faring any better. He had heard word from the other captains that James had decided to set the dories out in Placentia Bay, fishing grounds about twenty-five miles west of Cape St. Mary's bay. *Plenty of fish to be caught there, me son, but keep an eye out for the reefs and the sunkers.*

Paddy filled the barrel with water and looked to the north. Not long after he and the boys returned to the vessel, they'd be sailing across St. Mary's Bay to Cape Pine. There before sunset, they'd lower the dories over the rail. Paddy would give each of the six dorymen a course, "Four hundred strokes to the east, four hundred to the west" and the fellas would fish all night, setting and hauling trawl until Sunday dawn broke, a day that Catholic fishermen refused to work. Fearing the wrath of God, the dorymen dared not fish on the Lord's Day. Paddy would allow them a bit of rest then, time to repair their gear and share a few yarns and songs.

Aye, that might cheer Frankie up, some sea stories and music. And with some luck maybe the hold would be filled with the codfish by then. Paddy knew the men were dog tired; he had worked them for seventy-two hours straight; the weather had been fine, the sky clear and blue, the sea smooth as oil. 'Twas no reason for sleep or slackin' off, when the conditions were this good. "The sooner we catch the fish, b'ys," Paddy had told them, "the sooner, we sail for home."

Paddy dragged the barrel of springwater from the cliffs to the dory. His boots crunched the shells beneath his feet, reminding the captain of his own childhood. A boy of twelve, he had raced along the sand with his own dogs and brothers. Pushing his cap back from his head, the skipper wiped the sweat from his brow. One of the lads who owned the dogs waved and walked toward the skipper. The boy knew Paddy from previous journeys, and he had heard plenty of stories about the captain's fearsome nature and rough-and-tumble character.

"Aye, Skipper Paddy, how's the fishing?" the boy asked.

"Not so good, son. The fish are scarce off Cape St. Mary's. We'll be off before dark for Cape Pine. We'll see what we can land there."

"Aye, good luck, sir."

Paddy nodded farewell and hauled the barrel into the boat.

"C'mon sons, time to get back to the schooner," Paddy shouted.

Frankie and Jerome ran to their father with the older of the two dogs at their heels.

"Da, they say we can keep one of their dogs," Frankie pleaded. "They can barely feed 'im. His name is Trey. He's a fine fellow, Da."

"Please, can we keep him, Da?" Jerome asked. "Please?"

Paddy looked at the grins on his sons' faces. Frankie hadn't looked this chipper since the Lady Day garden party when he soared in the box swing.

"Alright," Paddy agreed, "Get 'im in the dory."

"C'mon, Trey, C'mon, boy," Frankie hollered.

The dog bounded for the boat, leaping through the water and landing in the dory with a thud that shook the planks.

"Jaysus, hold onto him so he doesn't capsize us," Paddy warned.

Jerome and Frankie sat on either side of the dog, their arms holding tight to their new companion. "Thanks fellas!" they shouted to the boys who remained in the cove.

The three brothers returned the farewell, their eyes following the skipper, his sons, and the black dog who barked at the seagulls flying overhead. Despite the dog's added weight, the dory cut through the water quickly with Paddy's steady strokes. The boat rose and fell gently in a sea that had turned golden with sunlight.

Two hundred miles south, there was no sun to be found. The sky was dark as ink, and rain flew sideways as the gale roared toward the southeastern shores of Newfoundland. A fast-moving mass of ferocious winds, the storm would arrive without warning. The weatherglass would drop quickly marking the fall in air pressure. The current would run like a river, the sea would swell, and then the demon would descend. Mountains of water would rise from ten to thirty to forty and fifty feet within hours. The combers would strike with a force that would splinter boats to kindling and sweep men, masts, and everything else on deck overboard into the cold and raging sea.

CHAPTER 16

CHASING ANCESTORS—MARYSTOWN, JUNE 2003

P addy Walsh's house is cold. Our footsteps echo on the wooden floors. The smell of damp wood and musty air lingers in the shuttered rooms.

"Mind the boards here," Alan Brenton tells us, pointing to the floor in the kitchen.

My father, sister, and I step gingerly, careful not to fall through one of the rotting planks. Despite the disrepair, we walk through the 120-year-old home as if we were in a museum, awed by the parlor's mahogany ceilings, the scrolled stairway banister, and the mammoth front doors framed by a stained-glass transom.

This was Paddy Walsh's house.

Not long after she enters the home, Joanie is struck by an odd sensation, as if Paddy's force, his formidable nature along with Lillian's worry and angst, still breathed within the century-old walls.

"There was a heavy vibe when you walked through the door," she will later tell me.

My father's engineering and pragmatic eye appreciates the home's solid construction, its walls and corners that remain sturdy, square. In my mind, I am pulled into the past; each room represents a stage, a scene for the stories I have collected, the details I have recorded. From the dining room window, the waters of Marystown's bay reflect the blue sky. I picture Lillian sitting on a velvet-covered chair, her eyes on distant coves, watching for the returning sails of her husband's ship. In several other windows, the thick and wavy glass that Lillian once peered through has been boarded up, victims to decades of wind and the young vandals who have broken into Paddy's home.

In the kitchen, plywood covers the window that faces east. Lillian and Paddy sat beneath this window and sipped tea on the evening before the skipper journeyed to Cape St. Mary's. The window would have shone clean and bright years ago, its view marred only once, when the evening grass and dirt flew against the pane: a sudden whirlwind spitting sand—the first of Lillian's omens.

In the darkened hallway leading to the kitchen, Alan tugs on a trapdoor beneath the stairs. He laughs as he tells us, "Paddy used to hide his bootleg liquor down here."

Here, the skipper hid his jars of rum among the root vegetables in the dark, cool cellar, defying the customs officer and anyone else who dared enter his home to search for the illegal spirits. We continue through the house into the dining room with its marble fireplace and blue-flowered wallpaper that is torn and peeling. Brenton pulls off a piece of the paper, showing us the layers of material hidden beneath: horsehair and sheets of newspaper, insulation to keep out the cold. I rip some of the paper to keep as a memento of my great uncle's home. The date on the yellowed newsprint reads 1903. A news item reports: *Colonel Willard Glazier of Albany has returned to his home after a successful trip to Labrador, for purpose of learning more than is now known about the topography and the inhabitants of the Great Lone Land . . . ten mountains, fifteen islands, six rivers, and four bays were noted and charted.*

I picture Paddy reading about such adventures as a young man and decades later sitting by his cookstove, sharing stories with his sons about his own far-reaching journeys. I see my grandfather, too, visiting Paddy on a cold January evening, the two of them warm by the fire, Paddy sharing yarns about the sea and Ambrose voicing his desire and dream to leave, to immigrate to the Boston States.

Alan Brenton's voice pulls me from my reverie. "You talk like Ambrose," he tells my father. "You have some of the same mannerisms."

Alan has watched my dad wave his hands in the air as he spoke. He has quietly observed this American stranger who reminds him of his deceased relative and friend.

"He kept pictures of you and your brother Billy in his wallet," Alan continues. "You were both young in the pictures, small boys."

The notion that my grandfather preserved pictures of my father and uncle in his wallet surprises and confuses me. I search my father's face for clues to his thoughts. He seems caught off guard, puzzled, too. Did my Nana send Ambrose those pictures years after he left? Or did Ambrose tuck them in his wallet the November night he slipped out the door leaving behind two sons and a wife in Brooklyn?

"He bragged about you and Billy," Alan explains to my father. "He'd talk about how smart you were and the good jobs you had."

His hands dug into the pockets of his khakis, my father is silent, weighing Alan's words. Later, his voice irritated and laced with resentment, he will tell Joanie and me, "I don't know what the hell Ambrose was bragging about me and Billy for. He had nothing to do with us."

Alan leads us to the second floor on stairs that creak with each of our footsteps. I run my fingers along the banister that has been worn smooth by the hands of Paddy's seven children. We wander through the five bedrooms on the second floor. They are small, and two of them have fireplaces. A white cast-iron bed frame remains in one of them. I picture Frankie and Jerome wrestling beneath the covers before they fell asleep; in another room, I see Little Lillian playing with her dolls, her eyes occasionally drifting toward the water below, hoping for a glimpse of her da's schooner.

Downstairs again, Alan pulls the back door shut, and we step into the meadow beyond Paddy's home. The grass is knee high, and the field is filled with buttercups. The June sun warms our faces, and we take in the panoramic view of the inlet as it flows from the west and then meanders east toward the sea. Marystown's shipbuilding factory and warehouses loom on the banks of the town's northern shore. To the left of the commercial buildings is a vacant lot where the Sacred Heart Church rectory once stood. Father McGettigan was but a quick dory or skiff ride across the bay from his friend Paddy. The two men could see each other's houses, their kerosene lamps lit up in the dark.

"This is some nice view," my father says looking east to Little Bay.

"Not bad, eh?" Alan agrees. "Years ago, they could see all the schooners coming and going. The women did a lot of watching and waiting. Could be days or weeks 'til ye knew whether someone was lost or shipwrecked."

"Well ye best be off for yur appointments," encourages Alan's son, Jack, who has helped us arrange interviews with retired dorymen and family whose fathers sailed on board the *Annie Anita* and *Mary Bernice*.

"Good luck and we'll see ye later," the Brentons tell us.

The footpath from Paddy's home leads down a small hill to the street. I follow my father and sister, reluctant to leave, to part from this home that connects me to my ancestors' past. Like Joanie, I sense lingering emotions in Paddy's house. What would this silent witness share if its walls could recount the memories, the celebrations and births, the music and song, the mourning and loss?

Once one of the grandest homes in Marystown, Paddy's house looks desolate now, forlorn with its boarded windows and crumbling chimneys. There is no hint of the front porch from which Lillian spotted a lone black cloud in the night sky and begged Paddy to postpone his sail 'til morning. The white picket fence that once adorned the front of the house is long gone, too. The garden that bloomed with daisies and roses, plum and apple trees, is thick with weeds and brush.

Despite the home's historic past, its future, Alan has told us, is uncertain. After buying his Uncle Paddy's home five years ago, he has yet to decide whether he will sell it or tear the house down and rebuild. I cringe at the thought of the home demolished, destroyed.

In my mind's eye, I see Lillian in the parlor window, her slender fingers wrapped around prayer beads. The schooners are gone, the *Annie Anita* and *Mary Bernice* sailed four days past. Lillian does not sleep while Paddy and her three sons are at sea. Dreams of storms and gales rob her of rest, and on August 24, she sits for hours by the window, waiting and praying for their return. Her eyes on the bay and her hand on her heart, she whispers, "Look after them, Paddy. Bring my sons home, safe ashore."

CHAPTER 17

"THERE'S A DIVIL COMING!"—NEWFOUNDLAND FISHING GROUNDS, AUGUST 1935

S trange things began to happen in the sea.

Anchor buoys marking the dorymen's fishing trawl sank and then shot back to the surface. The lines curled and twisted as if they were caught in a whirlpool fathoms below. Fishermen eyed their gear and the sky. Aside from the orange glow of sunset, no dark clouds loomed. The ocean did not swell, and the wind did not breeze up. Still, the seasoned dorymen knew the sea was not right; the current beneath the dories ran like a river. Something fierce was coming.

West of Cape St. Mary's, *Mary Bernice's* crew hauled cod from the shoal reefs along Placentia Bay. Bent over the dory gunnel, Dennis Long dragged his fishing line into the boat. The catch was good on this August evening. The gray-haired fisherman pulled a fish from nearly every fourth hook. Long reckoned they could haul a thousand pounds of fish by midnight, but the fifty-five-year-old doryman did not like the peculiar shift in the sea. He had taken to the dory when he was just nine years of age, and more than four decades on the water had taught him to mind the subtle changes, changes that portended deadly storms.

Long glanced at the pile of cod; the dory was only half full. He could stay out and fill the boat, but getting caught in the shoal waters, twenty and thirty fathoms deep among clusters of rock and reef, would be treacherous in a storm. And if a gale, an August gale, was coming, she would come fast. They would have little time to row back to the *Mary Bernice*. Long worried, too, about the young captain James Walsh. A maiden voyage was rough enough without fighting an August gale. And the lad had been a bit distracted, fretting no doubt about his wife giving birth while he was at sea. Long knew James would need some help at the helm, if a fierce storm struck. Paddy had asked Long and Dick Hanrahan of Little Bay to keep watch over the young skipper, and there would be hell to pay if James did not return ashore. Long turned to his dorymate, a greenhorn who was eager to prove his fishing skills. "Sorry, son, it's time to haul the gear and head for the schooner. A fierce storm is drawing near."

The younger doryman stared up at the clear night sky and began to argue, but Long's stern gaze silenced the fisherman's protest. The two men pulled their trawl into the dory, the hooks cartwheeling beneath their hands. Not caring where they landed or if they tangled, the dorymen tossed the lines in the bait tub and reached for their oars. Long sat down and prepared himself for a rough row back to the vessel. He rubbed the religious pendant beneath his shirt for comfort. The cloth scapular depicted the Blessed Virgin, and he never ventured upon the sea without it.

"Pull hard, son," Long told his dorymate. "We've not much time."

Throughout Placentia, St. Mary's, and Trepassey Bays, foghorns wailed as schooner captains signaled their crews to return to their vessels. Crosses pressed against their palms, the dorymen rowed against a current that seemed to push them backward. As the southeastern wind breezed up, they pulled with a strength they did not know they possessed. There was no time for slacking off. A hurricane wind or a series of broadside waves would flip their dories like matchsticks, tossing them into the frigid sea. Their fate would be a doryman's most dreaded end: Weighted down with their leather jackboots and oilskins, they'd sink like stones, dragged to a watery grave. Swallowed by the sea, their bodies would forever disappear beneath the blue-green water. Their families would have nothing then, no corpse to bury, no body to mourn. Their loved ones would keep nothing but the knowledge that their da went to sea and was never seen nor heard of more.

Anchored off the coast of Cape Pine, the *Annie Anita* rocked on the swelling ocean. Concerned about the sudden breeze, Tom Reid searched for his own dorymen. The vessel's three dories had departed not long after dusk. Having fallen seasick like Little Frankie, Reid stayed on board. Paddy had relentlessly teased Reid as he retched over the rail, but then the skipper surprised Reid with an offer: "I'll take ye place in the dory."

Reid suspected the skipper wanted to keep close to his son Jerome, who had gone out with two other of the crew. The young fellow begged Paddy to let him fish. Though the captain was reluctant to let the boy go at night, Jerome pleaded, "I'm fourteen, Da. Ye were in the dory when ye were twelve!"

As the sky blackened, Reid looked for the dory torches, the small dots of light moving closer to the schooner. Skipper Paddy would have known it was time to return; he would have noticed the buoys sinking, the anchors twirling. He would know that the current had gone mad, a sure sign that a gale was coming.

Left behind to comfort Frankie, Reid tried to calm the boy. The lad fell silent, terrified of the waves that grew ragged and taller.

"Jerome and yur da, they'll be back soon, Frankie. Skipper Paddy knows the sea. He's been shipwrecked, stuck in ice floes, and caught in gales before. He'll be on board soon."

Frankie nodded, his eyes wide and glassy. The boy clutched the rigging tighter and called for his new companion to come sit by his side. "C'mere, Trey."

Reid knew the dorymen would have a fight to get back. They'd be battling the wind and the tide together, their boats loaded down with a thousand pounds of cod. Some of the crew would be tossing their fish into the sea, eager to lighten their load and quicken their pace. They would be fearing the skipper's fury for returning with an empty dory, but they feared an August gale more than Paddy's harsh temper.

Paddy would be raging, cursing God and the oncoming gale as he pulled the oars. He'd be cursing the weatherglass that hours earlier foretold of nothin' but fair weather, and he'd be cursing himself for letting his son Jerome set out for the night. The skipper, Reid knew, would not return until Jerome was safe on board. The Capt'n had assigned each dory a course; he would hunt for his son's dory, search for the boat's light as he shouted into the wind.

The skipper would also be worried for James. A hundred questions would be roaring through Paddy's mind. *Can we beat the storm and get back on board in time? Should we sail the* Annie Anita *out to sea or chance heading north east into Trepassey? Is James clear of the ragged Virgin Rocks in Placentia Bay? Will he get his men back on deck?*

Reid recalled the words he had shared with Miss Lillian before they left Marystown. "Not to worry, Lil. I'll look after Frankie, and Paddy will keep an eye on Jerome."

Jaysus, Paddy'd never come back in without his son. He would call down the Lord if he had to, but he would not leave his boy out to sea. Reid reckoned that it might be hours before Paddy returned. He readied the *Annie Anita* for the blow, battening the hatches, reefing the sails, and stowing gaffs, trawl, and bait tubs below, Still, once Paddy returned, they'd have some hard choices to make. *Annie Anita*'s position bore them few options. She sat five miles off Cape Pine, a treacherous site southwest of Trepassey Bay. With its sheer cliffs and sunkers, Cape Pine offered no safe harbors. The waters were shallow and littered with reefs. *In a gale, ye'd have no chance there, caught in the shoal waters with waves pounding ye; the vessel would be smashed in two.*

Reid cranked the schooner horn again and again, calling his men home. The haunting bellows beckoned in the dark.

"Where the hell ye at, Paddy?" Reid whispered.

Hundreds of strokes from the *Annie Anita,* Paddy rowed in the dark, his kerosene torch lighting a small patch of the sea. The dory rode up and down on the rolling waves. Foam spewed in spindrifts, circling the boat like spirits. The white horses, waves that curled and crested like a horse's mane, pounded the dory's bow. As Paddy's dorymate John Brinton bailed, the skipper struggled to keep the boat from turning crossways in the sea. The combers were almost as tall as the fifteen-foot dory, and she rose up with them and crashed into their troughs with a teeth-jarring jolt. Blood trickled from Paddy's hands as he gripped the oars and heaved his chest into every stroke. The skipper knew there was little time left to find Jerome and get back to the schooner. There was little time for them all. In the distance, Paddy could see a half dozen vessels racing for shore, their lights blazing on the bow and stern. A schooner hove to the wind, drew closer to Paddy's dory. As the vessel sailed within shouting distance, the captain hollered over the rail, offering to hoist Paddy and his dory on board.

Paddy recognized the skipper, a fisherman from Trepassey.

"Paddy, ye've got to get in!" the captain shouted. "There's a divil coming!"

"I know," Paddy bellowed into the wind. "We'd be gone in now b'y, but we've got a stray dory!"

The Trepassey skipper nodded, bid the Marystown captain good luck and God's blessing before pointing his schooner toward shore. Paddy pulled harder on the oars, his eyes blinded by the rain that lashed from a sky black as coal. Waves crested and broke, one after another, slamming the dory onto her sides. Paddy cursed the wind, the waves, and the gale that threatened to kill them all. He turned to the heavens and shouted: "Take me, ye son of a bitch! Just spare me boys!"

The captain's mind raced, wild with worry. He imagined Jerome terrified in a dory that pitched and rolled. The lad would be weeping, crying for the comfort of his mother and a warm bed at home. *Jaysus, Jerome, don't fret lad. The dorymen will get ye back to the schooner; we'll get out of this then. We'll pull the anchor and sail into Trepassey. Ye'll be okay, boy. Hang on to the gunnels. Don't let the seas wash ye overboard. Hold fast, ye'll be home at your mother's side soon.*

Paddy hoped the dorymen who took Jerome out had taken notice of the changes in the tide early. If they'd pulled their trawl at the first hint of the gale, they'd still have a chance to get on board the *Annie Anita*. Reid would be looking out for them; he'd keep the foghorn blowing, the lights bright. He'd keep the schooner steady and Frankie comforted until they returned. *And James, was he keeping* Mary Bernice *hove into the wind? Was he at the helm?*

Head out to sea, James. Get away from the sunkers and the shoal water, son. The waves there will rise up from the bottom of the sea and pound the vessel to bits with the force of a freight train. Lash yourself to the wheel when the gale hits. When it gets dirty and dark, ye won't be able to stand in the fearsome wind. And then the waves will come, one after another, combers that look like mountains. Keep 'er steady, take the waves as best ye can. Don't let 'em hit ye broadside; the vessel, she'll never right herself with the blow that will strike 'er. Ride with the storm, James, keep yur wits about ye and ride 'er out. You're a captain now, son, bring yur crew home. I'll see ye on Marystown's shores. We'll have plenty of yarns to share about yur first August gale, me boy. Ye will be telling stories until yur grandchildren tumble beneath yur feet.

The full wrath of the August gale was but an hour away. The hurricane would strike sometime after 10:00 p.m. over Cape Pine, Trepassey, Cape St. Mary's, and Placentia Bays. The southeastern corner off Newfoundland's coast would suffer the top right hand of the storm, where the waves and wind would be most fierce. The waters there would be caught in a deadly trapped fetch. Two types of wind—the counterclockwise velocity of the gale and the forward speed of the hurricane—would combine to blow waves into forty, fifty, and sixty-foot monsters. The seasoned dorymen would remember the sounds as the gale grew closer, the rumbling in the distance, the thunder of mountainous waves crashing in the dark.

Still awaiting her crew, the *Annie Anita* bucked into the heaving sea and crashed violently as her anchor pulled her back down. The waves were twenty feet tall now, and she could barely ride them out. If they grew bigger, she'd have no chance. Reid reckoned it was only a matter of time before the sea tore the anchor from the schooner, and then her bow would no longer point into the wind and waves. If she took a heavy sea crossways, she'd be doomed. Clinging to the rigging, Reid scanned the horizon. He could scarce see a vessel's length. Visibility was pitiful with the rain and sea spray. Even the light atop Cape Pine had disappeared. Still, Reid expected to see Paddy's dory bobbing on the waves. Hear the skipper's voice bellowing in the dark. Paddy had gotten them home in gales before. Surely, he'd do the same now.

Hours earlier, Reid had sent Frankie down below to his father's cabin. The boy was trembling, the tears streaming down his face. There was nothing left for Reid to do but join the lad. He could barely stand in the wind; if he remained on deck any longer, he'd be washed overboard himself. Securing the hatch, Reid made his way below. He found Frankie in his Sunday suit, prepared to meet God. The lad sobbed as he lay in his father's bunk, clutching the small Bible his mother had packed in his duffle. Reid sat down next to the boy and held the child as the vessel rolled violently to port.

"It's alright, son; here, let's read from yur Bible together."

Frankie nodded, and Reid read from the passage stained by the boy's tears. Reid and other Catholic fishermen knew the psalm well, St. Mark, verse 4:39, "And he arose, and rebuked the wind, and said unto the sea, Peace, be still. And the wind ceased, and there was great calm."

Reid rubbed the boy's shaking back and urged the lad to recite the Lord's Prayer. Frankie uttered the words, his voice trembling, "Our Father, who art in heaven . . ."

"Keep 'er going, Frankie. I'm going on deck for another look for yur Da and the rest of the crew."

Frankie nodded and reached for Trey. The dog whimpered as the schooner creaked and shuddered, pummeled by the waves striking her sides. In the galley, mugs, plates, and pots flew from shelves. Trawl tubs rolled and bounced in the hold, dorymen's boots tumbled end over end, and precious keepsakes—pictures of wives and daughters, sons and mothers—fluttered like confetti from cabin walls.

Outside, the wind roared like a church organ and the waves grew taller than a vessel's mast. On schooners and dories along Newfoundland's southeastern coast, captains lashed themselves to the rigging and the deck bolt below the wheel. Dorymen clutched lifelines and marked crosses over the giant combers, beseeching the Lord to calm the seas. Waves tall as three-story houses struck decks, breaking masts in two and sweeping men and everything else on deck into the raging sea. Vessels large and small foundered in the hurricane-ravaged waters.

Fifty miles east of the *Annie Anita,* the crew aboard the *Jane and Martha* struggled to stay upright. Waves crashed over the deck and battered the vessel with such force the schooner pitched on its side; its masts nearly flattened to the sea. The wind howled and the rigging shrieked. Captain James Bruce warned his crew "Get ready, boys, 'tis going to be a dirty long and god-fearing night."

Fishing since he was eight years old, the skipper had weathered many storms, but this gale would prove to be the captain's most fearsome challenge in his fifty-four years at sea. A few hours before midnight, the full force of the hurricane roared overhead. The winds gusted to sixty, seventy, and eighty miles an hour, battering vessels and splintering them to pieces. Belowdecks, Bruce's crew braced themselves in their bunks and prayed they would live to see morning. By dawn, the seas still heaved, and the winds continued to knock fishermen off their feet. Hoping to make it into harbor, Captain Bruce ordered the crew to rig the sails. As they headed for shore, they came upon a schooner in distress. She rolled back and forth in the giant breakers, exposing her keel before she righted herself. A Marystown man on board the *Jane and Martha* recognized the vessel.

"It's the *Mary Bernice!*"

The schooner's deck was stripped bare; her dories and sails had been washed overboard. Bruce searched unsuccessfully for the vessel's captain and crew. Caught crossways in the sea, walls of water pounded the schooner.

Oh God, b'y, James Bruce thought. *Those poor fellows are doomed.*

The skipper and his men watched as the schooner pitched and rolled. Slammed onto her starboard side, the *Mary Bernice*'s anchors and chains hung from her bow. Bottom up with the weight of her anchor holding her down, she'd have no way of righting herself now. Bruce knew the schooner's crew had no chance a'tall. If they weren't swept into the sea before the vessel capsized, they were certain to be drowned now, their bodies floating in the cabin, their lungs gasping for air as they begged the Lord for mercy upon their souls.

Bruce and his men whispered their own prayers as the schooner named for Paddy's lost child, Mary Bernice, disappeared in the roiling sea.

CHAPTER 18

MOUNTAINOUS WAVES AND MIGHTY MEN— MARYSTOWN, 2003

We do not get far from Paddy's house before a blue Toyota pulls up to our rental car. A red-haired man shouts out the window at us.

My father, Joanie, and I stand in the street wondering who the stranger is.

"Hello," he says with a broad smile. "I'm your cousin, Tom Reid."

Tom Reid as in Tom Reid, Paddy's second hand?

"I hear you are Paddy Walsh's relations," he tells us. "My grandfather, Tom Reid, sailed on the *Annie Anita* with Paddy's crew."

I nod and compare my mental image of Tom Reid to his grandson who now stands before me. Reid was stocky, tall, and like Paddy, known for his fierce, stern gaze. The younger Reid bears few of his grandfather's traits. He is shorter, bearded, and jovial, chatting with us as if we are neighbors and good friends. A barrel-chested man like his grandfather, he gestures to a buff-yellow dory in the bay, a boat Reid rows when the weather is fair. In his mid-forties, Reid is a few years younger than his grandfather was during the *Annie Anita*'s 1935 journey.

"The Reids lived there on Shoal Point, just before Little Bay," he says, pointing to a knoll a short distance up the road. "Reid Hill it used to be called."

George Reid, Tom Reid, John Reid, and Joe Reid built their homes side by side.

Other fishermen who crewed for Paddy lived a stone's throw from Tom Reid's dwelling. At sea, they shared dories and bunks. On land, their homes neighbored one another in a row along the bay. The families of Charles Hanrahan, George Mitchell, Dominic Walsh, and John Brinton grew up within shouting distance of one another. Their children played in each other's meadows. Their wives and mothers waved to one another across fences and comforted each other over cups of tea, hushing away bad dreams and premonitions.

"They had a tough old life," Reid tells us of his ancestors, "But the fishermen were tough, too; they had no fear a'tall."

"What about Paddy Walsh?" my father asks.

Reid smiles and shakes his head.

"Paddy was vicious. He'd go out to sea in anything; it didn't matter what storm was coming. He wasn't afraid of nothin'. He thought he was grander than God."

His grandfather, Reid tells us, also had a fierce nature. Like Paddy, Reid had no use for fear, the rules, or the law. In the woods behind Reid's home, he and the skipper made moonshine. Under the cover of night, they boiled molasses and yeast in stills, contraptions which occasionally blew up due to carelessness or too much consumption.

"They were big drinkers," Reid says, "and the best of buddies—until they fought. Paddy was a tough Irishman and my grandfather was rough Scotsman. They'd fight each other over anything.

"Hard men, they were. But they trusted each other. They knew they could count on one another at sea."

I imagine Reid strolling down the dirt path from Reid Hill, a duffle over his shoulder and a song on his lips. He is eager to sail, to make a good catch before the winter cold sets in. On his way to Paddy's wharf, he stops by to reassure Lillian. "I'll look after Frankie, and Paddy will keep an eye on Jerome," he tells her before boarding the *Annie Anita*.

Did Paddy ask Reid to stop by, to utter those encouraging words to calm his fretting wife's nerves? There was no one Paddy trusted more than Reid, his second hand. On that August evening, when the ocean tide ran like a river and the wind started to blow, the skipper knew Reid would do his best to keep Frankie from harm. But how do you keep such a promise when the seas grow higher than a schooner's mast and the sky turns black as coal?

Wishing us good luck with our gale research, Reid shakes our hands.

"I'll be glad to help ye in any way I can," he says, sharing his phone number and a hearty wave before disappearing up the road toward Reid Hill.

Tom Reid is not the only one in town aware of our visit. It seems we are well-known and much talked about. As we travel in our blue rental car along the back roads of Marystown and Little Bay, strangers wave to us like we are long-lost family. They know we hail from the States, and in the local coffee shop they swap details about our arrival.

"Did ye hear? Paddy and Ambrose Walsh's relations are here. They're wanting to know about the gale, the August Gale of '35."

It seems we are connected to most of the town. Our expansive Newfoundland family tree makes my head spin. Not only are we related to the numerous Walshes, we are kin to the Reids, the Clinches, and the Brintons. My father is either a first or second cousin to nearly everyone we meet. Several of the relations are quick to note that my father reminds them of Ambrose. They watch him wave his hands in the air as he speaks, and in their minds, they see Paddy's younger brother, the charming young man who sought adventure and a new life in the Boston States.

"You bear a strong resemblance to him," they say.

As Tom Reid explained when he took in the sight of my dad's dark eyes and hair, "I could tell you were a pure Walsh."

Reid's words echo in my thoughts as we drive along the water, looking for the home of Jim "Pad" Kelly, a doryman caught out in the August Gale. We know little about Kelly before we step foot into his home, but we will later learn he is a bit of a legend in Marystown. Stories are told and retold in kitchens throughout the small town about his courage and might.

As most of the men who fished from the small dories, Kelly often found himself separated from the schooner, blinded by curtains of relentless fog. On two of those occasions, Kelly rowed more than a hundred miles home from the Grand Banks fishing grounds. For seven days, he pulled the oars, sustaining himself with little more than hardtack and sips of water. During one of the journeys, the winter wind blew and the cold numbed the doryman's hands. After rowing five days, Kelly's dorymate dropped the oars in exhaustion.

"I can't go on," the younger man cried.

"Well then give me yur damn mitts!" shouted Kelly, who had lost his own. "Because I'm not ready to die."

We find Kelly's house at the end of a dead-end road. Expecting our visit, Mrs. Kelly invites us into their kitchen where her husband waits. Eighty-five years old, Kelly's chest is still broad from years of rowing dories at sea. His hair, once thick and dark, is now white and thinned with age. His hands are large, palms that gripped dory oars for more than four decades.

Kelly was seventeen in 1935. He is one of the few survivors who can offer a firsthand account of the gale, and though his memories of the storm are vivid, his hearing is limited. On this June afternoon, my father, Joanie, and I are mesmerized by the fisherman's voice as he recounts the night the August Gale struck the southeastern coast of Newfoundland.

"You need to talk loud," his wife whispers to us. "He can't hear very well."

My father and I find ourselves hollering, trying to pull details from the doryman's memory to recreate the night the "devil" descended.

"It was my first year fishing," he tells us. "That was a bad old night. We were out on the *Hilda G. Reeves*. She was a schooner with three dories."

Kelly knew Paddy and James Walsh were out in their vessels, too.

"James was behind us in Placentia Bay, and Paddy was over by Cape Pine."

Kelly and his dorymate Bill Hanrahan had set their trawl west of Cape St. Mary's in Placentia Bay. Hanrahan, an eighteen-year-old man from Little Bay, was a greenhorn, too. He had never been to sea before.

"We set the lines, and our buoys got pulled with the tide. Not long after she breezed up, our boat busted an anchor cable. It was time to get out of there."

Kelly had never felt such a force.

"We had some job," he says, "getting back to the schooner. If we'd a'waited any longer, I don't think we would 'ave made it."

For the next two hours, the two men struggled to row back to their vessel. Neither spoke as they pulled the oars. They had a mile to row, and it seemed like twenty.

"When we got back to the schooner, all hands were on board. We pulled anchor and ran before the wind. We come right down the middle of Placentia Bay."

Kelly would never forget the walls of water and the shrieking wind when the brunt of the gale hit sometime after midnight.

"If ye were on deck, ye had to have a rope around ye. The waves, they were going over the mast."

His hands carving an imaginary crest in the air in front of him, Kelly explains, "The schooner she'd go up 'em, then come down and pop out over the waves."

"Did you see the *Perfect Storm?*" my father hollers to Kelly, referring to the movie about the 1991 hurricane that killed several Gloucester fishermen off Newfoundland's coast.

Kelly nods.

"Were the waves as big as in that movie?"

Kelly nods again, this time with a grin. At one point, he tells us, a monstrous wave rolled toward the sixty-foot vessel. Kelly shouted to his dorymate, Hanrahan, who was also tied to the rigging. Hanrahan's eyes grew wide at the sight of the giant comber thundering toward them.

"He nearly had a heart attack," Kelly says. "The water rushed in at us, mountains of water. We were some lucky to get in that night."

Shaking his head, Kelly adds, "A lot of the crowd didn't get in. It was a rough old night. Plenty has been said of them that got in out of the gale. Ye didn't have no equipment. All ye had was a big sail and the weatherglass. Ye didn't have much of a chance. Not a'tall."

Kelly falls silent, his blue eyes focused on something we cannot see.

"No," Kelly whispers, "a lot of the men, they never was seen no more."

CHAPTER 19

PRAYERS AND APPARITIONS—MARYSTOWN, AUGUST, 1935

Thunder rumbled, and lightning lit up the bay outside the Sacred Heart Presbytery. From his parlor window, Father McGettigan eyed the whitecaps and the waves that pounded the shore. The sea surge pushed past the fish wharves, tearing dories and schooners from their anchors. The priest sipped rum from his glass and shuddered. If the gale was this fierce inland, eight miles from the sea, McGettigan could only imagine the hellish conditions offshore.

Though it was well after midnight, lamps burned in the homes along the northern and southern shores of Marystown. Few would sleep on a night such as this. McGettigan knew that the fishermen's families—every mother, child, and wife—were on their knees. Clutching their Rosary beads, they'd be asking for miracles, beseeching the Lord and the Blessed Mother to protect their men at sea. *And 'twould surely take a miracle to bring the fishermen home, to see them through a gale that would show them no mercy, no respite.*

For much of the night, the priest had paced the parlor floor, uttering his own pleas for Paddy and his crew. Again and again, he recited the fisherman's prayer, his hands folded, his eyes closed in concentration: *Heavenly Father, We pray to You for those on the perilous ocean that You will embrace them with your mighty protection. Grant them grace in the hour of danger to commit their souls into Your hands. Oh Lord Jesus Christ, who can rebuke the storm and bring it to silence, and lay the roaring waves to rest, show them who call to You out of the deep that You hear their prayer and will save them.*

McGettigan pictured the *Annie Anita* riding the wind, her planks pounded by unrelenting waves. *Would the Lord grant Paddy another chance to conquer the sea, or would He pull him into the deep, claiming the captain's soul? And James, dear God, his first voyage as skipper. Would the Heavenly Father offer the young captain grace, guiding him and his crew safe ashore, or would he, too, vanish beneath the blue-black waters? Between the* Annie Anita *and* Mary Bernice, *ten of Marystown's men and two lads were in the Lord's hands. Two other of the crew hailed from Little Bay and Fox Cove. How many would return? How many would sail onto these shores again?*

McGettigan reached for another glass of the amber liquor to quiet his nerves.

"May the Heavenly Father be with you all," he whispered.

The priest drew the parlor curtains aside and gazed at Paddy's house across the bay. The lights blazed on each of the home's three floors. Lillian would be out of her mind with worry, and there would be no calming the woman until telegrams or fishermen offered word of her husband and sons' fates. Beyond the priest's meadow, the hurricane tore hundred-year-old trees from their roots; it smashed windowpanes and ripped roofs from housetops. Rain pelted windows like nails tossed from buckets. Deep into the night, the gale would rage, and in between the desperate prayers, dreams would haunt and visions would appear, tokens of spirits, sailors who breathed no more.

On Reid Hill, Shoal Point, in Marystown, Fox Cove, and Little Bay, families gathered beneath the lamplight. The Reids, Mitchells, Hanrahans, Farrells, Cheekes, Walshes, Longs, and Brintons knelt on kitchen and bedroom floors. "Pray for yur poor Da," their mothers urged. "Pray to the Lord to save his soul."

Ernestine Walsh winced at the thunderclap and the lightning flash that lit up the kitchen. The girl of nine closed her eyes, praying for the noises to cease, for the wind to calm, and for the bad things to stop. Rain pounded their roof and leaked in torrents onto the kitchen floor; gusts off the bay had blown out their kitchen window, sending shards of glass flying across the room. They had all screamed in the middle of their prayers at the sudden crash. Mother had nailed a quilt over the jagged opening, but the wind still found its way inside, shrieking like a wounded animal.

The remaining kitchen window rattled, and Ernestine searched out the glass pane, looking for her father Ernest's schooner. Like her Uncle Paddy, her da had set sail a week before the storm. *Please come home, Da! Don't let the gale take you.* Ernestine worried, too, for her cousins, Frankie, Jerome, and James, and of course, for Uncle Paddy. Out of father's five brothers, Paddy was her favorite. He could be a devil, drinking and carrying on, but he always looked after her and her family when Da was away. If one of them fell ill, Uncle Paddy was there to make sure they had enough food, enough medicine, and wood for the fire.

Out on the bay, small globes of light caught the girl's eye. Ernestine spied two schooners sailing through the whitecaps. Lights fastened to the rigging, illuminating the boats' bow and stern. Ernestine shouted, recognizing the vessels.

"Mom! Uncle Paddy is back. And there's James behind him!"

The schooners veered to the north side of Marystown, near the presbytery.

"Why are they on the north side, Mother? Why aren't they coming up to the southern shore by Uncle Paddy's wharf?"

Her mother shook her head and did not speak. Ernestine turned back to the window for another look at the vessels, but the boats were gone.

Beyond Reid Hill farther east in Little Bay, Richard Hanrahan's small home shuddered against the wind gusts. Bride Hanrahan hid beneath her bedcovers as the sky crackled and lightning burst like balls of fire. From the kitchen, Bride could hear her mother sobbing as she murmured the Rosary. Earlier in the night, Bride and her four siblings had knelt by their mother's chair, chanting Hail Marys for their father. When the clock tolled two in the morning, their mother had put them to bed, urging them to rest, but Bride feared sleep and her dreams. When she dozed, the images came to her. She saw her father thrashing in the sea. His mouth was open in a scream, but the roar of the wind silenced his cries. Weighted down with his oilskins, the waves crashed over his head, dragging him under; and then there was nothing but walls of black water, cresting, crashing. In the foaming sea, a flash of yellow appeared, her father's jacket sleeve. He shouted her name, his hand reached for her, for anything to hold on to. Hollering against the wind, she shouted to him. "Here, Da! I'm here!" Her small hand searched for her father's palm. But his body had vanished. There was only the sea, the mad, wild sea. She could hear his cries no more.

Lucy Walsh stifled her own screams as labor pains tore through her abdomen. It seemed the storm had brought on the young woman's contractions, and now, at the height of the gale, her pains grew more rapid, more fierce. Selena Gaulton held her daughter's hand trying to calm the soon-to-be mother. A midwife, Gaulton had delivered hundreds of babies in Little Bay, Marystown, and the surrounding outports. But this birth would bring its own complications. The thunder, lightning, and roaring wind had whipped Lucy into a fit of hysteria. She was beside herself with worry for her husband James.

"He'll never see the baby now, never!" she cried.

"Hush now, James and his crew will be fine," Gaulton told her daughter, though the older woman did not believe the fishermen stood a chance. She had never seen a storm this vicious in all her years. Gaulton could only imagine the horror James and his crew faced at sea.

"Ye've got to focus on yur baby now, m'dear," Gaulton told her. "Yur child will be here soon."

Overhead, the rafters groaned, and Gaulton prayed the roof would hold. *Lord spare us from difficulties with this birth tonight.* The doctor would never make it across the bay in conditions this rough. Sterilizing cloths for the birth, Gaulton uttered more prayers. As she headed back upstairs to her daughter's bedroom, she struggled to return to Lucy's side. Invisible forces, shapes stood in front of her, spirits who wanted to be present, to witness the birth of Lucy's child. Gaulton made the sign of the cross over her forehead, fearing James and his crew had passed on. *Dear God, James is just a young man, and his wife, barely turned twenty herself. Married only three months they were. Lucy's heart would surely break in two if he never returned.*

The midwife pushed the dark thoughts from her mind and focused on her daughter and the baby that was coming fast. "Push Lucy, you're close, now."

Pink and robust, the child emerged without complications and oblivious to the gale that roared outside. "It's a girl," Gaulton announced, handing the infant to her daughter. The child, Lucy quickly decided, would be named Jamie after her father. Swaddled and searching for her mother's milk, the infant wailed, and Gaulton sensed a presence behind her. She turned to the sea chest that rested by her daughter's bed. There sat James, a vision in the dark. The midwife gasped at the sight and then the realization struck: *My dear Lucy, ye've become a mother and a widow on the same eve. Yur husband is gone now, girl. May the Lord watch over ye and yur new babe.* The shock of it, Gaulton knew, would not leave Lucy for a good, long while. She only hoped that her daughter would not look upon Little Jamie as a reminder of death and loss.

Across the bay, Father McGettigan tried to settle himself beneath layers of quilts and blankets. Though he had finished several glasses of rum this evening, the liquor offered little solace. Concern for Paddy, James, and their crews gnawed at his every thought. Cursing the wind that continued to shriek like a banshee, the priest blew the flame from the kerosene lamp and recited another prayer. *Mary, Mother of God, guide them through the dark and roaring sea. Offer them your blessings, your benevolence, and your protection. Amen.*

From the third-floor attic, he could hear the maid, the young girl, Lizzie, shifting in her bed. *Sleep will not come for any of us tonight,* the priest thought. Moments later, McGettigan heard an odd pounding. The knocking continued and grew louder before he realized someone was at the door. *Who could be out at such an hour on such a wretched night?* Relighting the lamp, McGettigan made his way downstairs and opened the Presbytery door. There on the stoop, stood Paddy and his crew. Dressed in their oilskins, the men remained silent, solemn. Before the priest could speak, before he could embrace Paddy and praise the Lord for a miracle, the fishermen disappeared, leaving McGettigan alone in the blinding rain.

"What is it, sir?" Lizzie asked from the stairs.

McGettigan turned to her, his face white as chalk.

"They're gone; they're all gone. We'll never see, nor hear of them again."

Leo and Ambrose Walsh in Staten Island circa 1926.

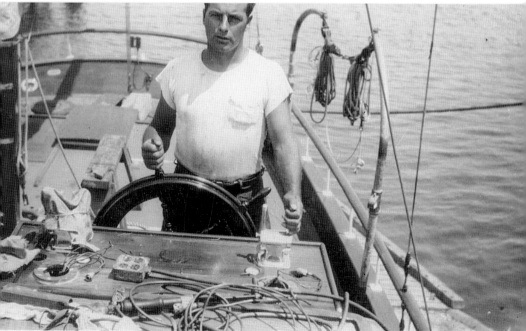

Ambrose Walsh at the helm of Florida yacht circa 1947.

Ronald Walsh's First Communion circa 1941.

COURTESY OF THE
WALSH FAMILY

Marystown funeral procession circa 1930s.

COURTESY OF THE
WALSH FAMILY

In mourning: Lillian Walsh and her daughters, left to right: Theresa, Lillian, and Loretta circa 1936.

After the gale: Paddy Walsh Jr. sitting on backyard fence post circa 1936.

Southern and northern shores of Marystown circa 2000.

PHOTOGRAPH BY DENIS THIBODEAU, COURTESY OF MARYSTOWN TOWN HALL

Vacant and boarded up: Paddy Walsh's house in June 2003.

PHOTOGRAPH BY BARBARA WALSH

Marystown Sacred Heart Cemetery, gravestones of Paddy Walsh and his family.

Marystown Sacred Heart Cemetery, gravestones of Paddy Walsh and his family.

Ronald Walsh and his daughters, Barbara (left) and Diane, circa 1962.

Patricia Walsh and her sons, Ronald (left) and William, gather for a birthday celebration circa 1980.

The Walsh sisters during the author's 1996 wedding, left to right: Janice, Jackie, Diane, Barbara, Laura, and Joan.
PHOTO BY WILLIAM PATRICK WALSH (UNCLE BILL)

The Walsh family at a New Orleans wedding in 1999. Left to right: Jacqueline, Barbara, Janice, Patricia, Ronald, Laura, Joan, and Diane.
PHOTOGRAPH BY PETE GREVEMBERG

William Patrick Walsh and his family, Pamela, William Patrick Jr., and Margaret.
PHOTOGRAPH BY PETE GREVEMBERG

Ambrose's children from his first and second families during a 2003 summer gathering in New Hampshire. Left to right: Kathy, Ronald, Donnie, and William Walsh.
PHOTOGRAPH BY PAMELA WALSH

CHAPTER 20

"MY POOR DADDY WAS LOST"—MARYSTOWN, 2003

We travel east, following the course Paddy last sailed on that August morning when skies were clear, the wind calm. The sky on this June afternoon is also cloudless, a brilliant blue. As our car crests Reid Hill, we glimpse views of the water below, vistas where children and wives long looked for a familiar sail, a returning vessel.

Here from the southern shores of Marystown, the children of the gale waited and watched, praying that their fathers would survive the storm. I imagine the strange happenings that night, the terrifying sounds, the unexplained omens. Ernestine Walsh, her face pressed to the windowpane, her eyes wide, envisioning Paddy and James returning in their schooners, kerosene lights guiding the phantom boats through a tempest of roaring wind and lashing rain. The baby, Jamie, a wailing infant born amidst a howling gale as her father's spirit stirred in the room. Bride Hanrahan's dream, the images of her dad, his frantic hand reaching for her as he disappeared beneath the angry sea.

Of the dozens of children who prayed that night, forty-two would never see their fathers again. Some would remember their last farewell, their father's kiss, the touch of his calloused hand. Others would hold on to the image of their dads' broad backs, sea bags slung over shoulders, dories drifting away in the dark. I imagine my father's memories of Ambrose vanishing, disappearing in the night. On the dark streets of Brooklyn, Ambrose closes a door, softly stepping into the cold November air. And in the morning, a boy of eleven learns, "Your father's gone."

Like the children of the gale, my father carries memories: how he was never far from Ambrose's side, following him to the Staten Island playgrounds and to the ship-rigging lofts of Brooklyn; how Ambrose's strong hands wrestled him to the living room floor or braced his wobbling bicycle; how the two of them took car rides alone, father and son, Ambrose at the wheel and his boy Ronnie standing on the seat beside him, his small arm wrapped securely around the shoulder of a man who kept him safe, held him close.

How many times did my father wish for Ambrose's return, pray that his family would be whole again? How many times did he wonder: Why did my father leave us?

For decades the children of the gale have asked those same questions. Despite the passing of sixty-eight years, their sorrow lingers. On this June afternoon we seek the gale children, men and women who are now in their seventies and eighties and live in Marystown or nearby. Paddy's niece, Gertrude Walsh, has agreed to share her stories with us. The eldest daughter of Ernest Walsh's seven children, Gertrude was fourteen in 1935. With a few hastily scratched directions to her house, my father, Joanie, and I venture east along Marine Drive, the road that leads from Marystown to Little Bay and the sea. There are few markers in the small village of 160 people, and naturally we get lost—several times. Short on patience, my father utters a "Jesus Christ, where the hell is this place?" moments before we find Gertrude's driveway.

Eighty-two-year-old Gertrude and her daughter invite us into their kitchen. Gertrude sits in her rocking chair and leans forward to hear our conversation. Her daughter has warned us that her mother tires easily and may have difficulty talking with us. But when Gertrude speaks, her voice is strong and clear. She has no trouble recalling the storm and shakes her head at the memory of that August night.

"Gales, gales, gales," she says closing her eyes. "The wind howled! Oh, it was awful. Mother lit the candles as the wind came through the windows.

"It was a terrible night. We gathered by Mother's feet and said the Rosary with her. We prayed for Father and we prayed for Uncle Paddy. The rain and the wind lashed down, and the water poured in through the roof. We never had a leak like that before."

Like many of the fishermen's children, Gertrude dreamt of her dad. In her mind, she saw his hand on the helm of the *J.R. Rodgers,* his back bent to the wind as he sailed into the harbor.

"I dreamt my daddy came in and anchored his boat. But when we got up the next morning, he wasn't there. Uncle Paddy hadn't returned either. We were worried sick for them both."

"Can you tell us some stories about Paddy?" I ask.

My request stirs a grin and a glimpse of a girl who admired her uncle's rambunctious nature. As with her memory of the gale, her stories of "Uncle Paddy" are vivid. Crossing two fingers, she presses them to her chest and explains, "My dad and Uncle Paddy were just like that. Close as could be. Uncle Paddy was my favorite. Oh, he was a character. I loved him.

"He was a good man but tough, the worst of all the brothers. He could argue about anything, but when he was fighting, all you had to do is put your arms around him and say, 'Uncle Paddy, be quiet now.'"

Paddy, Gertrude tells us, enjoyed music and song, but he could not carry a note. "I think I was his favorite because I used to sing dirty songs for him. He'd give me a quarter when I was done. 'Go get candy,' he'd say.

"After the gale," she says, her voice dropping to a whisper, "I never sang those songs again."

Gertrude closes her eyes, and her daughter nods to us, worried that her mother has worn herself out. Thanking her for her memories, I reach for Gertrude and hug her good-bye. We let ourselves out the door, and I wonder if Gertrude has any stories of my grandfather. Over the past few days, at kitchen tables, on living room sofas, and even in the local funeral parlor (where we stopped to pay our respects to Winnie Walsh, Ambrose's sister-in-law), we have heard several tales about Ambrose. His nieces, nephews, and old neighbors spoke about his charm, his ability to talk easily and convincingly at length on any subject, his knack for putting people at ease within minutes of meeting them.

"Your dad was a good man," these relatives told my father. "Everyone loved Ambrose. He had a great personality."

Sometimes my dad did not reply. Other times he shared his ill feelings, the memories that still haunt. "He deserted us," he explained. "I don't hate him. But I cannot forgive him for what he did to my mother."

Not fond of sympathy, my father also wants his relatives to know he has lived a good life, that his dreams of owning his own home, raising a family, have been fulfilled. "I am the luckiest guy in the world," he explains. "I have six beautiful daughters and a wonderful wife."

My father smiled beneath his Navy baseball cap when he spoke those words, and though I knew he *truly* believed that he is the luckiest man in the world (a sentiment he had shared numerous times when offering a toast at birthday, Christmas, and anniversary celebrations), I also understood these conversations with his Newfoundland family were not easy. In his heart, my father cannot call Ambrose a "good man." He cannot forget the past. He cannot erase what happened in Brooklyn or San Francisco.

"It's like they want me to forgive him or something," he tells Joanie and me in the car after one encounter. "They sure seemed to like him. They all thought he was wonderful."

As we drive along the quiet and curvy roads from Gertrude's Little Bay home back to Marystown, I replay the comments about Ambrose in my mind. *Are our relatives saying kind words about my grandfather to make us feel welcomed? Like my father's half sisters, Donnie and Kathy, our Newfoundland kin saw the good in my grandfather; he was well loved, well liked. Would I have liked him? Would I have found him charming, enjoyed his stories? Would I have forgiven him for deserting my dad?*

Winding past the cluster of houses along Reid Hill, we look for the home of Michael Farrell, whose father crewed for James Walsh on the *Mary Bernice*. A short distance from Paddy's home, we spot the small white house that sits along the bay. A bachelor who lives alone, Farrell has been waiting for our arrival. A thin, dark-haired man, he welcomes us from his doorstep. "God Bless ye. Come in," he hollers.

Cats, nearly a dozen of them, roam the yard. A few scurry inside the house. Not fond of felines, Joanie heads back to the car, explaining that she will pick us up later. My father and I follow Farrell inside where he pulls kitchen chairs out for us. In the dimly lit room, Farrell begins to talk. The words tumble from his mouth quickly. He is excited to share his stories, but his Newfoundland accent is thick, almost incomprehensible. I glance at my father's eyes and I know he is thinking, "Oh, brother." Still, Farrell has something to say, and we want to understand him.

Our conversation evolves into an odd charade. Farrell speaks a few sentences, and my father and I try to select words that we recognize and repeat them back. This goes on for ten minutes before we figure out that Farrell was a year old at the time of the storm, he had three older siblings, and his mother's name was Victoria. Farrell begins to talk about the night of the gale, and my father and I lean forward.

"The wind," Farrell tells us, repeating the word again before we have the chance to do so. "The wind was fierce that night. My gosh. The old people thought the roof was going to blow off."

Farrell says something about his mother, explaining that she saw a token. "Token?" my father and I ask, unfamiliar with this word that we will later learn means a vision, a portent of death. Ignoring our question, Farrell continues his story and we discern the words "hallway" and "boots." We utter the words back to him and Farrell patiently tells us the story again, this time slowly. The night of the gale, his mother heard noises in her second-floor hallway.

"Me mother could hear someone walking in the hall," he tells us. "She got up from her bed and saw me father in his oilskins and boots. He was walking back and forth in the hall."

"Your mother saw his spirit?" I ask.

Farrell nods.

"She kept shouting his name, but he would not answer. He just kept pacing the floorboards. She knew then, my poor daddy was lost."

Barely a toddler at the time of the gale, Farrell has no memory of the father he was named after. He cannot recall his father's voice, his face, his dad's large calloused hands. "All I knew when I was a boy was that my poor daddy was lost. Drowned. Gone forever. I used to feel terrible about it. I wished I knew what happened. How he went."

Farrell falls silent, and my father and I are quiet, too. From the window, I see Joanie pull into the driveway. Knowing we have garnered as much as possible from Farrell, I stand telling him, "Thanks for talking with us. I am sorry about your father."

He shakes our hands, appreciative that we listened to his stories. As we head out the door, he bids us another, "God bless ye." I smile at Farrell and return his blessing.

My father, who, like Joanie, is not fond of cats, walks quickly to the car. Farrell continues to wave good-bye, and I sense his sadness, a son lonely for his father. Sixty-eight years after the gale, his sorrow lingers. His words echo in my head, "All I knew was that me poor daddy was lost."

I follow my father's footsteps, taking in the sight of his back, the broad shoulders that have carried his own loss for much of his life. As he slips into the passenger seat, I wonder which is worse: To have no memories of your dad before he vanishes in a roiling sea, or to be deserted on a cold November night by a father who was your hero, your idol for the first eleven years of your life?

CHAPTER 21

SHIPWRECKED SCHOONERS AND BODIES
SWALLOWED BY THE SEA—NEWFOUNDLAND, 1935

S wamped with water and stripped of her masts, the schooner
drifted off Cape Pine. From the shore, fishermen watched
the forsaken vessel pitch and roll. As the waves continued to
pound the schooner, she struggled to stay afloat. There would
be no survivors, the men knew; the crew was most certainly
drowned, victims of a gale that showed no mercy and heard no
prayers.

"Yis b'y, 'tis certain to be all hands lost," a gray-haired doryman murmured. "There be many that won't come home from
this dirty weather. No, the sea, she'll be keeping plenty of souls,
she will."

The fishermen nodded and rubbed the religious medals
in their pockets, knowing this August gale would be forever
remembered and long mourned. There would be stories told,
songs penned, and homes where grieving would carry on until
widows turned gray and old.

In the days following the hurricane, as the winds calmed
and the waves grew smaller, the counting of the dead and missing began. It seemed no vessel, big or small, had escaped the
hurricane's wrath. The schooner floating off Cape Pine was but
one of several derelicts that littered the sea. The phantom boats
drifted, devoid of life, their decks robbed of dories, masts, sails,
and spars. Scores of other schooners were reported missing or

wrecked, smashed to pieces on sunkers and jagged cliffs. Hatch covers, spars, and planks from broken-up vessels washed ashore or floated on the sea.

Captains and crew who returned spoke of a gale fiercer than anything their eyes had ever seen. *'Tis like the divil rose up from the sea. The water, she boiled up, and crashed upon us like mountains. The wind she was blowing wicked to the world. 'Twas nothing to do but lash yurself to the rigging or go down below and pray. Yis, b'ys, 'twas the most vicious gale I've ever been through in all me years. When we got ashore, I never felt so lucky in me life. And a lot of souls, they weren't so lucky. No, they'll never be seen no more.*

On land and along the coast, the gale wrought thousands of dollars' worth of damage. Hundreds of dories, schooners, and motorboats were ripped from their moorings and sunk or smashed. Gale winds of fifty-nine miles an hour with ferocious gusts tore telephone poles from the ground, ripped one-hundred-year old trees from their roots, and blew roofs from houses and barns. The hurricane's violent winds, and waves stirred even the dead—the bodies of two fishermen and a young lad drowned several months past—rose from the ocean floor. Barely identifiable, their corpses washed up along three different shores, remains that would, to their families' relief, now receive a proper grave, a final place to rest.

In small outports and villages, the mourning and prayers would begin anew for sons and fathers, men whose bodies had vanished in the gale, victims whose final fate would remain a secret of the sea. Throughout Newfoundland, constables and parish priests received reports of doomed vessels and lost crews: *Schooner* Walter L. *plunged to the bottom of Trepassey Bay, Captain Butcher, his three brothers, and a fifth crew member suspected washed overboard or gone down with the vessel.* Elsie J. *wrecked in Placentia Bay, Captain John Gallet and crew of five presumed lost with all hands.* Annie Young *wrecked on Fox Island, crew of eight feared dead.*

Norman Wareham *wrecked in Fortune Bay, crew safe ashore.* Lizzie E. B. *wrecked in Indian Harbour;* Eureka *destroyed in Herring Neck.* Helen Healy *missing, no trace of crew. Wreckage of the* Carrie Evelyn *picked up, no sign of her five men.* Schooner Reginald Anstey *believed lost with all hands, board bearing the vessel's name picked up at Baie Verte.* Phyllis West *dashed on the rocks, crew abandoned vessel and took to their dories.*

Like dozens of other vessels, the fate of the three Walsh schooners from Marystown and their crew remained uncertain. Annie Anita *and its skipper, Paddy Walsh, and crew unaccounted for. Schooner* Mary Bernice *believed to be floating bottom up near Virgin Rocks in Placentia Bay; no sign of Captain James Walsh or the other four fishermen. The* J.R. Rodgers *reported missing, no word from Captain Ernest Walsh or his crew.*

The fortunate schooners that survived the gale limped ashore, battered and barely afloat, their sails torn to ribbons, anchor chains ripped from bows. The Nova Scotia schooner *Beatrice Beck* arrived in harbor reporting a crew member swept overboard along with four dories and everything else moveable on deck. The *Senora Dosandi,* a Portuguese schooner sailing from Greenland to Newfoundland, shared a similar tale; a giant comber plucked one of its dorymen into the sea and critically injured two others.

Newspapers in London, New York, and the Maritime Provinces chronicled the death and destruction. NEWFOUNDLAND COAST LASHED BY FIERCE STORM. AUGUST GALE KILLS MORE THAN 40 NEWFOUNDLAND FISHERMEN; FEARED LOSS OF LIFE MAY EXCEED HALF HUNDRED.

On August 26, the day after the gale swept across Newfoundland, the Canadian government dispatched the S.S. *Argyle* and S.S. *Malakoff* to look for bodies and survivors. Monday evening and Tuesday morning, the steamers searched Placentia, Trepassey, and St. Mary's Bays with little luck. Their only find: a waterlogged dory marked with its schooner's name—the *Annie Anita*. Later that day, the fishermen of a small village sighted another casualty of the gale. The tides had carried the derelict schooner from Cape Pine west to Hazel Cove. Standing on the headlands above the inlet, three fishermen from St. Shotts spied the vessel as the waves drove the craft ashore. Like their ancestors before them, the men were accustomed to wrecks and bodies drifting onto their beaches. With its severe tides and ragged cliffs, St. Shotts was known among sailors as the "Graveyard of the Atlantic."

Set between the cliffs of Cape St. Mary's and Cape Pine, hundreds of schooners fished the waters surrounding the small village. At night, the sea glittered like a city with scores of lights reflecting on the water. And when the fog rolled in, thick and black, the schooner horns wailed like banshees as captains called out to their stray dories. The sunkers and cliffs were deadly then, hidden by curtains of fog. Scarcely a season passed without a vessel wrecking on the reefs or rocks. There weren't more than a hundred people living in St. Shotts, but each had seen their share of sorrow and death, and on this day, Alonzo Finlay feared they would see more.

A man of twenty, Finlay had heard the stories about vessels that had wrecked and souls who had been lost. Steamers, mail boats, schooners, cargo ships—they had all met their doom in the waters here. Some of the old fellas spoke of the hundreds of victims they had buried, their bodies carried one by one up over the headlands. Whenever possible, the dead had been sent home for burial, but several of the foreign crews, fishermen from Portugal, Holland, and Britain, had been laid to rest in the soil of St. Shotts.

One of the more sorrowful tales Finlay could recall was that of the HMS *Harpooner*, a ship filled with British troops and their families. Traveling from Quebec City to England, the vessel, which was transporting many crippled or injured veterans back home from the War of 1812, struck a reef of rocks. Half of the 411 passengers—women, children, and soldiers—drowned in the frigid breakers as the ship sank. But then there were those who had been rescued, too, off St. Shotts's shores by the local lads who had risked their own lives ferrying the victims to land. In the past, fishermen had taken to their boats to save livestock: a cargo ship in June of 1894 wrecked on the rocks, and one thousand sheep had been driven up the village cliffs to safety. Finlay had listened to many a yarn from his ancestors who had been well fed by cows, hens, and sheep that had been plucked from a sinking ship. And there was no denying that nearly every home in St. Shotts, Finlay's included, had been built from the planks of a doomed vessel.

Some of the villagers, Finlay knew, believed the waters off St. Shotts were haunted. On storm-tossed nights, they saw ghost ships, sunken vessels sailing and then disappearing in sheets of fog. They heard the screams of dying fishermen, spirits still looking to be rescued, resurrected from the blue-green waters. Far too many coffins had been built on these shores, and Finlay hoped that this August day would not bring more despair and death. Slowly, he and the other two men made their way down the cliffs to scavenge planks from the wreckage. Nearing the beach sand, Finlay saw that the schooner was battered and broke in two. Her spars and masts had been ripped away. Looking to the stern, he noted the vessel's name: the *Annie Anita*.

The fishermen shook their heads at the sight of the ruined vessel and boarded her splintered deck. Finlay climbed down below to the cabin. In the darkened wreck, he found broken boards, rocks, and piles of sand—sand that had been dredged by waves striking the sea's bottom. Finlay had begun collecting wood when a flash of yellow caught his eye. He dug through the wreckage and glimpsed a face. A man in his yellow oilskins lay on his side. "Paddy!" Finlay shouted to his brother-in-law. "There's a body below."

Finlay and the fishermen carried the corpse from the cabin. The body was heavy and big, nearly six feet tall. They laid the dead sailor on the grass and returned to the vessel. Unable to move through the cabin filled with debris, the fishermen cut a hole in the deck. Crawling down below, one of the men hollered, "I see a rubber boot!"

Finlay reached between the boards and felt the boot. Inside was the foot of a young boy. Clearing more wreckage, the fishermen discovered a small hand protruding through the rubble, as if it were reaching for help, for someone to hold on to. Finlay gently uncovered the body and found a lad dressed in his Sunday suit, prepared to meet God. Near the child's corpse, lay a small Bible with the boy's fingerprints embedded in the pages. "Jaysus," whispered one of the men. "The poor fella must have been terrified."

The fishermen carried the lifeless boy from the schooner and laid him on the grass next to the sailor's body. On the child's chest, they placed the Bible he had clutched in the moments before his death. Covering the corpses with a shroud of torn canvas, the men uttered silent prayers. Noting the grim discovery from the village above, a crowd of fishermen soon joined them at the beach.

"Aye, 'tis John McNeil's old boat," hollered one of the men.

The vessel had once belonged to Capt'n John McNeil of Trepassey who had named the boat after his two daughters, Annie and Anita. McNeil, the fishermen knew, had sailed the schooner for a few years before selling it to Capt'n Paddy Walsh of Marystown. Pulling the canvas from the bodies, the men examined the large sailor that laid still and silent on the grass. "Aye, that's Capt'n Paddy," noted one of the fishermen. "Big and blocky he was. Jaysus, he was a fine skipper. Some gale it 'twas to kill 'im."

Within the hour, news of the tragedy traveled up the cliffs and along the headlands, across fences and onto doorsteps. One by one, the local women gathered as their mothers and grandmothers had done before them, to tend to the bodies. "The two of 'em washed up from the gale," the women explained to one another. "A father and son they are. Aye, at least they'll be buried together, a proper farewell for their families, so."

By afternoon, a horse and cart had carried the two corpses along the dirt path to the local church. There, in Our Lady of Fatima, a small sanctuary overlooking the sea, the skipper and his son were laid on wooden pews. As the sky darkened, the women lit candles and knelt before the cold bodies. They pulled Rosary beads from their pockets and began to pray for the departed souls. Outside, the men began their own ritual of gathering wood for the coffins and the local constable put the tragic words to paper. In a telegram to Marystown he informed Father John McGettigan: Annie Anita *wrecked at Hazel Cove. Bodies of Capt'n Paddy Walsh and his son have been recovered. Remaining crew missing.*

Not long after McGettigan received the grim news from St. Shotts, two motorboats towed another derelict schooner to shore. The vessel had been found bottom up near the Virgin Rocks. Their motors straining, the boats dragged the *Mary Bernice* toward Haystack Harbor, a small inlet in the northeast corner of Placentia Bay. There, a crowd of fishermen pulled the schooner onto the beach and righted it from its beam-ends. Unlike the *Annie Anita,* no bodies, no sign of Captain James Walsh or his crew were found in the waterlogged cabin. The local lawman penned another telegram destined for Father McGettigan: *Vessel* Mary Bernice *towed to Haystack. All hands feared lost.*

CHAPTER 22

"THE WHOLE TOWN JUST STUMBLED INTO SHOCK"— MARYSTOWN, 2003

Mary Brennan eyes the field of buttercups separating her doorstep from the deserted home with the peeling paint and crumbling chimneys.

Through thick glasses, her brown eyes gaze past the tall grass. "Three steps up and three steps down," she says, remembering the wooden step ladder that helped them across the fence separating her family's land from Lillian and Paddy Walsh's property.

"Their home was lovely, and they were wonderful neighbors to us," Mary explains. "Lil was an angel, soft-spoken, kind. Mr. Paddy was a fine-looking man but a rough man, a sea person. When his boat would dock, you would hear him. He had a loud voice. You'd know he was back in town."

Standing at the doorstep of the home where she has lived since she was a small girl, Mary conjures memories more than six decades past when the house across the field was freshly painted and filled with furnishings from around the world.

"There were lots of good times," she says. "They really enjoyed living, Paddy and Lil did."

The daughter of Albert and Elizabeth Brennan, Mary was nine years old when the 1935 hurricane rattled her roof and kept her father from crossing the bay. Known as the local ferry master, Albert Brennan operated a small motorboat that transported customers across Marystown's harbor. He often took Skipper Paddy over to Baird's store or to call on Father McGettigan.

"Paddy and my father were good neighbors and good friends. It was a terrible thing when the news came about the *Annie Anita* and *Mary Bernice*."

Of the forty Newfoundland victims to die in the storm, fourteen were from Marystown and its two neighboring villages. Rimmed in black and bearing death notices, the two telegrams from St. Shotts and Placentia Bay forever altered a town that relied on the Blessed Mary and good fortune to bring their sailors safe ashore.

"I remember Father McGettigan coming around, all in black, going door to door. Almost every home on the south side of Marystown had someone lost. The whole town just stumbled into shock."

Forty-two children on the south side of Marystown were suddenly fatherless. The news of fishermen's deaths crippled the community of three hundred. Widows collapsed on doorsteps, screams echoed across the water, toddlers clutched their mothers' skirts, and the whole town shuttered itself in grief.

"On the south side of Marystown, every house was affected," Mary tells us with a sigh. "Most everyone lost someone. If their son or husband didn't die, they lost an uncle, a cousin. It was an awful time. There were no maybes; the August Gale was the worst thing to hit Marystown."

And there was no one more stricken than Lillian Walsh. Mary shakes her head at the thought of her neighbor's misfortune.

"Miss Lil, she lost half her family. She lost her husband and three sons. It was heartbreaking."

Good friends and close neighbors, Mary's parents did what they could for Lillian; they crossed the field at all hours of the day and night to offer comfort to Paddy's widow. Three steps up the ladder, three steps down, over the fence and back, they wore a path in the grass. Now sixty-eight years later, Mary eyes the field where she can still see her father retreating in the night to sit by Lillian's side. Hours passed before he would return, his face ashen, his own eyes red with grief.

"My mother and father spent many nights with Lillian for I don't know how long. She'd be crying hysterically. My father would come home, and he'd look so worn. He would have a drink of brandy and talk about her screams."

The screams, Mary tells us, the suffering of the Marystown widows continued long past the summer of 1935, but there was little time for grief. The women worked dawn till dusk trying to provide for their fatherless children. They raked hay, planted vegetables, washed fish, and fed their families what they could. The government Marine Disaster Fund provided $115 annually to the widows. The $2.21 a week was barely enough to keep a family of six or seven from starving. Several mothers reluctantly packed up their youngest sons and daughters and sent them to live in the orphanages in St. John's.

"The women worked like dogs," Mary says, "and there was little help for them or their children. They had to make some awful hard choices."

I imagine the widows trying to stifle their own sobs and hush the cries of their children. A stanza from a Newfoundland song, its author unknown, replays in my head. The lyrics have haunted me since I read them months before our trip.

> *"Oh, Mother dear," the children cried,*
> *"Where is our father's boat?*
> *He said that he was coming home*
> *The last time that he wrote."*
> *Grief-stricken was the mother's heart,*
> *The father and his crew,*

For they're cradled in their ocean bed
Beneath the ocean blue.

So many fishermen, so many fathers cradled in the ocean blue. Thousands of ships—some ten thousand vessels—are estimated to have foundered, sunk, or disappeared in Newfoundland's waters over the past four centuries. The mourning, the anguish of untold wives, mothers, sons, and daughters is unimaginable.

Decades after the gale, Mary would come to understand such sorrow. She had only been married a year when she lost her husband, William Power, to the sea. On a fog-shrouded October night, a vessel collided with Power's schooner, killing him as he lay sleeping in his bunk. Days later, his battered body washed ashore.

"We lost him near the French Island of St. Pierre," she tells us. "My son, William, had just been born. He was a month old when his father died."

As with the August Gale widows, Mary worked many long hours to provide for her son. She planted vegetables, tended gardens, and put in a full day behind the counter at her family's general store.

"You just did your best and went along," she tells us. "There was nothing else you could do."

Before we leave Mary's doorstep, I ask to take her picture. She readily obliges and moves closer to my father. My dad places his arm around Mary, and they both smile into the camera. I stare into the viewfinder and a wave of recognition washes over me. Mary's wavy white hair, her gentle voice, and pragmatic nature remind me of my Nana. Paralyzed and in shock after the San Francisco trip and Ambrose's second betrayal, my grandmother did what was necessary to provide for her two sons. A down-on-her-luck single mother, she scrubbed pots, pans, and dishes in the local restaurant to earn a paycheck and dinners for her sons. With little money to buy her boys winter clothing, she often stayed up through the night knitting sweaters, mittens, and hats.

And despite the opportunity, she never remarried. As the Marystown widows forever looked to the sea, mourning their lost husbands, Patricia Walsh held grief and hope in her heart. She believed that one day, Ambrose, her first and only love, would return. There would be a knock on the door or an unexpected phone call, and suddenly, a husband, a father would reappear, reunited with his wife and two sons.

CHAPTER 23

MCGETTIGAN'S GRIM TASK—MARYSTOWN, AUGUST 1935

The priest's black robes rustled in the breeze as he stepped into the skiff. Father John McGettigan eyed the homes that hugged the land across the bay. He had comforted many grieving families in the twenty-two years since he had been ordained, but on this August day he would knock on the doors of a dozen houses. Many of the fishermen's widows had several children. A few were pregnant or had just given birth.

McGettigan's thoughts turned to Lillian Walsh. How would he break the news to Miss Lil? *How do you tell a woman that the sea has claimed three of her sons and her husband?* The priest studied the dark water as he steered the boat to the southern shore. The motor cut through the bay drawing him closer to his grim task. The local constable sat next to McGettigan; he had agreed to accompany the priest and assist in delivering the death notices. Lost in their own thoughts, neither man spoke. McGettigan made a mental list of Marystown's dead: Paddy, James, Frankie, and Jerome Walsh, Michael Farrell, Edward Cheeke, Dominic Walsh, John Brinton, Charles Hanrahan, George Mitchell, Tom Reid, and Billy Reid. And then there was Richard Hanrahan from Little Bay and Dennis Long from the neighboring village Fox Cove. Another Marystown father, James Keating, a doryman on board the *Jane and Martha,* had also perished in the gale. McGettigan bowed his head and uttered a silent prayer for the drowned men. *Requiem aeternam dona eis, Domine—Grant them eternal rest, O Lord.*

From the presbytery kitchen window, Lizzie Drake followed the boat and the priest's silhouette in the morning sunlight. His face had paled, his voice stunned into silence since he received the telegrams about the *Annie Anita* and the *Mary Bernice*. The young maid had thought McGettigan would tumble to the floor from the shock. The reverend had been queer enough with an odd, vacant look in his eyes since the night of the storm, and now this tragic news further rattled the priest. In her years washing floors, scrubbing potatoes, and cleaning up after McGettigan, she had feared and sometimes grew angry at the priest, but she had never felt sorrow, pity for him. Yet on this August morn she would not trade places with McGettigan for all the gold in the colonial governor's coffers. *No, 'twould be a day that priest and the whole of Marystown would never forget.*

On the south side of the village, children and their mothers watched as McGettigan's boat drew closer. The sight of the priest prompted fear and dread. The women crossed themselves as if to ward off an evil spirit. "Whose house will he be going to?" they whispered. "Surely, he has terrible news. Word of the men missing in the gale."

McGettigan and the constable spoke to no one as they stepped from the skiff. The priest turned away from the women and their faces pinched in worry. He pressed his own lips together and headed along the dirt path. McGettigan walked west along the water, toward the home of Paddy's parents, where he knew Lillian waited for word of her husband and sons. In his mind, McGettigan formed words, *They're all gone, Lil. Paddy, James, Jerome, and Frankie. They are with the Lord now. At peace, by His side.* He would try to hold her, convince her that prayer was best in this time of unbearable sorrow and loss. But the priest knew he would not get far with that advice. There would be screaming, wails from a woman who would never be right again.

Down along the creek, below the home of Paddy's parents, Ernest Walsh's daughters held their breath as McGettigan passed them. "Does he have word of Da?" they asked one another. The priest did not acknowledge the young girls as he strode quickly by them. He continued on to their Grandmother Walsh's home. McGettigan disappeared inside but for a few moments before the screeching began. The door flew open and four men carried Lillian Walsh out in the wicker chair she had collapsed into. Her screams, shrill and constant, echoed across the bay. Her legs kicked the air wildly.

The ungodly shrieks pulled women and children from their houses. From their doorsteps, they watched the men carry Lillian along the dirt path, past the fishing wharfs and Paddy's pier, to the captain's home on the hill. As they neared her front gate, Lillian's cries grew louder, her hands clawed at the air as she shouted, "No, no, no!"

Mothers covered their faces and sobbed as their children asked, "What's wrong? Why are they hurting Miss Lil?" McGettigan and the constable pressed past the crowds of women and proceeded on their mission. Leaving Lillian with the neighbors who had rushed to her home, the priest and the officer walked toward Alice and John Brinton's house. Her head bent to the ground, Alice Brinton raked hay as McGettigan neared her dwelling. Her seven-year-old daughter Mary ran to her side. "Ma, the priest is here to see ye."

Alice Brinton knew before she heard McGettigan's words. Her husband, the poor soul, was dead, leaving her with two young lasses and an infant who was barely two months old. Alice gazed at the priest as if he were an apparition, a spirit from another world. She recalled the night before the *Annie Anita* and *Mary Bernice* had departed. Alice had been finishing her duties at the Walsh home, cleaning the dishes when Lillian had begged Paddy and her sons not to go. *The woman knew*

*they would never return. The dark cloud, the whirlwind, omens of
death. Lillian had portended the loss, the gale. And here we are, left
the torment of fourteen perished souls and scores of children without
their fathers. Blessed Mother of God, who will watch over us now?*

McGettigan sympathized with the young woman's concern;
the priest had his own worries. What would become of the widows? They had six, seven, and some of them, eight mouths to
feed. With cod prices cut in half, the families barely survived
when their husbands came home with their schooners filled with
fish. *How in the name of Jesus would they make it now?* There
would be little wood or coal for their stoves this winter, and
in their cold kitchens, the cupboards would be bare. Dinner
would be nothing more than a crust of bread, a few potatoes,
and a kettle of hot water. It would not be long before the cemetery would claim the children, one by one. The thought of
more death, more sorrow, in this small village stirred a chill deep
inside McGettigan's bones.

The priest offered a blessing and a prayer for Alice Brinton
and her three children before moving on to the neighboring
home of Margaret Walsh. "I've got poor news," McGettigan
told Mrs. Walsh. "The *Annie Anita* was found broke in two. All
hands were lost. Your son Dominic is gone." Margaret Walsh
dropped into the kitchen chair. Both she and her son had shared
ill feelings about the August journey. Dominic had paced the
floors the night before he boarded the schooner. Margaret had
begged him not to go. The poor lad was just twenty-two years
of age, building a home for his bride and planning to be married upon his return. How she wished she had held him fast,
forbidden him to sail. She had dreamt of Dominic the night of
the gale, seen the mountainous waves crashing against his dory.
"He's not coming back," she had told her other children that
next morning. They had scoffed at their mother's dream until
McGettigan knocked at their door.

Just after noon, the priest walked along the path to Isabel Mitchell's home. Her husband, George, had been on board the *Annie Anita*. From her kitchen window, she saw McGettigan and the constable veering to her gate. Her four children gathered around her as the priest spoke. "I'm sorry, me' dear, I have tragic news. The *Annie Anita* wrecked at St. Shotts. The bodies of Capt'n Paddy and one of his sons were found in the cabin. I'm afraid your husband, George, was lost with the rest of the crew."

Isabel did not speak, nor did she cry out; she would save her grief for later. McGettigan blessed the children and their mother and quickly stepped from the home. He could barely comprehend the words he spoke. *Capt'n Paddy's body found. The* Annie Anita *and the* Marie Bernice *all hands lost. They're all gone. Husbands. Sons. Gone. How am I to impart this wretched news when I can scarcely believe it myself?* The priest shook off his misgivings and climbed the hill leading to the home of Charles Hanrahan, George Mitchell's dorymate. He had notified four widows and he had another five more to inform. The Fox Cove pastor would console Dennis Long's family, and mercifully, Lucy's mother had agreed to tell her daughter of James Walsh's death. McGettigan could not face the young woman with a newborn in her arms, a child born the night her father died. *No, the Lord had given him enough already.*

McGettigan paused to light a cigarette and calm his nerves. He drew in the smell of the sea and conjured the pleasant memories of his youth, his seminary years at All Hallows in Ireland. With his love for Shakespeare, poetry, and song, the seminary choir director had tried to convince McGettigan to pursue a vocation on stage, to perfect his brilliant tenor voice. "Why, I'll make ye as famous as the Irish singer, Johnny McCormack," the director boasted. McGettigan had been flattered by the praise, but he quickly declined. His three sisters had taken their vows becoming brides of Christ, and so, too, would he serve the Lord. But he was naïve and innocent then, unaware of August gales and drowned fishermen, unaccustomed to despair and death.

Grinding his cigarette stub into the ground, McGettigan stepped toward Charles Hanrahan's door. He rapped softly, knowing Hanrahan's wife was waiting for him. He had seen her eyes upon him through the window, the fear tightening her face. He did not speak but a few words before Mary Hanrahan began to scream. Five months pregnant, the woman collapsed onto the floor and drew her young daughter and son into her lap. "Yur poor daddy's gone," she sobbed. The children pressed their faces to their mother's breast. Her wails terrified them, and they did not understand where their da had gone to. His voice unsteady and barely above a whisper, the young boy turned to the priest to ask, "When will my father be coming back?"

McGettigan reached for the child's hand and marked the sign of the cross over his forehead. The priest closed his eyes and recited a prayer, "May they sense Your presence in this hour of need. In Jesus' name, Amen." The constable followed McGettigan out the door and placed a hand on the priest's slumped shoulder. "We're near halfway done, Father."

McGettigan nodded. The thought of more stunned widows soured his stomach and brought on a queasiness that left him unsteady on his feet, dizzy as if he'd been struck too many times in the head. He heard his father's advice to him as a young man, his dad shouting as McGettigan sparred in the ring with his older brother, a boxer for the British Royal Navy. *Keep yur feet moving, yur hands up, and keep breathing. Breathe, John. Breathe!* A loud buzz filled his head now, as if his brother had landed a blow to his brow. McGettigan inhaled deeply, heeding his father's words.

From Reid Hill, several of Tom Reid's children spied the priest and the peculiar look on his face. McGettigan stood alongside the dirt path as if in a trance. "Why does Father McGettigan have such a queer look on his face?" they asked their mother. Jessie Reid gathered her children close. Held in a tight circle, they followed the priest's movements as McGettigan stopped at the bottom of the knoll and knocked at their aunt's door. Jessie pressed her hand to her heart, believing her sister's adopted son had died in the gale. But then McGettigan and her sister started up the hill together. The priest, Jessie realized, had wanted her sister to come share the grim news.

"Dear Lord, children!" Jessie Reid screamed. "It's yur da that's gone! My poor Tom!"

As dusk settled over the town, McGettigan stood before the door of the last home, the dwelling of Edward Cheeke, a dory-man for the *Annie Anita*. McGettigan waited in the dark on the doorstep. From the lamplight inside, he could see Cheeke's family, his five children and their mother seated around the dinner table. There were sparse bits of potato, cabbage, and carrots on their plates, hot water in their mugs. Through the windowpane, the priest met the gaze of a ten-year-old boy he knew as Vincent. The child stared at McGettigan with eyes that did not yet recognize his loss. The priest waited for the boy to inform his mother of his arrival. McGettigan could not knock on another door, nor could he face another weeping child. He had no more comfort to give.

CHAPTER 24

A FINAL VOYAGE—MARYSTOWN, 2003

I learn of my grandfather's dying wish as the sun sets over the blue waters of Mortier Bay. My father's cousin, Alan Brenton, shares the story as our car crests a hill overlooking the north side of Marystown.

"He called to tell me he wanted one last ride in my boat," Alan says. "'But this time,' he said, 'I'll be in a vase. I want my ashes scattered over Tides Cove.'"

At the time, in the spring of 1990, my grandfather was dying of colon cancer and had but a few months to live. He had chosen his final resting place in the inlet nearest the sea, the headlands where a lighthouse beacon had welcomed his brother Paddy home after hundreds of journeys and sails. I imagine my grandfather lying in his hospital bed, taking comfort in knowing his remains would drift in the waters where his older brother had often shouted to his crew, "We're home, boys!"

My grandfather had other sentimental ties to the cove. The inlet harbored a patch of land called Big Head, a rocky crop of turf where Ambrose's great-grandfather, John Walsh, first arrived after emigrating from County Wexford. Here in these waters, where the schooners of his grandfather and brother took refuge from the sea and a long sail, Ambrose's ashes, his physical essence, would remain. And as with his family and the Marystown fishermen who drowned in the August Gale, my grandfather would forever abide in the sea.

Along with desiring an ocean burial, Ambrose had another request: "Play 'When You and I Were Young, Maggie,'" he told Alan "while my ashes are thrown overboard." Written in the late 1800s, the song had been Paddy's favorite. The skipper often sang the lyrics (off-key and loudly) at parties or alongside the family piano. The ballad told of a tragic love story between a Canadian schoolteacher and his pupil, Maggie. The two fell in love and became engaged, but Maggie contracted tuberculosis. The couple was married a year before Maggie died in 1865. Their brief time together reminds me of the short time Ambrose spent with my Nana, the decade during which he fathered his first two sons. *Did the song stir memories of their years together in Staten Island and Brooklyn? Of his youth when he fell in love with the shy, blue-eyed girl, Patricia O'Connell?*

In his later years, when he returned to Marystown, Ambrose played the song repeatedly during his stay. "I'd come home from work and that tape was playing all the time," Alan tells us. "I don't know what it meant to him. He was always listening to it."

I imagine my grandfather, alone in Alan's home, the somber lyrics wafting through the parlor with Ambrose on the couch, reflecting upon the years gone by.

> *They say I am feeble with age, Maggie.*
> *My steps are less sprightly than then.*
> *My face is a well-written page, Maggie,*
> *And time alone was the pen.*
> *They say we are aged and grey, Maggie.*
> *As spray by the white breakers flung.*
> *But to me you're as fair as you were, Maggie.*
> *When you and I were young.*
> *And now we are aged and grey, Maggie,*
> *And the trials of life nearly done,*

Let us sing of the days that are gone, Maggie,
When you and I were young.

Life's trials and challenges had not yet touched my grand-father when he left Marystown as a young man of eighteen, his hair thick and black, his face unwrinkled by time and choices that would weigh heavily on his conscience. He would not return to his birthplace for nearly five decades. His absence remained a mystery to his friends and family, who thought he had van-ished from the earth. His mother, Cecilia, prayed nightly for him, fearing that her youngest son had gotten into some terrible trouble or was dead. And in the years after she lost Paddy to the August Gale, Cecilia continued to pray that Ambrose was safe, that some terrible fate had not claimed him, too. "She died not knowing if Ambrose was alive," Alan tells us, shaking his head. "Shocking that he never wrote his own mother, aye?"

For decades, Ambrose had no contact with Marystown; he wrote no letters and made no calls—until he needed help. He phoned his sister Donalda in 1974 to ask her if she would allow Ambrose's son Michael to live with her in Marystown to avoid the Vietnam War draft. Donalda agreed to take her nephew in, but only after she hollered long and loud at her brother for dis-appearing without a word to his family.

"My mother was furious with him," Alan says of Donalda. "For all those years, she had seen Granny Walsh suffer not know-ing where her boy Ambrose was to."

After his lengthy absence, Ambrose accompanied his son to Marystown. It was the first of several trips he would make to his birthplace, where he would reconnect with his family and child-hood friends, reminiscing about the dories he rowed, the rigging he climbed, and the journeys he sailed with his brother Paddy.

"Ye can take the boy out of the bay, but you can't take the bay out of the boy," Alan's son Jack would later tell me. "Where did he want to be buried? Where did he want his ashes spread? All those years after he left Marystown, he never talked Staten Island or Brooklyn or San Francisco. He talked about Marystown and what it was like before he left. This was always his home."

Marystown offered my grandfather a safe harbor, a haven with few complications, few memories, to remind him of his devastating decisions. Still, he carried the guilt and regrets with him. He rarely talked about leaving his first two sons and his wife Patricia, but he once confided to Brenton's wife, "Take it from my experience, people always think the grass is greener on the other side, but it isn't."

In the years before his death, Ambrose found work painting hospital offices. While on the job, he met a psychiatrist with whom he shared stories about his life, the family he had abandoned. The doctor offered my grandfather some free advice: "It would be good for you to talk to your sons to resolve your feelings."

Surprised at the sudden contact, my father reddened with anger when Ambrose explained, "A psychiatrist said it would be good for me to call."

My father's voice rose in disbelief. "But what about us? What about Billy, Ma, and me?"

Ambrose fell silent. He had no words to say.

On an August afternoon in 1990, my grandfather's last wish was fulfilled. Ambrose's daughters cast his remains into the sea while the melancholy song "Maggie" blared from Alan Brenton's boat. Kathy and Donnie wept as the familiar lyrics bade their father a final good-bye:

They say I am feeble with age, Maggie.
My steps are less sprightly than then.
My face is a well-written page, Maggie,

And time alone was the pen.
They say we are aged and grey, Maggie.
As spray by the white breakers flung.
But to me you're as fair as you were, Maggie.
When you and I were young.

"There wasn't a dry eye on board the boat," Alan remembers. "Geez, it was some sad."

My grandfather was a month shy of his eighty-second birthday when he died in a California hospital in June 1990. Thousands of miles away, my father and uncle were unaware of Ambrose's illness or his death. No one had thought to inform them of their father's passing. Weeks after Ambrose's ashes were tossed into the cold Newfoundland waters, my father received a phone call from Ambrose's brother, Leo, with the belated news. His father—the man whom he had worshipped as a child and resented as an adult—was gone. There would be no chance for final words, no chance to mourn, to reconcile.

As he hung up the phone, my dad shed his own tears, stung by a final abandonment: "My father died and no one told me."

CHAPTER 25

"'TIS THE QUEEREST WAKE."—MARYSTOWN, 1935

The boy knew the bodies were coming home.

Word spread quickly throughout the town, as if there were an invisible cord that connected them all. From the fishing wharves, to the kitchens, to the hayfields, to the shops, the news passed from mouth to mouth. "B'y Gad, Skipper Paddy and his son Frankie are coming home."

The talk had found its way to the small ears of the boy, and the words terrified Paddy Walsh Jr. His father and brother were not only returning to Marystown, they were coming home to the boy's house. They were going to be laid out in his family's parlor, and the thought of all this, the idea of bodies in his home, frightened the child. In his four-year-old mind, bodies meant no heads, no arms, no legs. He didn't want to see his father and older brother Frankie this way.

In the days since Father McGettigan had delivered the death notices, his mother's constant keening had shaken young Paddy, leaving the child nervous and uncertain. The priest had explained that his father and three brothers were gone, but the boy couldn't grasp the finality of what "gone" meant. He wanted his dad home, singing alongside the piano, his loud voice filling the room. He longed for the laughter of his older brothers, Frankie, Jerome, and James. But their bedrooms were empty and still now, and all this talk about bodies further confused Paddy. Seeking comfort, the boy ran into the kitchen hoping to find the woman who cleaned their home and tended the garden. "Please, ma'am," Paddy pleaded, grabbing hold of the maid's dress, "look after me."

Outside, dusk settled over the bay, stealing the last remnants of light from the summer sky. A few miles east, a schooner ferried Capt'n Paddy Walsh on his final voyage. The vessel sailed past the sights Paddy had eyed hundreds of times: the red lantern at Tides Point, the rocky coves of Beau Bois, and the green hills of Little Bay. As the schooner glided into Marystown's harbor, men, women, and children along the bay's southern and northern shores viewed the vessel as if it were an apparition. Women made the sign of the cross, whispering silent prayers. Fishermen removed their caps, still trying to reckon with the notion that Captain Paddy was dead. *B'ye Gad Almighty. Paddy Walsh. He had no fear of nothin'. He could find fish better than any of 'em. Yis b'y.*

A crowd of men gathered at Paddy's wharf, waiting to carry the coffined bodies from the schooner. Another group huddled at the wooden gate leading to the skipper's home. Billy Mitchell stood among them. One of Marystown's heftiest residents, Mitchell's face flushed red with the exertion of walking. His fondness for salt pork and beef "will be putting ye in an early grave," Mitchell's doctor had threatened. But the doctor's warning didn't concern Mitchell; not much did.

Unlike most of the men in Marystown, Mitchell didn't fish; he couldn't boast about how much salt cod he killed or how far he could row a dory. Mitchell earned his keep making barrels at the local mill, and his passion was spinning stories. He collected details like bits of string, saving them until he settled in at a neighbor's kitchen table, where he could entertain and be rewarded in food and drink. There were few better storytellers along Newfoundland's southern shores, and Mitchell wasn't about to miss out on one of the biggest yarns of his lifetime. He knew Paddy Walsh as well as the next fellow and was determined to see for himself if the notorious skipper was really dead.

As the men carried the coffins along Paddy's wharf, Mitchell angled his way toward the larger box. Before anyone could stop him, he opened the lid. Mitchell eyed the blackened and bruised cheeks, the face bloated by death and sea. "'Tis not Paddy Walsh!" Mitchell hollered.

Father McGettigan squared his shoulders and glared at Mitchell. The priest wasn't in the mood for the storyteller's theatrics. He had listened to widows and children wail and screech over the past three days. More difficulties he did not need. He turned to Mitchell and spoke louder than he wanted: "Don't be stirring up trouble, Mitchell! Mrs. Walsh has it hard enough without you creating stories."

"You can say what you like," Mitchell answered. "But the body 'tis Tom Reid. You're taking him to the wrong home, ye are."

McGettigan shot Mitchell a final warning before he ushered the men to Paddy's fish store, the wooden shed where the skipper stored and repaired his gear. Pushing aside the nets and fish tubs, the fishermen removed the bodies from the coffins and laid them on workbenches. They took in the sight of the blocky captain and the small boy. "Jaysus, ye think Mitchell is right? 'Tis it Paddy or Tom Reid?"

A group of local women nudged their way into the store, ushering the men from the room. "Hush now, and don't be daft with ye nonsense! We've work to do!"

The women blessed themselves and the bodies before they began preparations for the wake. As they removed the clothing, they noticed queer things. The initials notched in Paddy's belt buckle read *T. R.* His knitted wool socks and his underwear also bore the same letters. "Surely Paddy wouldn't be a wearin' Tom Reid's clothes, now would he?" they asked one another. The women weren't alone with their questions. One by one, men who had learned of Billy Mitchell's accusation entered the fish store to view the body themselves. They picked through the discarded clothes and stared at the face of a man they knew well: "Aye, b'y, 'tis Tom Reid," they declared.

Despite their suspicions, no one dared challenge Father McGettigan. They had witnessed the priest's wrath on Sunday mornings, the old boy pounding the pulpit asking for more money or chastising some fellow for cheating on his wife. *And surely now, didn't McGettigan have special powers?* They hadn't forgotten about the only man in Marystown who had refused to help the priest build St. Gabriel's Hall. The poor lad later lost his home in a sudden fire. It could have been a queer coincidence or it could have been an act of God, they reckoned. *And there was a lot more that the Lord's servant could do, couldn't he?* McGettigan, more than a few of them believed, could turn you into a goat if he so wanted. *Ye dared not cross the priest. No, they weren't going down that path a'tall.*

Pushing their doubts aside, the women continued their task, gently washing the bodies that were now cold and heavy. They cringed when they touched Frankie's bruised limbs. "Aye, the poor lad. His thin little bones took a battering. God bless ye child."

Outside in the fields and along the wharves, the rumors about Paddy's mismatched body circulated like seeds in the wind. And inside the house on the hill, the small boy listened to his mother's cries. Paddy Jr. sat in the corner of the kitchen, quietly watching his sisters and the maid scurry from one room to the next, preparing for the wake. The boy didn't understand what a "wake" meant, and the sudden transformation of his home bewildered the child. Dark pieces of cloth covered the mirrors; the clocks had been stilled, the window shades drawn tight. Darkness shrouded each of the three floors, shutting out the daylight and further frightening him. Paddy searched for the housemaid and the comfort of her worn apron. "Where are you, ma'am?"

From the water below, fishermen shook off reluctant shudders as they sailed past Paddy's home. It was as if the building had taken on a human quality of grieving; its eyes closed, shuttering in on itself. As darkness cloaked the village, the fishermen carried the coffins up the hill and into Paddy's parlor. Lillian's screams echoed from the hall as the men placed the boxes side by side on wooden chairs. Lanterns cast shadows onto the flower-papered walls and the bodies that were now dressed in their Sunday suits. A small Bible rested on Frankie's chest. The boy's fingerprint impressions marked the book's pages, evidence, his mother believed, of her child's terror in his dying moments. Lillian would not separate the boy from the Bible he had clutched so fervently as the gale raged around him. "I want him buried with it," she told the priest.

Dazed with exhaustion and shock, Lillian stood before the bodies in the room where she had served tea on silver platters, the parlor where she and Paddy had entertained guests, their laughter echoing off the mahogany ceilings. In the nearby dining room, mourners spoke in hushed voices. They did not want to upset Miss Lil; they knew she wasn't in her right mind. A circle of mothers eyed Lillian, careful to keep their words to themselves. "No, she doesn't even seem like she knows where she is, poor woman. Her eyes look right past ye. Losing three sons and a husband. Ye'd never stop thinking about it, would ye? It'd be a hard chore to accept it."

The lights had blazed throughout the night since McGettigan delivered the shocking news to Lillian. The neighbors heard her wail like she herself were dying. "My babies," she cried relentlessly. "They can't be gone." Now she stood before her son, Frankie, her shy, sweet boy, unnaturally still. She bent to kiss his forehead, like she had done a hundred times before as he drifted off to sleep. *Could he be sleeping now,* she wondered? "Wake up, boy!" she begged. "Please wake up, Frankie!"

Lillian herself had not slept since the priest came to her door. When she closed her eyes, the images appeared. Monstrous waves, walls of water crashing, sea foam spraying wildly. Schooners, dories overturned, rolling in the sea. And she saw their faces, Frankie and Jerome, their wide eyes and mouths open in screams. She imagined their terror as cold water swamped their vessels. She knew Frankie had died in the bottom of his father's schooner, but what had become of Jerome? Was he tossed from the *Annie Anita?* Drowned after capsizing from a dory? And her eldest son, James, caught in the gale on his first journey as a skipper. Where was his body? Did he try to stay with the *Mary Bernice,* captaining her till his last breath? And his first child, his own baby girl, born the night of his death. *This can't be real,* Lillian told herself again and again. *I'll wake soon and 'twill all be over, a tormenting dream.*

Lillian turned to her husband's coffin. He had always made it home through storms, shipwrecks, and schooners trapped in ice. He had scared her plenty on his voyages, and she had counted him dead many times. But he always came home. He had tried to reassure her before he set sail. "Don't worry, Lil, if I do die, and there's a way to come back to ye, I'll find it."

She waited now for a sign, a voice in the night, a token that he was there. Paddy had never broken his word to her. If she wanted something, he got it for her, no matter what the price. He knew she liked fine things: fancy shoes and big houses with plush drapes and imported settees. When she had admired the grand house on the hill, one of the largest homes in Marystown, Paddy saved enough money to make it hers. She remembered the day he took her by the arm to the old Molloy Hotel with its stained-glass transom, mahogany ceilings, and scrolled banister. "Do ye like it, Lil?"

"Yes, of course, Paddy," she told him.

"Well, good," he answered, "Because I just bought it for ye."

Now this giant of man was laid out before her. *Could this really be Paddy?* Lillian had heard the whispers, the rumors about the body favoring Tom Reid's looks more than her husband's. *But surely now, it was hard to tell the two of them apart in life, never mind in death.* Cousins by blood, they had the same build. *You could barely identify the two of them if they had their backs to you.* And even their faces looked alike, with receding hairlines and wide foreheads. Lil studied her husband's body. Five days had passed since the gale tore up the sea and broke Paddy's schooner in two. His face had been battered by the ship's boards as he and Frankie sought refuge belowdecks in their final hours. Death had also darkened Paddy's skin, mottling his cheeks black.

Lil eyed Paddy's chest, thick from years of rowing dories off Newfoundland's shores. She turned to his hands. Paddy had always kept his fingers clean, manicured. But the hands in the coffin were rough, the fingernails caked with dirt. And Paddy's wedding ring, the ring that wasn't gone off his finger since the day he was married, was missing. Lillian stepped back from the corpse. "'Tis not Paddy! This is not my husband!"

McGettigan's black robes rustled against the wooden floor as he coaxed Lillian from the parlor. He could see that she wasn't right; her vacant eyes, reminded McGettigan of a glass-eyed doll. The doctor's pills had calmed Lillian's nerves for a short time, but the priest knew that no amount of tranquilizers would make her forget this wretched loss. He spoke to her in a soft voice: "Meself and Paddy have been friends for years, Lil. Surely I'd know Paddy any time."

"You're wrong," Lillian replied, her eyes focused on something only she could see.

Over the next two days, hundreds of mourners journeyed on foot or horse and cart to pay their respects to Skipper Paddy.

They came from Marystown and its surrounding villages: Little Bay, Mooring Cove, Salt Pond, Fox Cove, and Beau Bois. One by one, they knelt and stood before the coffins. Many of them had heard the gossip, and they inspected the body to form their own opinion.

They each had their own memories of Captain Paddy. Bernard Butler had grown up hearing stories about the famed skipper. Fishermen measured their own catch against Mr. Paddy's. "By Gad, he's got so much fish," they'd lament. "Funny thing, why can't other men share his luck?" Paddy lived for sailing schooners and fishing from one end of the year to the other. *Aye,* Bernard thought, *he was a real fish-killer.* Bernard had tipped his cap many a time to Paddy out of respect and fear. He knew you didn't mess with Skipper Paddy. *No, you didn't trod on Paddy's shoes. No sir.*

Still, Paddy had a soft side. He never minded when Bernard and Paddy's sons boarded his schooners, climbing to the top of the rigging. No, Bernard recalled, he never minded that a'tall. The sight of Skipper Paddy dead before him now unnerved the young man. It had seemed that Mr. Paddy was immortal and now all this talk about the body being Tom Reid. *Maybe, Capt'n Paddy was still alive?* Bernard searched Paddy's cheeks, knowing they would tell him the truth. Like other skippers, Paddy often anchored his ship in Golden Bay to collect water and trap birds that flocked to Cape St. Mary's cliffs. Thousands of birds nested on the Cape's rocky crevices, and fishermen often brought home baby gulls to their children. During one of Paddy's journeys, he encountered a bird that had no intention of becoming a tamed pet. The large gannet pecked Paddy's face, leaving a scar on his right cheek.

Bernard studied the body's face. He eyed both cheeks. *'Tis not there! The scar is missing!* Bernard eased himself out of the room as Paddy's nieces, Ernestine and Gertrude, stood in line, waiting to pay their respects. Gertrude could barely stand from the shock of her favorite uncle's death. She couldn't imagine seeing Uncle Paddy with all the life and fight drained out of him. Gertrude also feared that her family might soon be preparing their own wake. Her father, Ernest, and his crew had still not been heard from. In the darkened parlor, Gertrude knelt before her cousin Frankie, offering prayers for the young boy and his two older brothers, Jerome and James. She turned to the larger body and gazed at the face, noticing that it was thinner than Paddy's and the hairline was a bit off. She gasped and answered her sister's wide eyes with a whisper: "That's not Uncle Paddy!"

Beyond the captain's doors, a crowd of mourners collected in the meadow surrounding Paddy's home. Men sipped rum from the flasks they'd hidden in their coat pockets and swapped stories about who they believed rested in the coffin. "Be Jaysus, 'tis not Paddy. No b'y. And Father McGettigan himself saying so. Surely the Missus would know her own husband, now wouldn't she? 'Tis the queerest wake I've seen. Aye, b'y."

The men lowered their voices as they watched Tom Reid's sons, Billy and Emile, slip inside Paddy's home. The boys had heard the rumors about the mismatched bodies, and they were not eager to set their eyes on their father's corpse. They nudged their way past the mourners and fixed their sights on the large man lying in the coffin. They recognized his ruddy cheeks, the thick arms that had rowed dories and hauled quintals of cod. Emile couldn't speak the words that bubbled from his older brother's lips: "That's Da!"

The reality of losing their father hit them in the face like the cold Labrador Current. No more would they stand on the hill beside their home, waiting for a sight of their da on board Paddy's ship. The boys remembered how their father always hugged and kissed his six children before he left for sea. "Take care of yurselves now," he'd tell them, their mother standing in the doorway, the worry spreading across her brow like a fever. Like many of Marystown's fishermen, Tom Reid had tried to ease his wife's fear. "The Blessed Mother will protect me," he told her. Their da never boarded the schooner without the Miraculous Medal around his neck. Billy and Emile took one last look at their father's face before blessing themselves. Silently they prayed that the Blessed Virgin had watched over their da in his final moments.

Uncertain of what to do next, they searched the faces of the mourners, their eyes pleading for guidance. *Is everyone daft? Doesn't anyone know this is our da?* The boys backed away from the coffins, looking for someone they could talk to. Still, they knew it would do little good. Who would believe them? Billy was barely eighteen, Emile, fifteen. Who would heed such an outlandish story from the sons of a penniless fisherman? Shaken and bewildered, the boys trudged down Paddy's hill, not eager to head back home, where their mother waited.

Other mourners weren't as solemn as they strolled out Paddy's door. Several couldn't help sharing a laugh at the irony of a poor doryman laid out in the King of Marystown's parlor. "Aye," they agreed, "Tom Reid's getting a fine farewell for himself."

The laughter drew the scorn of the women who had collected in the field. They shook their heads and rubbed their Rosary beads as they shared their own opinions. "There's not a thing to be joking about now, is there? The whole town's gone mad with all this talk of switched bodies. What's the difference when there are forty-two children left fatherless? How do they carry on now, with barely anything to eat and the long, cold winter ahead?"

Out of respect or grief, nearly every home on Marystown's southern shores had pulled its shades, mourning a son, a father, a brother, cousin, or uncle lost on the *Annie Anita* and *Mary Bernice*. Really now, the women agreed, wasn't Paddy's farewell a wake for them all? No matter whose body rested in the coffin, 'twas the only man the sea had returned.

CHAPTER 26

AMBROSE CONTINUES TO HAUNT—MARYSTOWN, 2003

Fine china and crystal decorate the dining table. We feast on silver capelin, potatoes, and prime rib, raising our wineglasses to toast our first journey "home."

A few nights before we are to leave Marystown, Alan Brenton has invited us to dinner. We sit—my sister, father, and I—in between Alan and Jack's family. Conversation spills from four corners of the table, and there is much laughter as stories are swapped about our respective families and lives.

Throughout our week, we have felt welcomed and indeed, as if we were "home." The Brentons have done everything possible to make our stay comfortable and help us connect with families who lost their kin to the August Gale. "They treated us," my father will later say, "like royalty."

Sufficiently satiated after cake and coffee, we settle into Alan's living room where Jack suggests we watch a video of Ambrose's eightieth birthday celebration in Marystown. Knowing that Joanie and I have never met our grandfather, Jack offers the film as a way for us to glimpse Ambrose, to get a sense of his personality. The impromptu suggestion catches my father by surprise. He is not eager to view the video, but he does not want to offend. Standing in the corner of the room, he is quiet, steeling himself for an unwanted visit with Ambrose. Joanie and I sit on the couch, curious about what the movie will reveal and concerned about how it will stir our father's emotions.

The video opens with a couple dozen people gathered around Alan's family room bar. Ambrose stands in the center of the crowd. At eighty, my grandfather is strikingly handsome, muscled and fit. His black hair is still thick and black with flecks of gray. Traditional Newfoundland music plays in the background, and Ambrose is surrounded by his family and friends. His dark eyes flash as he grins, savoring the attention. As Ambrose begins to dance, twirling a woman around the room, Joanie whispers to me, "This is bizarre."

I nod, mesmerized by the image of our grandfather, who is so alive, so vibrant; it is as if a ghost, an apparition has walked into the room. I glance up at my father knowing he is confronting his own phantoms. His lips are pressed tightly together, and he rocks back and forth on the balls of his feet. He considers leaving the room but forces himself to stay, to watch. A cake with numerous candles is presented to Ambrose, and he blows the tiny flames out amid cheers and clapping. "This is quite an honor and a surprise," Ambrose says, his laughter echoing in the room.

You son of a bitch, my father silently curses.

He has not seen Ambrose for fifty-five years. The last time was in 1948 before Ambrose stepped into a San Francisco bookie shop to bet on the horses. While my grandfather gambled, my grandmother lay in a hotel bed, threatening to jump out a window. I stare at my father's eyes. They are wide and dark with rage. I can only imagine his resentment, the contrasting memories that flicker through his mind. The images of his mother devastated, shamed, heartbroken and now the pictures of Ambrose jubilant, charismatic—the cherished hometown boy.

The room is suddenly too small. I hear Joanie's breathing, her sighs as she exhales her own confused emotions. *This is too much,* she tells herself, feeling guilty for asking our father to come to Newfoundland to relive a past he would rather forget.

I shouldn't have pushed Dad to come here. The film ends showing Ambrose on another day walking around Alan's pool with his grandson. Ambrose holds the child's hand. The boy is five or six, and I think of my father, once a young boy of the same age, his palm locked inside Ambrose's hand, safe, secure.

The screen dissolves to black, and someone shuts off the television. The Brentons realize the film has upset my father, and they apologize. "It's okay," he tells them, knowing they were trying to share a celebrated milestone in Ambrose's life. It is late, and we thank the Brentons for dinner and head outside to our car. My father's sneakers kick up stones from the gravel driveway, and the sound seems unnaturally loud in the still night air.

In the distance, Paddy's house is silhouetted in the dark. I consider my great uncle's wake, the contested and curious gathering to bid the skipper farewell. No matter whose body lay in the casket, friends and family gathered to pray, to mourn, to accept the death of a fearless and famed captain and his crew.

I recall Ambrose's final wish, his self-designed wake. Had he the chance, would my dad have attended? Listened to the stories, added his own memories before the wind carried his father's ashes into the sea? Would a wake have helped mark Ambrose's passing, providing finality, an easing of my father's animosity? Somehow my grandfather does not seem departed. There are too many emotions, unanswered questions, and mysteries to put him to rest. I breathe deeply and glance at the stars. I wonder if Ambrose's spirit, his soul, understands that we are here, in his home, resurrecting the past.

A few years before he died, Ambrose speculated about his journalist granddaughter, musing that maybe I had inherited his loquacious manner, a trait that would have benefited me in my reporting career. He marked my progress through my Nana's correspondence. She sent him the stories I wrote and informed him about the 1988 Pulitzer Prize my newspaper won for articles on escaped first-degree killer Willie Horton Jr. and Massachusetts's flawed prison furlough program. I was one of two principal reporters who had worked on the yearlong series, and my Nana had proudly shared this news with my grandfather. Intrigued by my journalism career, Ambrose harbored hope that maybe, one day, I would grow curious about my California grandfather, track him down, and visit. "I wonder would she come this way and try to look me up?" he had asked a family friend. "But then," Ambrose quickly added, "I suppose she would have no reason to."

Thirteen years after he drew his last breath, I want to talk to my grandfather, to ask him questions, to seek resolution and understanding. I wish I had sought him out, realized that one day I would regret not meeting, never knowing him.

The scent of the Newfoundland sea fills the air as I turn to the night sky. From Alan Brenton's driveway, I gaze at the string of stars, the gauzy stretch of the Milky Way. *I am here. I've come looking for you. What do you want me to find? What do you want me to know?*

CHAPTER 27

DIGGING UP THE GRAVE—MARYSTOWN, 1935

The fishermen followed the boy with the white cross.

Dressed in their tattered Sunday suits, the men pulled a wooden cart along the dirt path. They took small steps and kept a careful eye on their precious cargo—the two pine coffins that cradled the remains of Paddy Walsh and his young son Frankie. The church bell tolled, marking their solemn procession. Outfitted in their long black dresses and dark jackets, men, women, and children formed a ragged line behind the wagon. More than two hundred had come to pay their final respects to Captain Paddy. Many rose before sunrise, walking distances of five, ten, and twenty miles from the villages of Fox Cove, Spanish Room, and Burin. Families from Little Bay, Beau Bois, and Duricle crowded into their dories and rowed along Mortier Bay to the northern shore of Marystown.

The mourners' faces were somber beneath their caps and black veils, yet their eyes couldn't hide their disdain and disbelief. They nodded to one another, declaring their contention in hushed voices. *Queerest thing to be carrying on this charade. Burying Tom Reid as Paddy Walsh. No sense of it a'tall.*

Despite their doubts, they filed through the doors of the Sacred Heart Church careful to keep their grim humor hidden from Father McGettigan's ears. The Walshes, Brentons, Powers, Reddies, and the Reids made their way toward their wooden pews, the hierarchy of their wealth, or lack of it, placing them in their proper seats. Billy and Emile Reid climbed the stairs to the church balcony and settled in their places, farthest from the altar and the coffins. The young men had not spoken to their mother about what they had witnessed at the wake. They couldn't find the words to tell her: "Ma, they've made a mistake. They're burying Da!" She would have cuffed their ears and scolded, "Stop your nonsense and say a prayer for your poor father."

Their mother hadn't stopped sobbing since McGettigan came to their door with the grim news. They didn't dare push her further into grief. Still, none of this made any sense. The boys wished they could ask their da for help. He was a strong and stubborn Scotsman who had worked long hours at sea to put food before his family. In the years before his death, dark circles permanently smudged their father's eyes. A weariness clung to him like the scent of cod that lingered on his boots. No matter how many barrels of fish he caught with Skipper Paddy, it never seemed to be enough. It had been several months since they had tasted a bit of beef or butter. Like many of Marys-town's families, the Reids survived on the cabbage and potatoes, carrots and beets that grew in their garden.

"Count yur blessings, boys," their mother often told them. Now that their father was gone, the boys didn't feel so blessed. And the struggles their da had endured to provide for the family would now fall on their young shoulders. Their mother had already confessed to her sons that she might have to put one or more of her children in the St. John's orphanage. "There are too many mouths to feed," she'd told them. "Too many, dear God."

Now, as they eyed the coffins resting before the altar, the boys prayed for their da and their family, knowing the months ahead would test them all. Below the balcony, the bereaved fell silent as Lillian Walsh and her four surviving children slowly shuffled down the center aisle. Village women stifled sobs as they glimpsed Lillian's pale face, her slow, unsteady walk. "Aye, she still isn't with us," the women whispered. "She mustn't have a clue to where she is. God bless the poor thing."

As many of the mothers in Marystown had tried, Adella Power did her best to console Miss Lil. Adella understood the painful loss of a child. Her own son, Ernest, had drowned in the bay on All Souls Day. He'd taken over the wheel of the *David & Lizzie* while the captain had gone below. The boy was never seen again. The skipper believed the young man had somehow fallen overboard and drowned in the harbor, just a mile from his home. Adella remembered Father McGettigan and Dr. Chester Harris coming to her door, their faces pinched, hands folded. She had collapsed onto the kitchen floor after they had told her Ernest was gone. Two years had passed since that day, but the grief still pierced her heart like a winter wind. Adella could not fathom Lillian's sorrow. *How do you carry on after losing three sons and a husband to the sea? There'll be no getting over it. Sweet Mother of God, you'll be driven mad.*

Father McGettigan stood before the pulpit uttering prayers for the souls of Captain Paddy, his sons, Frankie, Jerome, and James, along with the other eleven Marystown fishermen lost in the gale. The Latin words tumbled from the priest's mouth; he knew the phrases as well as Shakespeare's sonnets. *Requiem æternam dona eis, Domine; et lux perpetua luceat eis. Eternal rest give to them, O Lord; and let perpetual light shine upon them.*

As the priest spoke, the mourners silently mused about the charade unfolding before them. *A shame they're burying the wrong man. Aye. Can't make no sense of it a'tall. Tom Reid in Paddy's coffin. And soon to be buried in Paddy's grave.*

Young children squirmed in the church pews and covered their noses as the earthy scent of incense rose from the altar. Chanting Latin prayers, McGettigan sprinkled holy water onto each of the two caskets. Before he could return to the pulpit, a loud bang startled the priest and the church full of mourners.

The wooden doors of Sacred Heart slammed shut as a messenger boy walked briskly toward the front row, where Ernest Walsh's family sat. Knowing that the telegram could bear ill news of her missing husband, Cecilia Walsh made the sign of the cross and uttered a quick prayer. *Dear God, have mercy on us.*

As the boy leaned over the pew to deliver the small sheet of paper, McGettigan commanded from the altar, "Bring it here." Gertrude Walsh held her breath and prayed that the message did not bear news of their father's death. "Please Lord, spare our da," she pleaded. McGettigan fell silent as he read the small black words. He cleared his throat and informed his parishioners, "Let us thank the Lord for this welcome news. Ernest Walsh and his crew made safe harbor from the gale. They are alive in St. Pierre."

Gertrude and her sisters collapsed against one another, weeping with relief. Their mother quickly prodded the girls. Wiping away her own tears, she told her children, "Hush now! There are plenty of other families who aren't so fortunate!"

The girls turned toward their Aunt Lil, seated a few pews away. The widow's shoulders convulsed with sobs, her weeping muffled by the organ that echoed in the cavernous church. Women reached for their handkerchiefs as fishermen carried the coffins from the altar. Accompanied by Lillian's cries—which had grown to high-pitched wails—the men slowly made their way from the church to the burial grounds of the Sacred Heart Cemetery. Dorymen and skippers shook off sudden chills as the caskets of the twelve-year-old boy and Captain Paddy were lowered into the earth. The men couldn't get out of the boggy cemetery quickly enough. The screams of the skipper's widow would haunt them more than any of the gale winds they had heard at sea.

The bodies had been in the ground less than twenty-four hours when Lillian's mind began to clear from the tranquilizers;

the thought struck the widow like a sudden summer storm. *The scars! The scars will tell the truth.* As sure as Sunday, she knew that the body they had buried was not Paddy. The marks, she told herself, will end this travesty.

The morning after the funeral, Lillian sent a message to Father McGettigan: *The body in the grave is not my husband's. Either you exhume him or I will do it myself!* Soon after he received the note, McGettigan arrived at her door. Lillian explained that both her husband and Tom Reid had scars that would identify their bodies. A loose pinwheel from a boat motor had permanently disfigured one of Paddy's knees; a scar branded Reid's right shoulder, marking where he fell on his ax while chopping trees in the woods.

Lillian demanded that the priest dig up the body that rested in her husband's plot, and the widow had another request for McGettigan: "Please check on Frankie, too. What if the body in his grave is really that of his older brother Jerome?"

"Both your boys are gone, Lil," McGettigan told her, his voice sharp with irritation. "What's the difference which one is buried in the grave or in the sea?"

McGettigan's mood had soured since he had received Lillian's request. He wanted no part of exhuming a body that had been buried the day before. There had never been a body dug up in the history of Marystown, and McGettigan didn't want to be the first priest to oversee such a desecration. The whole town had gone mad, McGettigan thought. He couldn't walk the footpaths without meeting the eyes of a grieving widow or a fatherless child. The entire community slowed to a standstill. Several schooners had not left the bay since the storm. The shades of most homes remained pulled, the dwellings dark with sorrow. Many years would pass, the priest reckoned, before his congregation would recover from this terrible loss. Even McGettigan, himself, struggled to wake himself from a netherworld of shock and sadness.

The priest shivered at the thought of the roaring wind that had shaken the presbytery's roof. And there was no forgetting what he viewed on his doorstep the night of the gale. McGettigan knew that many of his parishioners believed in tokens, spirits that foretold of death. But the priest had little belief in such foolishness. The only spirit he believed in was the Holy Ghost, and he scolded himself for sharing his vision of Paddy and his crew with his maid. Now it seemed everyone in town looked at him queerly, thinking he was as daft as the town's grieving widows.

Still, there were other strange things that had occurred since the hard rain lashed his windows. The priest had begun to hear odd sounds as he walked through the church. Hooks like those hanging on the trawl lines rattled, unseen, hidden in the shadows. McGettigan had shouted in the darkened sacristy, "Who's there?" His voice echoed in the empty church, his fear rising to the rafters. He had departed from the building quickly, discounting the odd noises. *I just need a good night's rest,* he told himself. Still, he couldn't shake the image of Paddy on his doorstep, his old friend staring at him with vacant, unseeing eyes.

As if he weren't tormented enough, now Lillian was demanding that he dig up Paddy's body. Knowing he had little choice but to put the rumors to rest, the priest reluctantly gave in to the widow's request. McGettigan informed the local doctor and the constable of his decision. The three men agreed to examine the body the following day, before the flesh could further decompose.

Along the dirt paths, the fish wharfs, in shops and kitchens, word about the exhumation passed from mouth to mouth like a fire in the dry September woods. "Did ye hear, McGettigan's digging up Paddy's grave?" "Aye, the body never should have been buried there in the first place."

Predawn fog crept into the Marystown harbor, as men with pickaxes and shovels headed along the dirt path to the boggy woods of Sacred Heart Cemetery. A small motorboat cut across the bay, ferrying the doctor and the constable to the northern shores of Marystown. Two young lads, Hughie Ducey and Bernard Butler, sat quietly among the men. As the boat neared the mooring, the skipper cut the engine and warned the boys, "Ye stay here till this business is done."

Hughie and Bernard nodded. From their seats, they watched the men disappear over the hill leading to the graveyard. Once their backs slipped from sight, the boys jumped from the boat, running into the woods that bordered the cemetery. They settled behind trees for cover, hushing each other, as they eyed the crowd gathered at Paddy's grave. McGettigan stood by the freshly dug plot, cursing the dozen men who had shown up for the spectacle. Billy Mitchell placed himself at the front of the grave, his bloated face mocking the priest with a toothy grin. Three young men stood quietly with their shovels, waiting for McGettigan's orders. Tom Reid's eldest son, Billy, held his spade, nervously shuffling his feet, fearing whose body they'd find beneath the earth. The eighteen-year-old didn't relish the gruesome task ahead of him, but he couldn't stand the thought of his da resting in the wrong grave.

Shaking off the morning cold, the priest shouted to the men: "Get on with it!" The pickaxes and spades struck the ground, and the piles of dirt grew taller as the men removed the earth covering the two coffins. Mitchell took pleasure in the look on the priest's face; McGettigan's cheeks grew redder with every strike of the spade. The priest sighed as the pine boxes grew visible.

"Pull Paddy up," he ordered.

The men carried the casket to the grave's edge and removed the nails from the wooden cover. No one spoke as the crowd viewed the body. A few of the men stepped back and blessed themselves. They knew your luck could turn after touching a corpse, that strange things could happen to those who disturbed the dead. McGettigan glared at the superstitious fishermen and pulled a knife from his pocket. The priest bent over the coffin. His thick arms raised the body upright. Without a word, McGettigan slashed the back of the coat covering the broad shoulders. The ripped cloth tore to reveal a long red scar—the gash Tom Reid suffered from his own ax.

Billy Reid stared at the blackened face of his father. "Da!" he cried.

McGettigan dropped the body back into coffin and turned from the grave with a final command: "Carry him up the hill and bury him in the Reids' plot."

Tom Reid's sons carried their father's coffin up a small knoll and began digging their dad's grave. The boys would later build a large wooden cross to mark the plot where their mother would stand for hours, weeping and praying for her lost husband. While Reid's sons toiled in silence, two other men tossed dirt back onto Frankie Walsh's coffin. McGettigan wasted no time in leaving the cemetery and the dreadful mess behind him. Black robes slapping his heels, he retreated to the parsonage, where a bottle of rum waited. Billy Mitchell patted his bountiful belly and laughed. "Big Bull McGettigan won't soon forget this one!"

"Aye, Billy," muttered one of the grave diggers. "I'm sure ye won't be letting him."

Left alone to place the last shovelful of dirt on his father's grave, Billy Reid whispered a prayer for his da and his family. "How," Reid wondered, "do I explain this to Ma?"

Later in her kitchen, Jessie Reid, scolded her son: "'Tis a shameful thing, you at the wake and not knowing your own father!" Billy Reid dug the toe of his worn shoe into the kitchen floor, unable to meet his mother's angry eyes. Throughout Marystown and the rural outports beyond, word of the mismatched bodies traveled.

On fish wharves, in backyard gardens, at kitchen tables, and in huddled groups of schoolchildren, the stories were swapped, the details savored: "You should've seen McGettigan's face after he slashed the coat off Tom Reid's back. Shockin' angry he was."

Slumped into his parlor chair, the priest sipped from a tall glass of rum. McGettigan gazed at the midmorning sun sparkling on the bay. His thoughts drifted back to just a week past, before the gale had torn apart this small outport and his reputation. McGettigan knew there would be no forgetting this day: a Catholic priest digging up a corpse and swapping bodies from one grave to another. The sacrilege would be remembered for generations.

He reached for the decanter of rum, hoping to dull the memory of Billy Mitchell's face, gloating at the graveside. The priest had no doubt Mitchell would make his way from one kitchen table to another, drinking cold beer and greedily consuming platters of beef, as he offered the details again and again. *There would be no getting over this,* the priest thought. *No getting over any of it.*

CHAPTER 28

GRAVEYARDS AND REDEMPTION— MARYSTOWN, JUNE 2003

A lan Brenton leads us through the graveyard. He walks past dozens of white-washed, century-old markers. "It's over here," Alan says.

My father, sister, and I follow him toward the center of the Sacred Heart Cemetery, where two dark granite markers rise from the grass. We fall quiet, awed to be standing before Paddy Walsh's gravestone. The words etched in the polished granite read: CAPT. WM PATRICK LOST AT SEA 1887 – 1935. EVER REMEM-BERED; EVER LOVED. Next to Paddy's stone stands another similar marker: IN LOVING MEMORY OF JAMES, JEROME AND FRANCIS. LOST AT SEA AUG. 25, 1935. REST IN PEACE.

Mary Bernice, the baby for whom James's schooner was named, is also remembered on the stone with her name and AUGUST 20, 1920, death date. A third marker, rounded and whitewashed, bears the name of Lillian and Paddy's baby, Cornelius, the infant who died December 30, 1917, after a few short months of life. An etching of a small lamb and a cross cover the top of the stone, and the epitaph reads,

> THERE WAS A LITTLE FLOWER THAT BLOSSOMED BUT TO DIE
> TRANSPLANTED NOW IN HEAVEN
> TO BLOOM WITH GOD ON HIGH.

Nearby, there are several other grave markers for young children and babies, victims of a rural outport ravaged by poverty and disease in the early 1900s. A cluster of stones mark the loss of Paddy's younger brother Philip, who fathered seventeen children and buried six of them. One stone records four of the children's deaths: IN LOVING MEMORY OF THE DARLING CHILD ADRAIN WALSH, DIED NOV. 1933, AGED 13 YEARS. ALSO ALAN WALSH AGED 3 MOS. EDWARD WALSH AGED 5 MOS. THOMAS AGED 2 MOS.

On this June afternoon, Alan, my father, sister, and I are the only visitors to the cemetery. Scores of small, wooden crosses mark the flat, barren terrain, where tufts of grass struggle to grow. The bogs and scrub brush that once overran the graveyard are long gone. So too, are the woods where young boys once hid to watch the spectacle of Tom Reid's body being pulled from the grave. In my mind, I see a crowd of men gathered on this patch of dirt sixty-eight years ago; Father McGettigan stands among them. I imagine the priest's anger as the fishermen lift the coffin from the ground and the scar is revealed on Tom Reid's back. As the priest feared, the story of the mismatched bodies has lived on for nearly seven decades. Almost everyone we meet knows the tale. "Did ye hear," they ask us, "the story about Tom Reid being waked and buried as Paddy?" The peculiar wake and the exhumation (the only one to ever occur in Marystown) have become lore, legend, in this small town.

"Bit strange that Paddy's name is on the gravestone, but his body isn't there, eh?" Alan asks.

Though the names of Paddy and his three sons are listed on the stone, only one body lies beneath the earth: the remains of twelve-year-old Frankie. Like thousands of other fishermen, Paddy Walsh's body rests in the sea. I envision the skipper's final moments, the waves swamping his dory, the water filling his lungs. Before his last breath, did he cry out for help, seek redemption for his three sons and himself? Or did he die rebuffing God, like his younger brother Ambrose would decades later?

During his final days in a hospital bed, my grandfather shunned the Catholic priest who offered him last rites. "I haven't believed in God my whole life," Ambrose told the minister. "And I'm not about to give in now."

My grandfather did not want or receive the priest's absolution, yet I know he harbored remorse for his transgressions. His guilt weighed heavily on his conscience on March 28, 1989, the day of my Nana's funeral. That morning, Alan Brenton's first wife, Sybil Turpin, had flown to California to visit Ambrose and his wife, Arlene. Ambrose had just learned of my Nana's death through a family friend who lived in California.

While Arlene went to work, Sybil and Ambrose sat at the kitchen table. Staring blankly at the wall, Ambrose fell unnaturally quiet.

"He was never really what you call happy," Sybil recalled. "But on the day your grandmother died, there was a heavy sadness about him. I think his life was flashing before his eyes then—the choices he'd made. He never talked about leaving his first family, but it was always there, his regrets about what he had done."

From his wallet, Ambrose pulled the photographs that he had long kept hidden in his billfold. He handed Sybil two pictures, one of a toddler and the other, a boy of eleven. "These are my sons, Ronnie and Billy," he told Sybil. "Patricia did a good job raising them. They turned out to be better men without me."

That's a hard thing to admit when you're in your eighties and your life is nearly done, Sybil thought. Ambrose had never before talked to her about his sons or his first wife, but on this afternoon, his thoughts focused on the past. He spoke about his son Ronnie's visits to the ship-rigging loft in Brooklyn, and he talked about how Patricia often wrote him letters, sending him updates about the boys: the college degrees they had attained, the women they had married, and the children they had raised.

Ambrose also had something else he wanted to share. He insisted Sybil read a story about the shy, blonde-haired girl he fell in love with on Staten Island. He retrieved the story from his bedroom closet, explaining, "This is about Patricia; it was written by my granddaughter, the reporter."

Titled "Nana," the high school essay detailed how my grandmother doted on my five sisters and me, spoiling us with homemade chocolate fudge, strawberry shortcake, and Sunday dinners; how she taught us penny poker and pig Latin, told us spooky stories and took us for walks in the woods, where mounds of dirt transformed into castles, tree branches into witches' fingers.

"Ambrose treasured that story, he really did," Sybil explained to me years later during our trip to Newfoundland.

Why did he treasure it? I wondered. *Did it make him happy to know that Patricia—my Nana—had eventually found happiness? That she was adored by her grandchildren? Did the story ease some of his guilt? Or did it remind him of the young woman who showed him kindness soon after he immigrated to the Boston States?*

Not long after Sybil left California and flew back to Newfoundland, Ambrose discovered that the ache in his back signaled more than old age. He had end-stage colon cancer. Over the next several months, the pain and disease consumed him. He died a little more than a year after my Nana's death.

I think of my grandfather as I study Paddy's gravestone and the large bold Walsh surname engraved on the granite marker. Two decades earlier, Ambrose stood on this same plot of dirt. He made his own pilgrimages to Paddy's grave whenever he returned to Marystown. Alone, he visited the cemetery, sharing a silent conversation with his hero, the brother whom he idolized and sought to emulate. *Did he talk to Paddy about his poor choices, his regrets? Did he wish he had been more like Paddy, a loyal husband, a faithful father?*

Alan jars me from my thoughts, asking if we would like our pictures taken, a souvenir of this much-talked-about site. My father, Joanie, and I gather in between the polished stones. Fittingly, my dad is dressed in his Navy cap and sweatshirt, a salute to his Uncle Paddy and his love of the sea. As Alan focuses the camera on us, my father instinctively wraps his arms around Joanie and me. We smile, captured on film at our ancestors' burial site, photos that we will later pass around to our own family, furthering the Marystown lore, explaining, "This is where Tom Reid's body was dug up from Paddy's grave."

Handing the camera back to me, Alan offers to show my father the grave of his mother, Donalda. As they walk away, I linger behind to touch the stones and say a prayer for Paddy and his deceased children. Though his name is not listed, his grave not here, I also utter a prayer for my grandfather. *I hope you found peace before you died.*

"No one is good when they run off on their children," Sybil has told me, trying to explain my grandfather's character. "But down deep, Ambrose was a good man."

I breathe in the scent of the sea, the salty breeze of my grandfather's birthplace. Here in the stillness of the cemetery, I want to believe that Ambrose asked for redemption before his death, that he whispered, *I'm sorry.* Even if my Nana, dad, and uncle never heard those words, I want to believe my grandfather sought their forgiveness.

CHAPTER 29

THE STORM STILL LINGERS—MARYSTOWN, 1935

A pall, a darkness in spirit and hope, settled over Marystown like a black thunderhead. On footpaths, in classrooms, and in meadows, the fatherless children passed one another and nodded, the tears inevitably tarnishing their cheeks. No words did they share; each understood the loss that pressed like a stone on their hearts from morn till night.

Dressed in black from head to toe, their dyed stockings, aprons, and dresses cloaking them in grief, the August Gale widows carried their own burdens. The women worked from dawn to dusk. They raked hay until their hands blistered, washed and salted the cod until their fingers numbed with cold; they pulled beets, potatoes, and carrots from the ground and stored the vegetables in their cellars, hoping it could carry them through the cold months ahead. In between their work and worry, the widows often stared at the bay and sobbed. They spoke to the water as if it would somehow talk back to them, render the secrets of where their husbands' bodies lay hidden.

Five months pregnant, with a two-year-old daughter and a five-year-old son, Mary Hanrahan cried herself to sleep and lingered by the bay where her husband, Charles, had departed on the *Annie Anita*. "I wish we could find yur dad," she often told her children. "I miss him, the poor soul."

Like the other widows, Mary received $9.50 each month from the Marine Disaster Fund. With the thirty-one cents a day, she provided what she could for her son and daughter. Still, dinner was often nothing more than a crust of bread and a spoonful of molasses, a meal that did not satisfy and often ended with tears and protests from her children. "We're hungry, Mother!"

"My dears," she tried to explain, "We just got to put up with what we got; I've no more to give us."

From the presbytery meadow across the water, Father McGettigan watched the widows stand by the shore's edge, gazing at the bay as if they expected the sails of their husbands' vessels to appear. Day after day, the priest crossed the inlet in his skiff to visit the mothers and check on their children, who grew paler with each passing week. The sight of their gaunt faces sent shivers down his collar. *The young will not survive the winter. Their bones poke through their thin clothing like sticks.*

As the autumn days grew shorter, the widows grew angrier over their misfortune. They wanted explanations for the August Gale, reasons why the Lord swept their men to death in the cold, dark sea. "Why, Father?" the widows asked. "Why did God take our husbands?"

McGettigan shook his head and folded his hands in prayer. Surely, the Lord had His reasons for their fate, but even the priest wrestled with the magnitude of Marystown's loss, and he feared that more sorrow would befall the small outport and its young. The doctor and constable shared McGettigan's concern. Before the winter snows fell and the bay turned to ice, the law officer knocked on the doors of the August Gale widows.

Unwilling to hand over their sons and daughters, mothers pointed to pots of water boiling on cookstoves, a ruse that failed to satisfy the constable, who understood there was nothing to boil, nothing to cook. Her three-month-old baby on her hip, Alice Brinton confronted the officer's solemn face as he stood in her kitchen. The past few weeks had tested the young woman, but she was not ready to give up her daughters.

"Pack up your children," the constable told her. "I'll take them to the orphanage."

Alice reached for her daughters' hands. She could barely stand from the exhaustion and grief. Still, she would be damned if she would parcel her children off like packages.

"If they're going to starve," she told the officer, "then they'll starve at home."

Other widows with larger families and six or seven children to feed had no choice but to send one or two of their offspring away to the orphanages in St. John's. Tom Reid's wife, Jessie, reluctantly hugged her nine-year-old daughter Theresa good-bye.

"My dear girl, we will see ye soon," her mother promised.

Jessie also lost another child, her son, Bill Reid, to the law. The boy was arrested by the Rangers, the government police, for stealing a sack of flour to help feed his family. Angry over the injustice, Jessie pelted the officers' boat with wood and rocks as they hauled her son away to serve his time. Several other fishermen's wives grew so desperate they scattered their children in neighboring villages among families who could spare a bit of food and a bed. And though she could afford to provide for her four surviving children, Lillian Walsh's tattered nerves and grief left her in a daze; she could not console or control her seven-year-old daughter, Little Lillian. Tormented by her own heartache, the child thrashed on the floor screaming for her father.

"She'll be better off in the orphanage," Father McGettigan advised. "The sisters will look after her there and provide the girl with a good education."

The spirited young girl, who had often fished with her father and had pleaded to sail with him on his August journey, found herself in the red-bricked Belvedere Orphanage of St. John's. Supervised and taught by the stern and formidable Sisters of Mercy, Lillian took comfort in the familiar face of Theresa Reid, who had also been placed there. Just as her father had depended on his second hand Tom Reid at sea, Lillian now sought Reid's daughter for kinship and memories of home.

As the fall winds chilled the night air, Father McGettigan continued to visit and check on the widows. The vacant and worn look in their eyes alarmed the priest. Lucy Walsh particularly concerned McGettigan. She could barely hold her baby as she sat in her rocking chair, trembling. The young woman's mind was locked on the past, the days before her husband James set sail on the *Mary Bernice*. She had little interest in caressing or feeding her blue-eyed infant born the night of the gale. The child reminded her of death.

"She has a horrible case of nerves," McGettigan told Lucy's mother, Selena Gaulton. "Perhaps, it's best for her to go away."

Selena nodded. A midwife for many years, she knew her daughter might never recover from the tragedy. Before the spring snows thawed, Lucy would be gone, leaving Marystown and her baby, Jamie, behind.

In the home on the hill, Lillian concealed herself behind closed drapes and shades. At night, every lamp blazed, warding off the shadows and darkness. Lillian dared not sleep for fear of the images that settled in her dreams, visions of her sons screaming *Mother!* as the monstrous waves battered their vessels and pulled them beneath the malevolent sea. *My babies. My poor babies. Why did I let them go? Why?*

For hours, she stared at photographs of her sons and Paddy, talking to them as if they were seated on the settee next to her. One by one, she held the pictures to her eyes, studying the details, the moments of their lives frozen in the black-and-white images. Her fingers outlined the edge of Jerome's rounded face in a photograph taken in the priest's meadow during a Lady Day garden party. Dressed in a white shirt, tie, and the new brown breeches she had sewn for him, her boy grinned into the camera. Ten at the time, his hands stuck in his pockets, he balanced himself on a post, proud and confident. *Ye were always so sure of yourself, Jerome, so full of spirit like yur Da.*

Lillian picked up another picture of Frankie and Jerome. The two of them sat shoulder to shoulder in their uncle's rowboat. Caps on their small heads, they smiled, secure in the vessel that was safely moored on shore. *Ye were only five and seven then. Good little brothers, always at each other's side, looking out for one another. Sleep well, boys, take care of each other now until yur mother can hold ye close again.*

Turning to a photograph of Paddy, Little Lillian, and Paddy Jr., Lillian remembered the chilly Sunday it was taken. She had insisted they take a picture on that afternoon in 1934. The three of them posed on the side of the house. Bundled like a doll in his snowsuit, Paddy Jr. gazed downward, mesmerized by something in the grass. Outfitted in a dress and her Sunday coat and shoes, Lillian pressed close to her father's side. Her small hand wrapped around one of her father's large fingers. Dressed in a cap, suit coat, and tie, Paddy stared straight into the camera, his eyes defiant, a surly smile on his lips.

Ye were afraid of nothing, Paddy. Fearless of God and the sea. Always believing ye'd return. But now Little Lillian has no hand to hold, no father to take her fishing. And Paddy Junior, no da to look up to. How will we get on without ye, Paddy?

Her son James gazed at Lillian from the last photograph. Leather jackboots rose to his knees, the woolen sailor's jacket his mother had sewn covered his broad shoulders. His lips pressed together, he shared his father's stern, serious look. *Oh, me son, ye were ready to captain, ready to be a father. Ye would have done a fine job of both, dear boy. A fine job. Yur new baby has yur eyes, son. She'll be forever wanting to know ye. Forever missing ye, like yur mother. May the angels watch over ye, son.*

From the kitchen, Alice Brinton listened to Lillian's ramblings. If she hadn't known better, Alice would have thought James, Jerome, Frankie, and Paddy kept their mother company in the parlor. But the young maid understood how grief could change a woman, turn her daft with sorrow and heartache. Since Alice had lost her husband John off the *Annie Anita,* she had begun talking to her dead husband herself. *Are ye there, John? Can ye hear me? Is yur spirit settled? Are ye at peace, my poor soul? We miss ye, John, yur daughters pray for ye every night. They love their da.*

Though Alice kept vigil for her husband, she glimpsed no sign of him, heard no whispers from his phantom lips. Still, she knew such things could happen. She had witnessed plenty of odd occurrences at Captain Paddy's home since the skipper's death. One evening as she finished the ironing, she heard stomping on the stairs. Alice took the lamp into the hall and discovered a single brown shoe on the step. *Aye, that's Skipper Paddy's shoe. He always told Lillian if there was a way for him to come back, he'd find it. Dear Blessed Mother of God, the captain had kept his word. No wonder Miss Lil was afraid of the night.* "Go on now, Mr. Paddy, settle down," Alice whispered in the dark.

Another curious event startled Alice on a Sunday morning. She and the second maid were cooking dinner while Miss Lillian and her children had gone to church. The two women nearly jumped from their shoes at a loud crash in the dining room. Must be the cat knocking the dishes from the table, Alice thought. Searching for the wreckage, she found nothing out of order. The plates, silverware, and glasses remained in place, and there was no sign of cats or any earthly evidence for the noise.

Jaysus, something has the skipper out of sorts today, Alice reckoned, remembering Paddy's rage as he pounded the teakettle spout, angry over his late dinner. If she wasn't so desperate for the extra money and the secondhand clothes that Miss Lil offered, Alice would have steered clear of the captain's quarters for good.

"Don't be passing Paddy's house after dark," she warned her children.

Throughout the winter, into the spring and summer, the shades and drapes remained drawn on the house on the hill, and the lights continued to blaze from dusk to dawn. Inside, Lillian sat beneath the lamplight, shrouded in black, holding the photographs of her three sons and husband, her voice filling the parlor with hushed murmurs and memories.

CHAPTER 30

AUGUST THUNDER AND AMBROSE'S DAUGHTERS— NEW HAMPSHIRE, AUGUST 2003

The young man knocked on the door.

Ambrose did not recognize the surprise visitor—his second-born son, William Patrick Walsh, the child he had named after his beloved brother Paddy.

Bill Walsh eyed the man he believed to be his father. He had seen pictures of him, but still, he was not sure.

"Are you Ambrose Walsh?" he asked.

Ambrose nodded.

"I'm your son, Billy."

It was 1972, and my uncle had just completed his master's degree in social work. A few years earlier, Ambrose had surprised him with a phone call, wanting to talk. My uncle was excited about this unexpected connection with his dad. *Maybe he wants to reconcile with Ma, with us.* Unlike my father, my uncle had no memories of Ambrose. He was a year and a half old when Ambrose had slipped out the door in Brooklyn, and just a few years older when his dad abandoned his family again in San Francisco. My father was not excited about hearing from Ambrose after three decades of silence, but my uncle thought, *I just want to see him. I want to see my dad's face.*

When he arrived at Ambrose's California home without warning, my uncle did not consider the repercussions of his visit. Unflustered by his son's sudden appearance, Ambrose invited my uncle into the living room. As the two of them talked, Ambrose's daughters returned home. Twelve at the time, Donnie asked her mother, "Who is that man?"

"He's your brother," Arlene said, pulling Donnie into the kitchen.

"My *brother?*" Donnie asked. She had four older brothers, but no one had ever told her about this mysterious sibling. "What are you talking about?"

Ambrose's eldest daughter, Kathy glimpsed the man talking to her father. *He has to be related to us. He looks just like my brother, Jim.* For years, Kathy had wondered about Ambrose's other family after discovering two paintings in her father's closet. The watercolors depicted young boys, with curly light brown hair. "Who are they?" she had asked her dad. Ambrose shook his head, refusing to answer. "Who *are* they?" she persisted.

"They're my sons from my first family," Ambrose said quietly, refusing to say anything more.

Now, a decade later, Kathy stared at the stranger in her father's home. *That's got to be my brother.* For most of her childhood, Kathy had dreamed about her mysterious brothers. *I wonder what their lives are like.* After my uncle's impromptu visit, Donnie also began to consider her secret siblings and her connection to them. *Someday, I want to meet them. I want to know them. They're my family.*

❖

The August sky is dark and storm clouds threaten as the plane touches down at the New Hampshire airport. After the sudden connection through our August Gale research and multiple phone and e-mail conversations with my father, Kathy and Donnie fly three thousand miles east to meet the brothers they have long wondered about. They have no trouble recognizing my father at the airport terminal; he walks and carries himself like their brother Jim. Kathy's eyes tear up. *After so many years, I can't believe we're finally meeting our brother.* As my father helps them carry their suitcases, Kathy and Donnie stare at his hands. They are identical to Ambrose's. Over the next few days, they will watch my father wave his palms in the air as he talks, place his fingers to his forehead as he thinks.

"He's so much like dad. His mannerisms are identical," Donnie whispers to her sister.

"How," Kathy and Donnie will later ask themselves, "can he mirror Dad's characteristics so much when he was only with him for a short time?" Oddly, none of their other four brothers share Ambrose's traits.

As I drive south from Maine to my New Hampshire child-hood home, I imagine my dad and his half sisters together, getting to know each other after decades of separation. I consider my Nana, how she would have told my father, *It's the right thing to do. Invite them to your home. You're the oldest. It's your responsibility.* For most of my Nana's life, she bridged her two families— the first six siblings born to her mother—and the other seven children born to her stepmother. My grandmother quelled the feuds, mended the hard feelings, and was forever trying to link her brothers and sisters together. And now my father tries to do the same. "I don't hold anything against them," he says of Kathy and Donnie. "Why would I?"

Though my father has no qualms about meeting Ambrose's daughters, my mother, five sisters, and I still find this get-together surreal and strange. For most of their marriage, my mother had never asked about Ambrose. She knew my father did not want to talk about him, to resurrect the painful memories of his past. Protective of my father, my sisters and I are unsure of how we will feel in Kathy and Donnie's presence. They represent the family Ambrose chose over our dad; they symbolize the grandfather several of my sisters still resent. Still, we are curious. Will they look like us? Act like us? Will we like them?

Hours after Kathy and Donnie arrive, I pull into my parents' driveway. Overhead, storm clouds loom, growing larger, closer. They are black and thick and will soon thunder and spark lightning that will crackle in the afternoon air. I muse about Paddy and Ambrose, their spirits conspiring to create an August storm as a backdrop to this unexpected family gathering. Donnie and Kathy's visit comes so soon, six weeks after our trip to Marystown, and I wonder if their stay, their memories will flesh out the grandfather I am beginning to know. What stories will they tell, what details will they choose to share about their lives and Ambrose?

My parents' house is quiet, the kitchen, sunporch, and pool area empty. An uneasy feeling lurches in my stomach. *Where are they?* The living room is vacant, too. I head down the hall and open the den door. The air conditioner whirs on high, and my parents, Kathy, and Donnie are laughing at the black-and-white images that flicker on the television. They are watching videos of my sisters and me as young children. Our chubby legs pump backyard swings and attempt to climb a metal slide. My older sister, Diane swings, vigorously, upside down on the monkey bar. Kathy and Donnie laugh as if they have seen this video before, as if they are part of our family. I am struck by how comfortable they are, how at ease my parents are in their company.

I hug each of them, taking in their auburn hair, the color of their eyes. Kathy's are soft, hazel, and a bit guarded, watchful like my own. Donnie's brown eyes sparkle with light, reminding me of my sister Laura's luminescent gaze.

Not long after I arrive, my Uncle Bill and his wife Pam pull up to my parents' home. Despite having moved to Michigan in 1970, my uncle has often driven to New Hampshire for his six nieces' weddings, for momentous birthday and anniversary celebrations. And he was not going to miss this gathering, the chance to meet his half sisters.

As with my father, Donnie and Kathy tear up when they see my uncle. Later they will tell each other: *He's got the same facial features and build as our brothers Michael and Jim.* Kathy also appreciates my uncle's soft-spoken nature. She watches him listen intently to conversations. *He's like me,* she thinks. *A listener, a bit shy.*

That evening, after the dinner dishes have been cleared, Ambrose's children sit at the kitchen table sharing stories, piecing together the secrets of their father's life.

"My dad always told me that I was six weeks old when he bundled me in his coat and drove me and my mother from Brooklyn to Florida," Kathy explains. "A few months later, my mother and I took a bus across the country to San Francisco."

Ambrose, Kathy explains, arrived before them, on a yacht he was paid to sail to the fog-shrouded city. My father is stunned; he had not realized Kathy is the baby who suddenly appeared in their Mill Valley home.

"My mother took care of you," he tells her. "For a few months, you lived with us."

Kathy cannot understand or fathom why my Nana would care for her, knowing that she was the child of Ambrose's mistress. Though her mother Arlene will later refuse to talk about why my Nana temporarily cared for Kathy, she does tell her daughter, "She was good to you. I walked up to see you every day and had tea with her. She was really nice to me."

Kathy and Donnie wince as my father continues the story, explaining how Ambrose gambled away most of their money and eventually deserted them again.

"It was tough, really tough on my mother," he says. "She had a nervous breakdown."

Shaking their heads, Donnie and Kathy offer their apologies. They loved their father and never worried that he would leave them, but they understood how their dad's bad choices could cause chaos and pain. While raising his six children in California, Ambrose worked a variety of jobs—selling cars, painting commercial buildings, driving buses, but he often gambled away his paycheck, and sometimes he got fired for taking too much time off to bet on the horses.

"You probably were better off without him," Donnie says, sharing a sentiment that her four other brothers have voiced about Ambrose's first two sons.

My uncle and father fall silent.

Eager to console, Kathy offers some of the good memories, stories of the years before Ambrose left his sons.

"Before he died, my father opened up more about you," she tells my dad. "He talked about how close he was to you, how he bought you your first bike and taught you how to ride. He said the two of you used to go everywhere together. You used to stand on the car seat next to him as he drove, with your hand around his shoulders."

My uncle listens quietly to these stories; it is painful to realize there are few memories for him. Still, he knows Ambrose saved his life. My uncle was only a few days old when he came home from the hospital and caught the whooping cough. Ambrose and his wife, Patricia, feared their second-born son would die. They watched as the infant closed his fists and flailed his arms, coughing and struggling to breathe. Determined not to lose another infant like their daughter, who was stillborn, Ambrose swaddled his brother Paddy's namesake and took William Patrick to five doctors. "There's nothing we can do," they told him.

Ambrose refused to take their word. He sought out a chiropractor, who massaged the phlegm from his baby's lungs and told him to take the infant to the sea to breathe the cold, salty air. With several treatments, Ambrose's son overcame the cough and survived.

Still, for much of his life, my uncle lived with a void, an emptiness, no recollection of his father. Though the stories Kathy and Donnie tell are difficult to hear, my uncle understands that his half sisters are doing what they can to absolve Ambrose's wrongs. *They want to know that we're happy, that we're okay, and even though Ambrose left us, he still thought about and loved his first two sons.*

Before they leave to return home to California, Kathy and Donnie witness a raucous birthday celebration in which all of our family—my parents, five sisters and me, my uncle, his wife, eight grandchildren, four brothers-in-law, and even my Aunt Eleanor— all gather poolside for a barbecue. It is my father's sixty-eighth birthday that day, August 12; the following day is my forty-fifth birthday. Kathy and Donnie laugh at the insanity that unfolds around them. Kids jumping in and out of the pool, sisters brewing batches of margaritas, a Wiffle-ball game in the backyard. Growing up, they did not have these types of celebrations, and they are happy to take part, to be welcomed, to be considered family.

Before the birthday candles are lit, my uncle has a surprise gift for Kathy, Donnie, and my father: navy T-shirts with white bold block letters that read: WALSH. Pulling the shirts over their heads, they pose for pictures. They line up, Kathy and Donnie on either side of my uncle and father. They smile and instinctively place their arms around one another. As I focus my camera on them, tears well up in my eyes. Never did I think the August Gale, the desire to tell the story of my seafaring ancestors, would lead to this: to Ambrose's children hugging, sharing the apologies their father could not voice.

During the last few days of their stay, Donnie, the more loquacious of the two sisters, shares a wish with me. "I've always felt sad about your father," she says. "Out of all the brothers, he was the closest to my dad. And then his father leaves. You never get over it. That wound stays with you all your life.

"I thought maybe by visiting him, we could resolve some of his heartache. I know he cannot quite forgive, but to let go of that anger would be the best thing."

I nod, knowing my father has unburdened some of his bitterness, some of the anger. He has talked about Ambrose more in the last few months than he has over the past five decades. I think about the conversation my dad shared with me on a winter's night about the August Gale—how a storm that wrought so much grief and loss could result in calming another tempest, the squalls and sorrow my grandfather stirred.

CHAPTER 31

"LEFT IN A DREAMLAND"—NEWFOUNDLAND, 1935–2005

Bride Hanrahan still dreams about her father grasping for her as he thrashes in the roiling sea. Her hair is white, her eyes failing with age, but the vision she had as a young girl remains vivid: the flash of yellow oilskins, her father's face disappearing in the ragged waves.

"It's the same dream I had the night my father drowned," Bride says. "I always see his hand reaching for me as he cries for help."

Seventy years have passed since the 1935 August Gale, but the thought of her dad alone, sobbing in the sea during his final moments, still torments Bride. She cannot bear to look at her father's picture; the portrait makes her too lonesome for his company. She cannot smell or view the sea without shivering, and she cannot erase the memories of the gale or the days following the storm.

"I still see Father McGettigan coming to our door," she says. "My mother knew. 'Get the candles,' she told me, 'so we can pray that yur poor father is in heaven. Ye'll never see yur dad no more."

"Of course we will, Mom," the young Bride argued. "Da is going to come home!"

A month later, her family received another unexpected visit from Father McGettigan. The priest handed Bride's mother a letter from the constable in Harbour Buffett, a village in Placentia

Bay. The note explained that a body had washed up on in Keating's Cove, a beach not far from where the *Mary Bernice* had capsized. The dead fisherman wore his yellow oilskins, a green hand-knit sweater, and his Kingfisher hip boots. The middle finger on his right hand was crooked, bent from a previous injury. A small gunny bag hung around his neck. A cloth pendant of the Blessed Mary and a medal of the Virgin's mother, St. Anne, were tucked inside.

"My mother knew it was my father from his crooked finger and the sweater she had knit for him," Bride remembered. "He was so long in the water. His body was broken up, so they just put him in the grave there."

Decades later, Bride and her sister visited her father's burial place in Port Royal, a small community near Coffin's Cove and Haystack, the village where the *Mary Bernice* had been towed to shore. Bride and her sister sat by their father's grave, boiled tea on the beach rocks, and prayed.

"My daddy used to like his tea, so we had our cup with him and cried. He always said, 'If I drown, I don't want to be buried at sea.' After all his suffering, at least his body made it to shore."

Now eighty-six and living in a senior citizens' complex in Boston, Bride pulls the picture of her dad from a drawer to show a visitor. She eyes her father's face, his smooth, youthful skin. The photograph was taken when he was in his thirties, two decades before his death.

"A long time has gone by, but I'm always thinking about him and the gale, and the other poor souls who went down with him. I always wonder what would my life have been like if my poor daddy hadn't drowned."

Like Bride Hanrahan, the August Gale children and widows pondered the same question, lamenting how their fate would have been different if the hurricane had veered away from Newfoundland on that summer night in 1935.

"They were all left in a dreamland," says Gerald Hoffe, who married Paddy Walsh's youngest daughter, Lillian. "The families had two lives: before the gale and then after. For many of the survivors, it was harder being left behind. They were stuck in time, trapped by memories and grief."

Less than a year after she was placed in the St. John's Belvedere Orphanage, Lillian Walsh returned home to Marystown. A picture of her taken soon after she reunited with her family shows her standing in a field of daises outside her house. Her aunt, uncle, and younger brother Paddy Jr. stand with her in the garden. Lillian wears a dress and a slight, forced smile. In her hand, she holds a bouquet of flowers that she has picked—a gift, perhaps, for her mother.

For the most part, her older sisters Lottie and Tessie looked after Lillian and Paddy Jr. while their mother continued to grieve. Eventually, after Lillian completed her grammar and secondary education, she left Marystown to study nursing in St. John's. She worked in the operating room and supervised her own floor of hospital patients. She earned a reputation as a skilled and unflappable medical professional. Like her father Paddy, she did not shy away from a challenge or a patient who needed calming or a stern word.

A stroke victim later in life, Lillian ended up in a nursing home, in pain and unable to control her limbs. Shortly before her death, she bemoaned her crippled body and the tragedy that had claimed her beloved father and brothers. For years, she wished that her dad had taken her with him on that fateful journey. Depressed and distraught, she cried to her husband, "I wish I had sailed with my dad and brothers that day. I wish it was me in that boat."

Lillian's younger brother Paddy Jr. struggled with his own sorrow and confusion over the tragedy that claimed his father and three brothers. He grew up in Marystown shadowed by his dad's legacy. The young boy became accustomed to fisher-men's voices trailing his footsteps. "Aye, that's Captain Paddy Walsh's son. Only Walsh male not taken by the sea." Out of respect for his father, Paddy Jr. received special treatment from captains, who allowed him to board their vessels and climb the masts. Still, the boy longed for his dad and three older brothers. Surrounded by women in his home, he was lonely and bereft of male companionship. In a photograph taken soon after the gale, Paddy sits on a fence post in the corner of his yard. His hair is curled in ringlets that obscure his face. His gaze is cast down-ward, forlorn. Facing east toward the ocean, his small body is framed by the bay as it reflects the summer light.

For two years after the storm, he woke at night screaming, unsure of where he was or what terrified him. Unable to cure the young boy, the local doctor suggested his mother Lillian ask the priest for help. Reverend John Fleming, who would replace Father McGettigan, stopped Paddy on his way to school one morning. He rested his hands on top of the boy's head and uttered several prayers.

"You will be fine now, Paddy," the priest explained.

Paddy never had another bout of nightmares or hysteria. In the years that followed, he dreamt about captaining a schooner like his father, but Paddy never pursued a life on the sea because he knew such a decision would break his mother's heart. Instead, he continued to row the family dory across the bay to attend the Catholic school located on Marystown's northern shore. There in the five-room school run by the Sisters of Mercy, Paddy earned his high school diploma. Eventually, he left Marystown and settled in Calgary, where he became a stockbroker, married, and had three daughters of his own.

In 2001, sixty-six years after the August Gale, Paddy's eldest daughter decided Marystown would provide a fitting backdrop for her father's seventieth birthday. With the approval of Alan

Brenton, who owned Captain Paddy's former house, and the local mayor Jerome Walsh, a party was planned in the meadow where the skipper's cows and sheep once grazed. On a warm August afternoon, scores of relatives—grandchildren, cousins, nieces, nephews, and other gray-haired men and women who had lost their fathers to the 1935 hurricane—gathered to celebrate Paddy Jr.'s birthday and to remember the gale that forever changed their small community. Tables and tents were set up in Skipper Paddy's old field. Music played, memories were shared, and the legendary doryman Jim "Pad" Kelly sang sea shanties and told stories about the "devil" that danced on the water that summer so long ago.

When the local newspaper reporter asked Paddy how it felt to be "home," he explained: "When you leave a place you love, you can take a little bit of it with you, and you leave a little bit of it behind, but it will always be home."

Among the seventy people attending the reunion was Jamie Walsh, the baby born the night of the gale. Like Paddy, Jamie relished the opportunity to be among family, to remember the town where she had lived as a young girl. Birthed the night her father Captain James Walsh drowned, Jamie never recovered from losing both parents at an early age. After her mother Lucy abandoned her at the age of six months, Jamie was raised by her grandparents in Little Bay. Seven years passed before Jamie's mother returned to Marystown.

"That was the first time I had ever seen her," Jamie recalled. "Then she left again for the States. My grandparents could not have been any better raising me, but I always had an insecure feeling, like someone would always be leaving me."

Jamie would wait another eight years before her mother remarried and could afford to take her to California. Fifteen and used to living in a small outport of eight hundred, Jamie was overwhelmed with the cars, crowds, and the noise in her new home. She also felt like an unwelcome stranger in her mother's company. Her mother Lucy could not look past the cruel irony: As her daughter drew her first breath, her husband took his last.

"She always resented me for it," Jamie remembered.

While her mother refused to talk about Marystown, her deceased husband, or anything connected to the sea, Jamie collected model schooners, lighthouses, and pictures of sea captains and sailors, and she always wondered: *What if my daddy had lived? Would he have held me and sung to me? Taken me fishing on his schooner?*

Three weeks after Paddy Jr.'s party, Jamie and several other August Gale children gathered for a memorial service on August 25, the anniversary of the storm. Doryman John Brinton's daughters, Mary, Sadie, and Theresa, and fisherman Michael Farrell's son Michael Jr. sat in the front pew of the Sacred Heart Church with Jamie to remember their fathers. The gray-haired men and women held each other and wept as the service concluded. "None of us ever forgot the loss," Jamie said. "Ever."

Like her granddaughter, Lillian Walsh carried the memories of the August Gale close to her heart for the remainder of her life. She also chose to remain single. "I'll never find another man like Paddy," she told relatives. "So, I'm not going to bother trying."

For the first five years following the gale, she continued to wear black and spent much of her time isolated in her home. After countless hours staring at the bay watching for Paddy's returning sails, she could no longer bear to view the water. She moved the parlor couch and chairs away from the windows, turning her back on the tides, the rhythm of the sea that she had grown to know so well. Rarely did she venture outside, preferring to remain in her darkened rooms, sewing and conjuring memories of the past.

"For a long time, she didn't know if she was in this world or the other," her son-in-law Gerald Hoffe recalled.

Her two eldest girls, Lottie and Tessie, watched over their mother and tried to pull Lillian from her stupor. The summer after the storm, the three of them sat on a wooden bench outside their home. Flanked by her daughters, Lillian wore a black dress, stockings, and a large, dark bow around her neck. Her mournful attire is stark against the white picket fence and her daughters' light-colored dresses. I imagine that someone had coaxed Lillian outside for some fresh air, sunshine, and a family portrait, but it is clear that she was there reluctantly. In the picture, her lips are pressed together tightly, her white hands folded in her lap. Lillian's daughters wrap their arms around their mother's shoulders, holding her close, trying to boost her spirits.

"Don't ever believe that you can die from a broken heart," Lillian often told her family and friends. "Because if it were true, I'd be dead."

In 1950, she sold the home on the hill, the old Molloy Hotel that Paddy had bought as a surprise for her. She lived with her daughter Lillian for several years in Chapel's Cove, and she told stories about the August Gale over and over to anyone who would listen. She recounted her premonitions the night before her husband sailed, the terrible deaths that befell her three sons and husband, and the misidentified body that led to Tom Reid being buried in Paddy's grave. When her husband's youngest brother Ambrose finally returned to Newfoundland in 1975, he visited Lillian.

"The two of them sat at the table telling stories till the air turned blue," Gerald remembered. "They were both fond of talking of the past. Neither one of them got over losing Paddy. He was Ambrose's hero and Lillian's one and only love."

Two weeks before she celebrated her ninetieth birthday, Lillian died of cancer. Her body was returned to Marystown, where she was buried next to her son Frankie's grave.

Not immune to the sorrow that gripped his community, Father McGettigan found himself caught up in his own grief following the gale. He continued to hear odd noises in the church, a rustling like the sound of oilskins. His parishioners noticed the dark circles beneath the priest's eyes and his haunted gaze. McGettigan could barely look at Paddy's empty, abandoned wharf. The priest knew there would be no more shouting, cursing, and singing from the skipper as he set sail or returned home. Paddy's voice, like the voices of the other August Gale fishermen, was silent, still now.

Soon after the first anniversary of Marystown's tragedy, McGettigan received orders to serve in St. Mary's Bay, along the southern coast of the Avalon Peninsula where the *Annie Anita* had washed ashore. Several in the Marystown congregation were eager to see the gruff priest depart, while others mourned his exodus. Before he left, he stopped to say good-bye and offer a prayer for Paddy's widow, who he knew would struggle for a good long while. Picking up Paddy Jr. in his arms, McGettigan encouraged the five-year-old boy to behave as best he could. "Be good to your mother, son."

Though he desired to put the sorrow of the August Gale behind him, misfortune and poor luck followed the priest. The second anniversary of the August Gale had barely passed when a storm struck St. Mary's Bay. McGettigan's young maid, Lizzie, who had moved with the priest, stood outside the presbytery admiring the last summer roses as the sky darkened. Suddenly, she heard a loud crack and saw a flash of light. A thunderbolt struck the rectory. The lightning shattered the chandeliers and blasted the bedroom where Father McGettigan brushed his hair, preparing for Mass. The bolt blackened the priest's bronze bed and knocked McGettigan face-first to the floor. Outside, the lightning burned a ribbon of grass down to the bay. Shaken and temporarily stunned, the priest recovered, but he became especially wary of dark skies and summer storms.

Before his retirement, McGettigan served in two more parishes, and he found himself delivering several more death notices to widows who lost their men to the sea. Yet he never faced another catastrophe like the August Gale. In the years before he died, McGettigan returned to live in St. John's where he enjoyed the city's fine restaurants and plays. In his quiet hours, alone before the parlor fire, he sipped his rum and reminisced about his time in Marystown and his surly and fearless friend, Captain Paddy. When the memories of the gale overwhelmed him, the priest sought solace from the books that lined his walls. Often, he read works from the British poet, Alfred Lord Tennyson. One poem in particular captured his emotions and sorrowful recollections of the storm. He read the words so often he could recite them by heart:

Break, break, break,
On thy cold gray stones, O Sea!
And I would that my tongue could utter
The thoughts that arise in me.
O, well for the fisherman's boy,
That he shouts with his sister at play!
O, well for the sailor lad,
That he sings in his boat on the bay!
And the stately ships go on
To their haven under the hill;
But O for the touch of a vanish'd hand,
And the sound of a voice that is still!
Break, break, break
At the foot of thy crags, O Sea!
But the tender grace of a day that is dead
Will never come back to me.

The Marystown fishermen's voices had been stilled, their hands forever vanished in the sea. Yet one voice still resonated in McGettigan's mind, one image still held strong. The priest saw Captain Paddy, his hand on the helm; he heard the skipper's shouts commanding the crew, "Heave up the anchor! Hoist the sails! We're away again, lads!"

Fair seas to you, Paddy, the priest whispered. *Rest in peace, in the waters that you loved.*

CHAPTER 32

ONE LAST JOURNEY—
BROOKLYN AND STATEN ISLAND, OCTOBER 2006

My father walks along the Brooklyn pier. The October wind is brisk off the New York Harbor; whitecaps dance on the gray-green water. Decades past, a wooden wharf stood here, the pier where my grandfather awaited the Staten Island ferry on an August afternoon in 1935.

Somewhere nearby, in the waterfront neighborhoods of Brooklyn, Ambrose sat on a bench, eating his lunch as a breeze carried a newspaper to his feet. I imagine the terror that gripped my grandfather as he read the New York newspaper headline: AUGUST GALE KILLS MORE THAN 40 NEWFOUNDLAND FISHERMEN.

Scanning the story further, he found the words that caused him to cry out:

> The hurricane that roared across Newfoundland over the weekend swept away forty lives. Tragedy concentrated in some cases on individual families. Captain Patrick Walsh and his son were found dead aboard the Annie Anita when she drifted into Hazel Cove on her beam ends. Six other men and another of Walsh's sons were listed in her crew and they were almost surely drowned.
>
> That was only part of the Walsh family tragedy, however. Captain Walsh's eldest son was skipper of the schooner Mary

Bernice. *Today, the vessel was found drifting bottom up in Placentia Bay, her crew missing.*

Along this gritty waterfront, my grandfather sat alone, collapsed in grief, sobbing for the death of his hero, Paddy, and his three nephews, James, Jerome, and Frankie. Distraught, he made his way here to the Sixty-ninth Street wharf to await the ferry home to his wife, Patricia, and his newborn son, Ronald. The news of the tragedy broke something deep inside my grandfather. "He went beserk," a relative told me. "Screaming and shouting. He totally lost it."

Five years have passed since my father shared the story of the August Gale with me. Here on this pier, a sudden and persistent breeze carried the prophetic newspaper to my grandfather's feet. *What if that story had not been remembered, retold decades later by my father, voiced to me on winter night? Would my grandfather have remained a stranger, my father's childhood a mystery?*

On the horizon, the Statue of Liberty rises up toward the blue October sky.

My father gazes across the bay to Staten Island. *His story began here too. His memories, the good and the bad, resonate here.*

Surprisingly, it was my father's idea to visit the homes, neighborhoods, and churches of his childhood. "I thought it might be good for you to see them," he tells me. My two younger sisters, the twins Janice and Joan, and my mother decide to accompany us; they realize this is a once-in-a-lifetime trip, and they do not want to miss it.

Yet this sojourn, like our Newfoundland journey, has triggered yet a new round of emotions in each of us. The night before we drive to New York, my dad reminisces about his younger years. The story of Ambrose's deadly street fight in Bay Ridge stands out in his mind. Ironically, it is one of my father's good memories.

At the time, in 1944, my Nana, father, and Ambrose lived in Bay Ridge, in one of the many apartments they rented during the post-Depression years. On the day of the fight, my father is nine years old and sent to buy milk at the local market. The dark-haired boy runs along Sixty-ninth Street. The grocery is a couple of blocks away from his family's home. He eyes the candy shelves as he enters the store, wishing he had a few spare pennies. He grabs the milk and pays for his purchase. Sprinting from the store, he races down the sidewalk. Up ahead, the entry to a Greek restaurant's cellar storage is open. The boy doesn't see the metal door, and his foot catches its edge causing him to trip. The milk bottles shatter, scattering dozens of shards. He falls, his hands splayed out in front of him. Before he gets up, he worries about the milk that pools on the sidewalk, and then he notices the blood that runs down his left hand like a little river.

"He needs seven stitches," the doctor later tells Ambrose. "You need to take him to the hospital for ether."

"He doesn't need ether," Ambrose says. "Stitch him up here."

The boy winces but says nothing. He knows his father doesn't like crying or weak men. In Newfoundland, Ambrose grew up without painkillers or hospitals. Ronnie falls quiet as he watches the doctor thread a large needle that reminds the boy of a fishhook. The doctor pulls the needle in and out of the boy's hand, six times. The child has never felt pain like this. But he sighs now, thinking it is over. The doctor eyes his work.

"We need one more," he says.

This stitch would hurt more than the first six. Still, he does not cry. Later, Ambrose takes his son home and leaves to confront the Greek restaurant owner whose open sidewalk vault caused the accident. "You hurt my son!" he yells at the owner. "You need to pay for his doctor's bill."

Affronted over the accusation and this brazen dark-eyed man, the owner hollers, "Get out!"

When Ambrose refuses to leave, the owner grabs a butcher knife and chases him into the street. There is shouting, screaming; strangers stop to stare at the man who shakes the silver knife in the afternoon air. Ambrose eyes the blade; he could outrun this man, but he does not. During the Depression, he fought as a middleweight to earn extra money, and like his brother Paddy, he refuses to back down from a challenge. He punches the restaurant owner in the head as the knife is raised. The man falls to the street, and his skull strikes the curb with a loud crack.

The wail of ambulance and police sirens grow closer, and soon the dead body and Ambrose are taken away. Days later, a judge frees Ambrose, ruling that the lethal punch was thrown in self-defense.

As my father retells this story, the details that linger in his memory are not the fight or a man's death, but the seven stitches and Ambrose's pride.

"He was so proud I didn't cry," my father tells us.

Ambrose's son had suffered like a man. He bragged about his boy at poker games and to relatives. My father will carry those words, Ambrose's love and respect, close to his heart for the next six decades.

Absentmindedly on this October evening, my father rubs the scar. The gash on his left hand is faded now, the crescent moon mark barely visible. The sun dips below the trees outside as my two younger sisters and I try to visualize Ambrose, his bravado, his pride for our father. Would we have grown close to our grandfather, forgiven him if we had had the chance?

"I don't know if I would have liked him," Janice says.

"I probably would have hugged him if I met him," Joanie adds.

My father shakes his head at the thought of his daughter embracing Ambrose.

"He's still my grandfather, our blood," Joanie says. "He had to live with the guilt."

The conversation pauses as my father tries to explain his animosity, the memories of his mother who struggled to feed and clothe her two sons. One vision continues to haunt him, the image of his mother bent over a sink, scrubbing dirty pans in the back room of a restaurant.

"Every night, Billy and I had to sit at the counter and eat our dinners there while she washed dishes," my father says, his voice breaking. "It was painful as hell."

The memory ends there. My father wipes tears that we have never seen before.

"I'm sorry all this happened to you, Dad," Janice says. She, too, is now crying.

The room is still. My sisters and I are beginning to realize how much hurt lingers. My mother sits quietly, by my side. She, more than any of us, knows how long my father has buried his feelings. For most of my parent's marriage, my father refused to talk about Ambrose or his childhood memories. "It has affected him his whole life," she has told me. When she met my father in 1956, she was a raven-haired striking young woman, working as a secretary at the Raytheon Company in Bedford, Massachusetts. One of her jobs was collecting time cards, and the dark-eyed young man who stocked the shelves immediately caught her eye. "We just looked at each other, and it was love at first sight."

Just out of the Navy, my father's confidence and good looks enamored the young woman from Lowell, Massachusetts; my mother's laughter and bright eyes captivated my father. Within a year they were married, in February 1957, at a wedding in which the guests were told Ambrose was dead. "I don't want to talk about him," my father explained to my mother. "I don't want to hear his name."

For the next forty-nine years of their marriage, my mother respected her husband's request, and now on this fall evening, she is keenly aware of how far my father has come in sharing, relieving the burden he has carried for decades.

The following morning is cold, brisk, and the October breeze swirls leaves into the air as we walk along Brooklyn's Sixty-ninth Street. My father searches for the street door that tripped him and prompted the deadly brawl. "I want to show you where the fight was," he says.

Hands stuffed into his khakis, he looks for the familiar details of his childhood. Much is different now. He does not recognize the apartments built over the years. Tall buildings replace the vacant lots where boys tossed balls. The stores and restaurants have changed hands and names. Yet, there are two crimson metal doors. My father walks to them, trying to remember. He stops to stare at the two sheets of metal pressed into the sidewalk. Could this be the street vault he tripped over as a small boy?

Inside the nearby deli, a young man in a baseball cap pours coffee. A middle-aged man stands behind the counter. "Excuse me," my father says. "I used to live here more than sixty years ago. Do you know if a Greek restaurant used to be here back in the 1940s?"

The two men cannot help my father recreate his past. They do not know if this deli was a Greek restaurant years ago. Still, there are the crimson metal doors outside. We step back outside and stare at them again. I see my father, a small boy running down this street, two milk bottles in his hands. I hear glass shattering and the sound of a boy's surprised cry as he eyes the blood running down his palm.

"This must be it," my father says, staring at the doors, lost in his reverie of the past.

As we drive away from the street with the crimson gates, away from the water, I consider my father's scar, a symbol of his lesson learned as a child. The tender palm of a boy stitched together with a needle, large and shaped like a fishhook. Ambrose knew that his son had to endure, to accept pain. He had witnessed many a Newfoundland fisherman, his own brother Paddy, suffer through festering fishhook wounds, wrists swollen and blistered from the salty sea. *Pain is being lost in your dory on the Grand Banks with nothing to eat and your hands bleeding from pulling on the oars day and night in the cold curtains of fog. Pain is drowning in the sea, with a gale roaring overhead, a gale that you know will take you and your three sons to a watery grave. Pain is part of life, boy.*

At sea, Ambrose knew there were no doctors, no quick cures for infection. The Newfoundland fishermen had their own ways of dealing with pain. Afflicted with a fishhook in their hand, the superstitious and religious dorymen often pressed the hook three times into their wound, three times in honor of the Holy Trinity, three times to heal. Unknowingly, my father carries out his own ritual. Often, he presses his fingers into his palm, absent-mindedly rubbing the scar, touching the wound to remember. *It taught me a great lesson. It toughened me up, taught me how to tolerate pain.* Ironically, the man who taught him the lesson would later provoke the deepest hurt.

The afternoon sun loses its warmth, and the light fades behind the tall buildings as we hunt for one more church, one more apartment, and the last place my father lived in Brooklyn. After getting lost for two hours, which exasperates all of us and stirs several "Jesus Christs!" from my father, we park alongside the Visitation of the Blessed Virgin Mary Church in Red Hook. The church and its presbytery are mammoth, intimidating gray Gothic buildings that span the block. The steeple and bell tower loom over the treetops and a nearby park, an icon that once drew the families of Irish and Italian fishermen to Mass.

My father climbs the twenty steps to the rectory and rings the buzzer. From the sidewalk, he appears small, dwarfed by the towering church walls, the large double doors of glass and wood. A priest answers on the intercom.

"Hello, Father, I was an altar boy here sixty years ago. I'd like to talk to somebody and see the church."

Minutes later, the priest answers the door with a smile and welcomes us inside. Father Carlos Valencia is slim, dark-haired, and young. He is eager to help, and he offers us a tour before the Saturday evening Mass begins. The church was built by Irish fishermen, he tells us, the cavernous ceiling constructed to resemble the hull of Noah's Ark. I eye the church's ceiling and think of wooden schooners, of Paddy Walsh and the August Gale. My Nana sat in one of the oak pews here, Rosary beads in her hand, a beret on her head. She came here often to pray and watch her son perform his duties on the altar. My grandfather did not join her.

"He came here once to see me," my father remembers, his voice soft and low.

At the front of the church, to the left and right of the altar, small red votive candles flicker. Nana often took my sisters and me inside churches to light these candles. She slipped quarters inside the metal boxes and lit the tiny flames, praying silently for her sons, her grandchildren, and for Ambrose.

A statue of the Blessed Mary hovers near the candles. A blue cloth cloaks her head, her face radiates peace, forgiveness. I think of Nana's soft cheeks, her kind blue eyes. *She forgave Ambrose. After all his hurt, horrible choices, and betrayals, she forgave him. She prayed for him, wrote him letters and kept him informed about his sons, his grandchildren. She forgave.*

Sunlight filters from the stained-glass windows illuminating a row of pews. I sit down in one of them and close my eyes. I make a mental list of the good in my grandfather: the years he supervised fifty men at the ship-rigging loft during the war, the afternoons he played catch with my father and taught him how to ride a bike. The years that he provided for his family, was a loving father, a loyal husband. *I will never understand what you did, but you are my family. My grandfather. You are my father's father. A part of him and a part of me.*

At the back of the church, I hear my father's voice. He is talking to a few older women who were born in Red Hook and have belonged to the church since they were small girls. My father tells them he served as an altar boy in the church on Sundays and lived on Columbia Avenue in a three-story apartment building. A synagogue occupied half of the building's first floor. The women nod, remembering.

My father doesn't tell them that this is the home where Ambrose abandoned him, the apartment where he remembers eating onion sandwiches for dinner, where rats scrambled in the stairways, and the Mafia ruled the poverty-riddled streets. The women give my father directions to his old apartment, and we step out into the street. Birds swoop in the trees as my father strolls past the park where he played baseball many years ago. His head is bent against the wind as he walks along the brick sidewalk that leads to Columbia Avenue. Hip-hop music blares from a parked car as he crosses the street. Tattered chairs lean against a sidewalk bar. He eyes the deli on the corner and remembers a store where his mother sent him for groceries. Many times he paid with food vouchers, charity from the church.

He remembers the Italian parades that wound their way along this street and the Italian kids who dominated the neighborhood. Here, he had his share of fights. The Italian kids called him "Irish." Somewhere on this street, my uncle, a toddler at the time, tossed my father's new shoes onto the sidewalk from their window. They were stolen by the time my father ran down the two flights of stairs to fetch them. Continuing to the end of Columbia Street, my father shakes his head. The apartment building he once lived in is gone.

"It must have been torn down," he says, disappointed, still looking for something familiar, a street corner, a store.

I envision my grandfather carefully closing an apartment door, a shadow in the dark. Quietly he slips into his sister-in-law's car and drives away, stealing the car and $800 in cash, advance money for a paint job he would never do. Inside, his two sons and his wife sleep. The streets are quiet as Ambrose leaves, the car disappearing, turning away from Columbia Avenue.

Now on this October afternoon, I am glad we cannot find this home. I do not like to think of my father alone here, an eleven-year-old left to look after his mother and year-old brother. A boy left to wonder where his father went and why. Like the bulldozer that tore down my father's old home, I wish I could destroy these memories, the ill-fated trip to San Francisco and the night Ambrose disappeared from this street. But as with the August Gale children, the past remains present for my father. It is his to keep, his to remember, his to forgive or forget.

Not long after we return home, my father reflects on why he kept his childhood memories buried, concealed from me, my sisters, and mother. On the phone, he apologizes to me one evening.

"I kept this all inside me in the form of bitterness. I was wrong to keep it from you all. I just wanted to push those memories out of my life. I guess I was selfish. I dunno. I didn't want to burden you kids or your mother with this stuff. I didn't want you to think I wanted any sympathy or anything."

"It's okay," I tell my father. "We know the stories now."

My father sighs and falls quiet.

"I love you, Dad," I tell him, my voice cracking with the weight of my words.

"I love you, too," he says.

Months after our journey to Staten Island and Brooklyn, I find a picture taken during one of my father's birthdays. My father, uncle, and Nana gather around our backyard picnic table. A birthday cake with strawberries and whipped cream rests before them. My uncle sits in the middle, and his arms are wrapped around the shoulders of his mother and brother. He is a father himself now, with a son and a daughter, a loyal wife, and successful job overseeing a mental health agency in Michigan. He grins into the camera, and it is clear he is so happy to be among his family. *Happy Birthday, big brother. You were always looking after me, steering me in the right direction. And Ma, you sure took care of us through thick and thin. We were blessed to have your love and strength.*

Nana is in her early seventies, confident in who she is: a mother, a grandmother, a woman well-loved by her grandchildren and sons. She gazes toward the camera lens with a hint of a smile, and there is resoluteness in her blue eyes. *These are my boys, Ronnie and Billy. They turned out pretty good. We all came out pretty good.*

On the other end of the table, my father's arm rests against his younger brother's back. His lips are pressed together in a smile and his brown eyes shine. I have seen this expression many times before when he has attended the honor roll dinners, award ceremonies, and college graduations of his six daughters. Pride and love well up in his face on this summer afternoon. *My mother is something else. She worked so hard and went through tough times to keep us together, to raise us right. We each could have taken some bad turns, but we stuck together, and that made all the difference.*

I consider the turmoil, the internal storms they each weathered, how this picture, their lives might have turned out differently. Both my father and uncle could have taken darker, destructive paths, but my Nana held them close and they watched out for each other. Ten years younger than his older brother, my uncle looked to my dad for advice and support, once even giving him a Father's Day gift to show his appreciation.

"Your dad was the male role model in my life," my uncle tells me. "He taught me how to be a good father."

Throughout my childhood, my father espoused many rules and offered many pieces of advice to my sisters and me. But there is one saying that resonates. Whenever my sisters and I battled or we strayed too far from home in our travels or jobs, he would tell us, "Always remember that blood is thicker than water."

There was nothing more vital—even after his father twice abandoned him—than family. His mother and brother remained the center, the heart of his young life. Years later, my sisters, mother, and I would further cement his belief that there is "nothing, nothing more important than your family."

For as long as I can remember, my father has encouraged, cheered, and guided us all. Through the bad dreams, the disappointments, the milestones, the baptisms, the weddings, and the bumps in the road, he has always been there for his family, for me, for my sisters, and for my mother. His strong arms have always held us close, and I have always known that he would never, ever let us go.

ACKNOWLEDGMENTS

Like my Great-Uncle Paddy who gathered a strong and seasoned crew for the *Annie Anita* and *Mary Bernice,* I was fortunate to have my own team of friends, family, and experts to guide and encourage me through to the completion of *August Gale.*

To Con Fitzpatrick, a volunteer at the Marystown Heritage Museum and coauthor of *A History of Marystown, Mortier Bay,* who eagerly shared his knowledge of his town, its history and its seafaring culture.

To dorymen—Jim "Pad" Kelly, Bill Hanrahan, Jerome Walsh, Tom Roff, Richard Barry, and schooner Captains Hayward Hodder, Anthony Kelly, and Matthew Mitchell—thank you for sharing your adventures and perils at sea.

Extraordinary thanks to Ralph Getson, curator of education at the Fisheries Museum of the Atlantic in Lunenburg, Nova Scotia for his patience, wisdom, and kindness over the past year while he taught a landlubber about schooners, dories, and the salt cod fishery. His lessons (*a schooner is not a ship, it's a line not a rope, and it's a tub not a bucket!*) were invaluable.

To Captains Alex Green and George Pike, savvy and skilled Newfoundland and Nova Scotia fishermen, who taught me how to row a dory (despite the fact I had "dogfish strokes") and offered crucial insight into the mind-set of skippers and dorymen. They ensured that my details about hauling trawl, sailing the sea, and battling gales were accurate and true.

To Chris Fogarty, Canada Hurricane Centre forecaster and program manager, who helped me track and recreate the 1935 August Gale and instructed me on trapped fetches, extra-tropical transitions, and hurricane winds and waves.

To the men and women, sons and daughters of the Marystown fishermen, who shared their memories about the tragedy that forever changed their lives and their small rural outport. Scores of Marystown citizens and people from other Newfoundland communities also offered their recollections of the 1935 storm, and I could not have written this book without their assistance. This is by no means a complete list, and if I have forgotten anyone, I apologize. A heartfelt thanks to: Jamie Walsh, Jerome Walsh, Bernard Butler, Bride Hanrahan, Aloysius Brenton, Sybil Turpin, Mary Brinton Mallay, Lizzie Drake Pittman, Margaret Mitchell Lundrigan, Mary Pittman Hodder, Adele Hanrahan Fulford, Gertrude Walsh, Mary Brennan, Narcissus Walsh, Elsie Walsh, Evelyn and Tom Reid, Charles Walsh, Michael Farrell, Vincent Cheeke, Emily Long Roff, Alonzo and Marie Finlay, Sadie Brinton Kelley, Adele and Bill Pittman, Frances Hanrahan Mitchell, Val Morrissey, Ernestine and Loretta Walsh, Bride Coady, and Georgina Mitchell Kilfoy. Special thanks to Paddy Walsh Jr. who offered poignant and detailed stories about his father, Captain Paddy Walsh, and his mother, Lillian.

To the Newfoundland band Great Big Sea, whose song "Safe Upon the Shore" inspired me while I wrote about the centuries-old tradition of fishermen's wives worrying and waiting for their husbands to return from the cold, cold sea.

Much gratitude to my writing group: Pat Hager, Susan Casey, Nancy Brown, Gro Flatebo, Rick Wile, Steve Lauder, and Jean Peck, whose suggestions, critiques, and advice made this book infinitely better. Thanks also to Newfoundland authors Maura Hanrahan and Paul Butler for giving me a place to stay in their St. John's home and introducing me to several of their country's talented writers.

To my dear friends who read and reread *August Gale* and never wavered in their enthusiasm and encouragement:

MaryEllen Tracy, Janice Borghoff, Nanie Barnes, Mary Tippet, Becca Nazar, Kathy Gillis-Soltan, Diane Lade, Jean Kirpatrick, Kyle Chapman, Abby Philbrook, Victoria Brett, Jean Preis, Shane-Malcolm Billings, and Alan White.

To my wonderful literary agent, the unflappable Diane Freed, who guided me with a steady hand from the dreaded book proposal process to the book-selling adventure, and to my editor Erin Turner, whose devotion and talent made my first book-publishing experience an absolute joy.

And finally to my family:

To my relatives and the friends of my grandfather, who helped me to understand and come to know Ambrose Walsh, Thomas and Morris O'Connell, Raymond and Hilary Walsh, and especially my Aunt Eleanor Sumner who recounted stories about her beloved sister, Patricia O'Connell Walsh, and much appreciation to Donnie Walsh and Kathy Walsh Pope, who answered endless questions about their father—and my grandfather—with honesty, grace, and compassion.

Many hugs to my sisters—Diane Walsh Clancy, Jacqueline Walsh Coffey, Laura Walsh Upton, and Janice and Joan Walsh— for their support, love, and willingness to pop champagne and plan book-celebrating parties before I had even completed a chapter.

To my Newfoundland family, the Brentons—Alan, Jack, Jeanita, James, Diane, and Alan Jr.—who treated my father, sister, and me like royalty during our stay in Marystown and welcomed us "home" in every way possible.

To my Uncle Bill, my favorite and most loveable uncle, who cheered me on, chapter after chapter, and openly shared his own memories and emotions, patiently answering his niece's countless questions.

Much love to Emma and Nora, my precious daughters, who for months put up with a book-obsessed and stressed Mommy and created my "writing family," a collection of stuffed animals, butterflies, hearts, angels, and a small, plastic smiling monkey to keep me company while I wrote.

To my husband, Eric Conrad, who loved and comforted me even when I was supremely cranky and not "loveable." He bolstered and reassured me every step of the way on this nine-year book-writing journey. I could not find a more empathetic, generous, and giving husband.

To my parents, Patricia and Ronald Walsh, who have always stood by my side with an abundance of love and faith. I am proud to be their daughter and blessed to have been raised in a home where family always came first.

And lastly to my Nana, Patricia O'Connell Walsh: thanks for teaching me pig Latin, penny poker, and how to knit. I still miss and love you, and will forever admire your strength and kindness.

GLOSSARY OF NEWFOUNDLAND
AND NAUTICAL TERMS

August gales – hurricanes that roar up the North Atlantic and carry severe winds and waves. In the 1800s and early 1900s, hundreds of fishermen died off Newfoundland and Nova Scotia's coast during the month of August when the gales struck without warning.

banker or banking schooner – a schooner that fishes offshore banks. In the North American waters, these vessels typically stacked dories on their decks, which were then lowered over the schooner's side, allowing the dorymen to fish from trawl lines.

banks – an undersea elevation of land where fish feed and may be caught. The Grand Banks off Newfoundland's coast were among the most popular fishing grounds from the sixteenth century through the early 1900s.

banshee – ghost or spirit.

batten down the hatches – to make a vessel watertight. To prepare for gales, storms, or foul weather, fishermen secure their vessel's hatch covers with wooden battens so as to prevent water from entering the ship or boat belowdecks.

beam-ends – The sides of a ship. "On her beam-ends" means the vessel or schooner is on her side, listing forty-five degrees or more and about to capsize.

b'y – term for boy, man. *Eh b'y* is to agree with what someone is saying. B'ys would mean boys or men.

ceili – a dance accompanied by guitar, fiddle music, singing, and storytelling. The traditional dance originated in Ireland and Scotland and is common in countries where the Irish and Scots immigrated.

codfish – bottom-feeding fish found in the cold North Atlantic waters. The cod family includes many species; the North Atlantic *Gadus morhua* are typically forty-eight inches in length and twenty-six pounds. But much larger codfish have been caught. Cod has historically been considered "king" to Newfoundland and its economy. In 1497 during his discovery of Newfoundland, British explorer John Cabot noted the cod were so plentiful that they could be plucked from the sea with a basket weighted down with stone. In the early sixteenth century, fishermen from England, France, Spain, and Portugal began hunting for cod off Newfoundland's shores.

comber – a large ocean wave.

crosstrees – horizontal bars at the top of the mast that support the rigging.

dory – a flat-bottomed boat with flared sides. Dories were rowed and could also be sailed. The boats generally measured fifteen feet on the bottom but could be as short as eight feet and as long as twenty. The dories were used to fish close to the shore and on the Banks fisheries in Newfoundland.

doryman – a man who fished from a dory. Traditionally, two men or dorymates fished from a dory in the Banks fishery.

fathom – six feet in length.

fish flake – an elevated platform created with long poles and topped with tree boughs used for drying salted codfish. In the 1800s and early 1900s, fish flakes lined the shores of Newfoundland's harbors.

fish store – fisherman used this small wooden shed to store their gear, repair their hooks and trawl lines. The fish store was typically built near the shore or on the fisherman's wharf, and it was also a good place for a friend to drop in for a drink of rum.

forecastle – partial deck, above the upper deck and at the head of the vessel; traditionally the sailors' living quarters. Pronounced "fo'c'sle."

founder – to fill with water and sink.

gaff – a large hook attached to a pole used to toss fish from a dory to a schooner deck.

glass or weatherglass – a barometer that foretells the weather.

gunwale or gunnel – where the sides of ship and the deck meet.

greenhorn – an unseasoned or inexperienced fisherman.

grub – food.

gurry butt – a barrel used to hold the fish offal or waste.

hardtack – a hard and long-lasting dry biscuit, used as food on long journeys. Dorymen who found themselves separated from their schooners often ate the hardtack to survive.

mast – a vertical spar on a ship which supports sails or rigging.

mug up – small lunch break.

oilskins – clothing that protects fishermen from the elements. In the 1800s and early 1900s, oilskins were often homemade garments made of unbleached cotton treated with linseed oil.

outport – a Newfoundland coastal village.

port – the left side of a ship when facing the bow.

puncheon – a large wooden barrel used in the fishing trade.

quintal – a hundredweight of 110 or 112 pounds. Salted codfish was typically weighed by the quintal.

rigging – all the ropes, lines, and wires that support and control the masts, spars, and sails on sailing vessels and ships.

schooner – a fore and aft-rigged sailing vessel with at least two masts that traditionally carried stacked dories.

shoal water – shallow water that is a threat to navigation, schooners, and ships.

sou'wester – an oiled, waterproof hat with a broad brim and elongated back to keep a fisherman's head and neck dry in foul weather.

spar – a general term for all wooden masts, yards, gaffs, and booms on a sailing ship.

starboard – the right side of a ship when facing forward.

sunker – rocks or reefs that lie just below the sea's surface and pose a threat to sailors.

tholepin – a small round wooden peg inserted in the gunwale to hold the oars in place while rowing.

token – an omen, vision, or premonition of death.

trawl – the buoyed fishing lines used by dorymen. Baited hooks were set at three-foot intervals on the thick, tarred cotton line. The dorymen typically would set 7,200 feet (a mile and a half) of gear on the ocean bottom.

Sources: *Dictionary of Newfoundland and Labrador* and Fisheries Museum of the Atlantic.

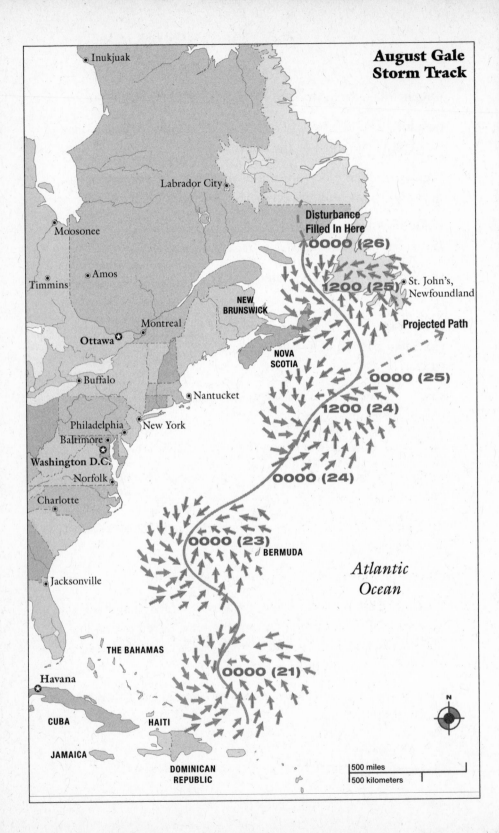

August Gale
Storm Track

Inukjuak

Labrador City

Moosonee

Amos

Timmins

NEW
BRUNSWICK

Montreal

Ottawa

Buffalo

NOVA
SCOTIA

Nantucket

Philadelphia   New York

Baltimore

Washington D.C.

Norfolk

Charlotte

Jacksonville

THE BAHAMAS

Havana

CUBA   HAITI

JAMAICA

DOMINICAN
REPUBLIC

Disturbance
Filled In Here
0000 (26)

1200 (25)   St. John's,
             Newfoundland

Projected Path

0000 (25)

1200 (24)

0000 (24)

0000 (23)

BERMUDA

Atlantic
Ocean

0000 (21)

N

500 miles

500 kilometers

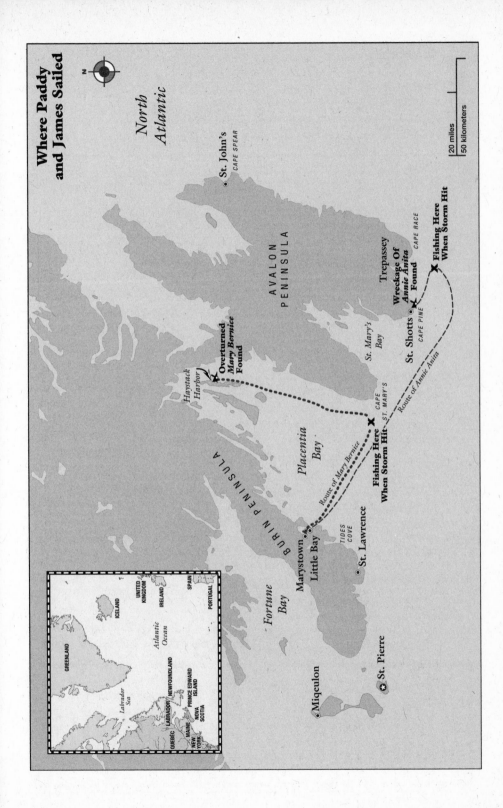

Where Paddy and James Sailed

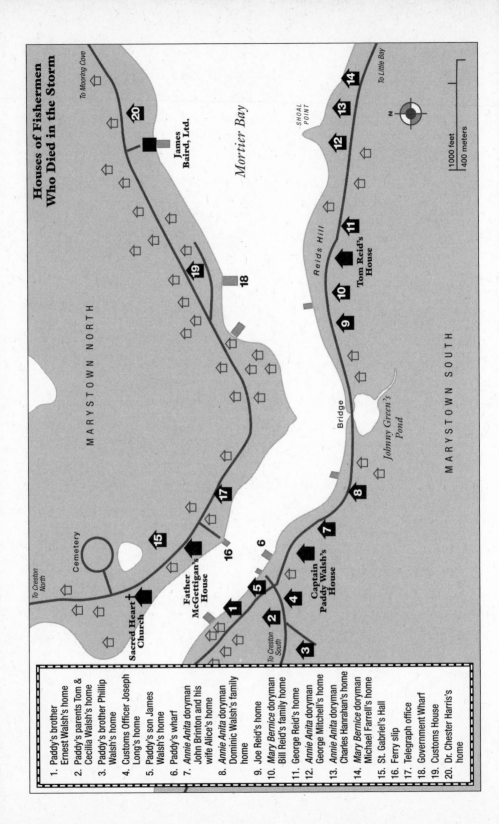

Houses of Fishermen Who Died in the Storm

Mortier Bay

MARYSTOWN NORTH

MARYSTOWN SOUTH

SHOAL POINT

Reids Hill

Johnny Green's Pond

Cemetery

To Creston North

To Creston South

To Mooring Cove

To Little Bay

Bridge

Sacred Heart Church

Father McGettigan's House

Captain Paddy Walsh's House

Tom Reid's House

James Baird, Ltd.

1000 feet
400 meters

1. Paddy's brother
   Ernest Walsh's home
2. Paddy's parents Tom &
   Cecilia Walsh's home
3. Paddy's brother Phillip
   Walsh's home
4. Customs Officer Joseph
   Long's home
5. Paddy's son James
   Walsh's home
6. Paddy's wharf
7. *Annie Anita* doryman
   John Brinton and his
   wife Alice's home
8. *Annie Anita* doryman
   Dominic Walsh's family
   home
9. Joe Reid's home
10. *Mary Bernice* doryman
    Bill Reid's family home
11. George Reid's home
12. *Annie Anita* doryman
    George Mitchell's home
13. *Annie Anita* doryman
    Charles Hanrahan's home
14. *Mary Bernice* doryman
    Michael Farrell's home
15. St. Gabriel's Hall
16. Ferry slip
17. Telegraph office
18. Government Wharf
19. Customs House
20. Dr. Chester Harris's
    home

THE WALSH TRAGEDY SONG

BY JOSEPH MURRAY

In nineteen hundred thirty-five on August twenty-one
Two fishing boats went out to sea from the port of Marystown
Headed for the Grand Banks, Cape St. Mary's fishing grounds
Among the fourteen men who sailed were a father and three sons

The skies and sea were calm and clear til August twenty-fifth
When a big nor'easter came ashore setting wharves and boats adrift
Uprooting trees and houses along the coast of Newfoundland
While out at sea two fishing boats were filling up with sand

Chorus

As the wind screamed thru the rigging and the waves rose mountains
high
Those brave men fought the hurricane and prayed to God on high
The ocean is a graveyard when those storms are at their height
Fourteen people lost at sea on that dark and stormy night

Narrative

Paddy Walsh was skipper of the Annie Anita *while eldest son Jimmy*
skippered the Mary Bernice
Other members of that ill-fated crew were
John Brinton, Edward Cheeke, Dominic Walsh, George Mitchell,
Richard and Charles Hanrahan,
Dennis Long, Michael Farrell, Tom and Billy Reid

Also on board were Paddy Walsh's 12 and 14-year sons Francis and
Jerome

As the thunder rolled and the lightning flashed across the banks of
Newfoundland
As waves crashed down upon the heads of that gallant little band
A baby girl named Jamie was born that night to Jimmy Walsh's wife
As her father fought the raging storm that finally took his life

When the dawn broke clear and bright next day across the fishing
grounds
No sign of the two small boats could anywhere be found
'Til a wreck washed up on St. Shotts' beach, half filled up with sand
The only sign of human life was a small boy's little hand

Chorus

Church bells rang out in Marystown as the news spread far and wide
Prayers and masses for the dead for the fourteen souls who died
Mothers wept and widows grieved while children tried to understand
How God in all his mercy had forsaken these brave men

The memory of that awful night back in thirty-five
Still haunts the hearts and minds of those who are still alive
When the August Gales each summer cross the banks of Newfoundland
They kneel and pray to God above, safeguard our fishermen

Chorus

ABOUT THE AUTHOR

Barbara Walsh is a Pulitzer Prize–winning journalist and magazine columnist who has chased many stories during her career; her work has changed laws, lives, and affected the 1988 presidential election. She is the author of *Sammy in the Sky,* a children's book illustrated by painter Jamie Wyeth and published in August 2011. Barbara lives in Maine with her two daughters, husband, and a Tennessee coonhound.